I. PRIMARY REFERENCE WORKS ON SHAKESPEARE

II. CRITICISM AND INTERPRETATION

    A. Textual Treatises, Commentaries
    B. Treatment of Special Subjects
    C. Dramatic and Literary Art in Shakespeare

III. SHAKESPEARE AND HIS TIME

    A. General Treatises. Biography
    B. The Age of Shakespeare
    C. Authorship

Series III, Part B

THE AGE OF SHAKESPEARE
VOL. I

THE AGE OF

SHAKESPEARE

(1579-1631)

BY

THOMAS SECCOMBE and JOHN W. ALLEN

VOL. I

POETRY AND PROSE

WITH AN INTRODUCTION BY

PROFESSOR HALES

 BOOKS FOR LIBRARIES PRESS

FREEPORT, NEW YORK

03

Reprinted 1971

INTERNATIONAL STANDARD BOOK NUMBER:
0-8369-5860-8

LIBRARY OF CONGRESS CATALOG CARD NUMBER:
74-160993

PRINTED IN THE UNITED STATES OF AMERICA

CONTENTS.

"NOUS sommes au centre même d'une des périodes les plus extra-ordinaires de la beauté tumultueuse et folle comme la mer. Il s'agit en effet de la mer, et du plus grand océan de poésie qui ait jamais battu les falaises informes de la vie quotidienne. Cet océan qui est vraiment le *Mare poetarum* des mappemondes spirituelles, la mer la plus puissante, la plus énorme et la plus inépuisable qu'il y ait eue jusqu'ici sur notre planète terre, est presque inconnu des lettrés."   MAETERLINCK.

INTRODUCTION.

By Professor Hales.

The popular saying that 'History repeats itself' has but little truth to recommend it. No doubt there are certain resemblances between important historical and literary periods, and the conditions that have fostered and that distinguish them, and such resemblances are well worth noting and considering; but they are often superficial rather than intimate, and they are always sporadic rather than complete. It would be much more accurate to say that History never repeats itself.

Between the great literary periods of the world it would be easy to point out productive influences and circumstances of a similar kind, as, for instance, between the Periclean period and the Elizabethan; but it would be easier still to point out essential differences and divergences. To confine ourselves to English Literature, it would be easy to point out resemblances in origin between our three chief poetic periods, viz., the Chaucerian, the Elizabethan, and the Wordsworthian; but in these cases also the dissimilarities are yet more striking than the similarities. In short, each great period, if we look beneath the surface, will be found to be unique and singular in respect of both its growth and its fruit, having no doubt some characteristics in common with other illustrious ages, but at the same time significantly marked by much that belongs peculiarly to itself and to no other age. And to the student a profoundly interesting subject is the investigation of the conditions and circumstances that have produced, or tended to produce, this distinguishing uniqueness, or, in other words, to differentiate one time from all other times.

Now the more the Elizabethan period is explored, the more separate and individual it will be discovered to be; the more clearly will it appear that the atmosphere in which it rose, so to speak, was such as had never existed before, and is not likely ever to exist again—cannot possibly exist again.

Like many—perhaps all—great literary epochs, it was a time when the spirit of the nation was high-raised and enthusiastic—was exceptionally elate, self-confident, sanguine; but the influences that acted upon this excited and ardent spirit were of a kind unknown before or since, at all events in any such degree of intensity, and so gave to its literary expression a development and a form of extraordinary fascination and of enduring excellence.

In no other century of English history was the national feeling more deeply roused and exalted than in the latter half of the sixteenth. In the earlier part of it there had been endless disquietude and uncertainty. There had been many so-called 'religious' antagonisms and controversies —so-called 'religious,' we say, because in their ferocity, their selfishness, their uncharity, 'religion' in the proper sense of the word was conspicuous by its absence, and Christ's Sermon on the Mount, the supreme document of Christianity, was signally forgotten. And there had been many other causes of profound anxiety and urgent alarm. Who could say which way England was drifting? Was it to go backward or forward? Was it to sink into insignificance amongst the Powers of Europe, or rise to a foremost place as the Sovereign of the Sea? Such questions had to be answered before the nation could feel undistracted and at its ease. A noble poetry could not flourish

amidst such doubts and misgivings as they implied.
Nothing is more paralyzing than insecurity. Singing is
impossible when one's fate is undeclared, and at any
moment one may be laid prostrate. Not till the accession
of Queen Elizabeth did a better state of things begin to
be. Not till then did the fortunes of England begin to be
decided. Not till then did there dawn a day that was to
bring safety, confidence, freedom from care. These blessed
results of the Queen's rule were not attained or manifested
at once. Some score years went by before the country was
conscious of the vast improvement both in its present
state and in its prospects. But slowly and with delight it
at last recognized the happy transition that had taken place,
and then began the great Elizabethan period of literature.

England had made finally its choice between Romanism
and Anglicanism—between Popery and Protestantism—
between Mediaevalism and the Reformation, or whatever are
the best terms to use to denote Roman Catholicism on the
one hand and the Catholicism of the English Church on
the other. There were still, no doubt, many adherents
of the unrevised ritual, especially in the rural districts;
but more and more it grew certain that any such reversal
of things ecclesiastic as had been attempted in the reign
of Queen Mary would not again be attempted, or, if
attempted, would have no chance of success. Perhaps the
most effective bringer-about of this ultimate election was
a Pope, Pius V. to wit, who in 1570 published a bull or
'sentence declaratory against Elizabeth, Queen of England,
and the heretics adhering unto her.' So little did this
pontiff understand the temper and mood of England that
he produced a result precisely the opposite of what he
vehemently desired. The 'heretics' of his blundering edict
clung all the more loyally to their sovereign; and the hope
of any Papal restoration died altogether away. Thus he

fanned the flames both of Anti-Romanism and of Patriotism till they burnt with an unquenchable brightness. Of
yet more service in fanning the patriotic flame was, quite
unintentionally, the King of Spain. Our bitterest enemy
proved our truest friend. His preparations, long threatened
and deferred but organized at last, deeply excited the in-
dignation and the defiance of the English people. At
first, it may be, they were regarded with some humility
and awe, though unquestionably they were the answer to
long provocations; but every year any such feeling more
and more gave place to self-confidence and daring. The
real weakness of Spain, however wide its dominion, or
rather because of the width of its dominion, was more and
more vividly realized. Philip II. was derisively styled 'a
colossus stuffed with clouts.' 'To singe his beard' became
a favourite pastime; and if the Queen had been willing to
give her sailors unrestrained liberty and licence, he would
have suffered yet fiercer treatment even in his own country.
But she shrank from an open rupture, though she connived
at many acts that were thoroughly hostile, as indeed also
did Philip on his part. Both sovereigns would fain have
avoided a deadly collision, and assuredly Philip did not
equip his great armament till he had no other choice.
But meanwhile the courage and audacity of his opponents
attained an irresistible vigour. Never were English seamen
bolder or more contemptuous. They were eager to anticipate
the Spanish invasion, and absolutely sure they could easily
suppress it, were only the royal permission granted. 'But
for her [the Queen's] positive orders of recall,' writes Major
Martin Hume,[1] 'Drake on this very voyage [the 'beard-
singeing' voyage of 1597] would have made the Armada

[1] See *The Year after the Armada*, 1896, p. 9. See also Prof.
Laughton's most interesting volumes on the *Defeat of the Spanish
Armada*, printed for the Navy Records Society, 1894.

impossible by destroying, as he was able and ready to do, all the ships preparing for it in Lisbon harbour.' When the Invincible Armada, to give it the title assigned it by one of Fate's little ironies, was on the verge of starting on its disastrous voyage, there were many offers to thwart and stop it—to effect its disablement and destruction at the very outset; and it is credible enough these impetuous offers, if accepted, would have been duly fulfilled. But that credibility does not now concern us; we have only to call attention to the fearless energy, the uncowed daring, the unfaltering assurance, which they so conspicuously manifested. The valour of England was just then over-brimming; it could not conceive itself defeated and shamed. It could only imagine itself coming and seeing and con-quering. It felt its strength in every limb. It could not dream of failure and ruin.

In material surroundings and comforts too there were great changes and improvements taking place. Commerce was making very considerable progress. Fresh means of wealth were being initially or fully developed. The dissolu-tion of the monasteries had helped to produce an economic revolution, which has not yet been sufficiently recognized. The contrast between the England of Henry VIII. and that of his daughter in respect of trade, manufactures and agri-culture is immense. The large increase in the national riches

' produced important changes in the mode of living. The standard of comfort became higher. Food became more whole-some. As agriculture improved and animals could be kept through the winter with greater ease, salt meat and salt fish no longer formed the staple food of the lower classes for half a year. Brick-making had been re-discovered about 1450; and by the time of Elizabeth the wooden and wattled houses had generally been replaced, at least among all but the poorest class, with dwellings of brick and stone. The introduction of chimneys and the lavish use of glass also helped to improve the people's dwellings, and indeed the houses of the rich merchants or the lords of the manors were now quite luxuriously furnished. Carpets had superseded the old filthy flooring of rushes; pillows and cushions were found in all decent houses; and the quantity of woodwork of this period shows that men cared for something more than mere utility in their surroundings. The lavishness of new wealth was seen too in a certain love of display, of colour, of " purple and fine linen," which characterizes the dress of the Elizabethan age.' [1]

These noticeable improvements in what may be called the external life of the country and the effects of them might easily be illustrated from the literature of the time; but we will content ourselves in this Introduction with quoting an excellent summary both of their causes and their indications from Mr. E. J. Payne's *Voyages of Elizabethan Seamen to America*, 1880. pp. x, xi :

'It has been truly said that all history rests on an economical basis ; and the great extension of English enterprise which the Atlantic voyages represent could certainly not have taken place unless it had been supported by a corresponding increase in the wealth of England. It is well known that such an increase took place in the reign of Elizabeth. The fertility of England's soil, the comparatively large number, the thrift, and the industry of the inhabitants of its towns, had always made of England a capital-making country ; and the stoppage of the continual drain of money to Rome, the dispersion of one-third of the land, previously belonging to monasteries, among the mass of the people, the cessation of wars, and the great reduction in numbers of the unproductive classes which these causes involved, had by this time increased its gross capital yet more.

---

[1] See Gibbins's *Industrial History of England*, 1890, pp. 104, 105.

All the trades of England increased, and many of them were connected with the shipping trade, and contributed to the increase of that also. London and other towns increased vastly in extent, a movement which statesmen in vain tried to check by Act of Parliament. Of the increase of personal wealth at this period the face of the land still affords ample evidence. The great country houses, the magnificent tombs to be found in churches, the costly furniture and pictures with which Englishmen now began to surround themselves, still remain to testify to it; and this increase of personal wealth accounts in some measure for the readiness of Englishmen to engage in remote and romantic enterprises.'

Thus about the middle of Queen Elizabeth's reign, *i.e.*, about the year 1580, England was greatly prosperous and greatly self-confident. The Queen's policy of fostering its gradual growth [1] had succeeded to admiration. Things had settled down in a wonderful way. The immediate future was no longer wholly obscure and to be mistrusted. Men saw the way before them, at least for a certain distance; no longer *ibant sub luce maligna*. And they were resolved to go triumphantly on the way they saw before them. They were conscious of their high destiny, and set themselves to fulfil it. They awoke from a broken slumber of restlessness and anarchy to find themselves a strong and an united people; for, indeed, the sectaries were comparatively but a slight and insignificant element. It was a supreme era in English history—a golden age—a time of exultation and joy.

But a suppression for the time being of 'religious' quarrels, a high excitement of national feeling, a large increase of riches—all these conditions were not bound to result in a great literature, though they provided a state of things favourable to such a result, should there be added

[1] See Creighton's *Queen Elizabeth*, 1899, p. 217.

to them influences tending in that direction. Happily, such influences were not wanting in the Elizabethan period; indeed, they were present in a remarkable degree. Both the intellect and the imagination were roused and stimulated as they had never been before, and have never been since. We say both the intellect and the imagination; for possibly at other times the intellect may have been not less awakened and not less busy, and there have been other times when the imagination has been deeply—though not so deeply—moved and inspired; but there has been no period in English literature when both the imagination and the intellect have at the same time been so profoundly inspirited and stimulated, and expressed themselves with comparable brilliancy. There has been no period that has produced side by side geniuses so strikingly diverse and yet so lofty and so consummate as Shakespeare and Bacon.

The special influences out of which came these effects were first what is called the Revival of Learning, and secondly what is closely connected with that Revival, and yet not wholly to be identified with it, the wonderful sense of emancipation that for various causes penetrated and quickened men's minds and souls. The Reformation in its early days, whatever its subsequent developments, was only part of a great movement for the enfranchisement of the human spirit. New ideas and new ideals flowed in a glorious stream before the eyes and into the heart of the sixteenth century. The old things passed away, and behold, all things became new. The intellect was fed by the new learning; and the imagination asserted its freedom, countenanced and encouraged by discoveries that far surpassed its wildest dreams.

It is difficult for us to estimate—almost impossible to overestimate—the consequences of the Revival of Learning. In the course of the Tudor period three magnificent literatures that had hitherto been very faintly and imperfectly known and appreciated were made familiar to the modern world, viz., the Hebrew, the Greek, the Latin, not to mention the more recent Italian poetry and that which was arising in France. Much might be said of the merely literary influence of what are specially styled 'the Scriptures,' or what is specially entitled 'the Bible' or the Book (though it consists of many very various books), when translations in the English of the day became common. There are endless evidences of the interest and the fascination the Prophets and Psalmists had for Elizabethan readers and writers—of the delight with which they refreshed themselves at those wells of the grandest poetry.

> ' The thirst that from the soul doth rise
> Doth ask a drink divine';

and such 'drink divine' was furnished by those unsealed fountains. Already, too, Hellenic influence was beginning to be felt, with the inevitable result that the general conception of the literary art was raised and ennobled. Already men were discovering what strange and unimagined heights of perfection had been reached in Drama and in Epic a thousand years before the age in which they lived. And the sight and even the report of such exquisite accomplishments were stirring in them new aspirations. Yet more deeply impressed on the Elizabethans was the influence of Latin literature—of Latin literature at its best, not as it had been chiefly known in the Middle Ages, at its second best or its third. However inferior to the Greek masterpieces, the great Latin writings were splendidly useful at a time when our literature very seriously lacked style. It was not void

assuredly; but it was without form. Good models were
sorely wanted. Our literary artists had many essential
lessons to learn, above all perhaps the lesson of self-
restraint, of temperance, of order, which is 'Heaven's
first law' and should be Earth's. They were carried away
by the very fulness of their geniuses. They were rivers
that knew no bounds, and so lost themselves in spacious
overflowings. The classical moderation was the one thing
needful. Μηδὲν ἄγαν or *Ne quid nimis*—this was the
motto that was supremely necessary for a time that had
so much to say, and was so alert—was so impelled to say
it, and was in danger of becoming indistinct and inarticulate in its impetuous utterances. Thus the service
done for the Elizabethan age by classical literature, as far
as that age was acquainted with it, was twofold; it both
inspired and restrained. But it is the former service that
now particularly concerns us—its putting before the
Elizabethans finished pieces of literary art, and pieces
that had won the approval and the acceptance of all the
critics England knew—that came heralded by the eulogies
of every civilized age and every civilized country of
Europe. Happily the profound admiration with which
Vergil and Ovid, to mention no other Augustans, were
regarded never sank into idolatry. The vigorous originality of the chief Elizabethans saved them from any such
servile folly. They read the *Aeneid* and the *Metamorphoses* with the warmest appreciation and not without
reverence; but they never surrendered their own personality. They did not sit at the feet of the great classical
authors, or pick up the crumbs that fell from their tables;
but rather they sat by their side, giving them with all
respect and courtesy the place of honour, but yet not
playing the part of parasites—listening with charmed
ears to their speeches and songs, but not in any wise

inclined to become mere repeaters and echoes of ancient melodies, however choice and immortal. There is no finer illustration of Elizabethan independence than certain lines of Ben Jonson, whose attitude to the Classics is commonly supposed to have been devout and adoring, and who certainly loved them as he tells us he loved Shakespeare, and honoured their memory, 'on this side idolatry, as much as any.' These lines occur in a poem well known, but yet not known well enough; for its value from more points of view than we have now the opportunity of indicating is not easily to be measured. It is one of the noblest eulogies of his great friend ever written. It is the first of the four—by Ben Jonson, Hugh Holland, Leonard Digges, and 'I. M.'—prefixed to the Shakespeare Folio of 1623, addressed 'To the memory of my beloved, the Author Mr William Shakespeare: And what he hath left us.' The writer says he would fain 'commit,' that is compare, his lost friend with his 'peers,' not with inferior 'Muses,' however eminent, such as Lyly, and Kyd, and Marlowe. Though Shakespeare was not much of a classical scholar in his judgement, yet he would venture to pronounce his tragedies worthy of the hearing of the great classical masters, and his comedies such as had no rivals in Greek and Latin literature. 'To honour thee,' he writes, 'I would not seek amongst contemporaries

> 'For names; but call forth thund'ring Æschilus,
> Euripides, and Sophocles to us,
> Paccuvius, Accius, him of Cordova dead
> To life again, to hear thy buskin tread,
> And shake a stage; or, when thy socks were on,
> Leave thee alone for the comparison
> Of all that insolent Greece or haughty Rome
> Sent forth, or since did from their ashes come.
> Triumph, my Britain, thou hast one to show
> To whom all scenes of Europe homage owe.'

It is no slight proof of the robust originality of the Elizabethan genius that it held its own against the enormous prestige of the Classics, which had so lately been born again and were now once more living and in their highest glory. Of the vast influence they exercised there can be no doubt. It was not overwhelming, because the age possessed a certain native energy and self-assertiveness, but it was an incalculable benefit in assisting the said age in its own education and development.

But not only the study of books, the classical especially, is to be remembered, if we would understand the Elizabethan period, but also the study of nature—the study of the earth and its domains and its creatures, and of the heavens and the bodies that bespangle them. The culture of this age was far from being only literary; it was also scientific. It was a time of boundless curiosity and of innumerable incentives to curiosity. All of a sudden the world presented itself to its inhabitants in a quite new aspect. Knowledge of its dimensions and its contents had seemed final and complete. To men's bewilderment at first, and amidst the conservative incredulity that always exhibits itself at such crises in human history, it was discovered that what had passed amongst the learned for geography was far from deserving the name—that the current ' orbis descriptiones ' described in fact only a part of the globe, and nobody could say how small a part; and it even began to be rumoured that the earth was not the centre of the Universe, but only one of the sun's attendant planets—that the lord of creation was after all only a servant. The effect of this wonderful revolution of ideas was unfathomable. The full significance of astronomy's revelations is not felt till the post-Elizabethan days, as those revelations were slow in finding credence. But the amazing fact, soon ascertained beyond all controversy, that what people had called the world was only a section of it acted immediately on men's minds. It is often observed how a wide view from some high eminence, hill or mountain, seems to widen one's mental outlook—that there is a certain broadening of one's mental horizons when the physical horizons are broadened. Our views are all apt to be local, or at the best provincial, if we do not enlarge our prospects; and, as we have said, there is a certain sympathy between our corporeal and our rational eyes. Horace's often quoted remark that

'Caelum, non animum, mutant, qui trans mare currunt,'

is true only in a sense. To travel has always been an invaluable item of an ideal discipline; or, if the student has been unable to travel himself, then to travel by deputy—to explore foreign countries through the experience and report of others—has been found an immense benefit. The English are a nation of travellers, and of readers of travellers' books. Now it is almost impossible for us to conceive the shock to common conceptions of the earth and its area when it was stated—when it was demonstrated—that the so-called world was only half the world, that the sphere was only a hemisphere. What infinite possibilities suggested themselves—of riches 'beyond the dream of avarice,' of extended dominion, and, in the nobler minds, of enlarged knowledge. It was as if the walls that had circumscribed movement and life within primeval and narrow limits had been suddenly overthrown, and immeasurable spaces had been laid open for men to traverse at their will. The imagination could now occupy itself with pictures of far away oceans, novel landscapes, strange races of astounding habits and features and faiths. A huge new volume seemed added to the library of mankind. What secrets that had for long troubled humanity might not now be solved! What havens of rest and peace might not be visited! What paradises might not be disclosed in the dim distances! A great victory had been won over nature. The curtain had been torn away that hid a great mystery. Who could say what farther victories might not be won, what other mysteries uncurtained? These thoughts inspired boundless hopes; and these hopes inspired infinite daring. No man could tell what tidings any day might bring forth—of vast continents annexed to knowledge as well as to the English dominion, of living creatures of extraordinary shapes and notions, of incalculable facilities for the expansion of the human, especially the English, race. New paths opened out in directions that seemed barred and blocked; new planets seemed swimming into mortal 'ken.' The stolidest natures must have been and were deeply roused by such a marvellous amplification of the habitable region. At this time, as at another, wonder came to life—a vigorous, eager life. All sorts and conditions of men were affected—affected variously—by this unveiling of the reaches of the sea and the tracts of the land—by their discoveries of all sorts and conditions of things. The merchant, the statesman, the man of learning— all were attracted to these newly displayed realms as providing fresh areas for markets and colonies, or fresh material for a more exact physiography. Some at least of the great sailors of the age were prompted by ambitions that were not merely mercenary, though the prospect of acquiring riches was no doubt a common motive enough. Some at least there were

> 'Yearning in desire
> To follow knowledge like a sinking star,
> Beyond the utmost bound of human thought.'

There was no lack of a career for any true son of that age.

'The world was all before' him, 'where to choose.' He might well devote himself to the splendid, however arduous, profession of maritime discoverer. Shakespeare reckons this amongst the lines a young man might take up. To Proteus's father in *The Two Gentlemen of Verona* Panthino says that Antonio wondered Proteus should be allowed to waste his precious moments, when there were so many things to do :

> 'He wonder'd that your lordship
> Would suffer him to spend his youth at home,
> While other men, of slender reputation,
> Put forth their sons to seek preferment out :
> Some to the wars, to try their fortune there ;
> Some *to discover islands far away* ;
> Some to the studious universities.
> For any or for all these exercises
> He said that Proteus your son was meet,
> And did request me to importune you
> To let him spend his time no more at home,
> Which would be great impeachment to his age
> In having known no travel in his youth.'

There are many passages in Shakespeare's plays, to say nothing of his contemporaries, in which is vividly shown the influence on the imagination of the terrestrial explorations carried out with such passionate and triumphant zeal in his day. Men could not rest from travel. The spirit of enterprise was everywhere,

> 'Et mens praetrepidans avet vagari.'

What emphasis that they have now lost to us must many of Shakespeare's phrases that relate to maritime matters have conveyed to Elizabethan ears—how underlined, so to speak, they must have seemed to the reader, how strongly accentuated to the hearer.   When Juliet declares,

> ' My bounty is as boundless as the sea,
> My love as deep,'

the metaphor must have had a freshness that has now somewhat decayed.   To those that first heard that verse the ocean was verily illimitable.   When Rosalind in *As You Like It*, impatient to hear what Celia has to tell, exclaims that ' one inch of delay more is *a South Sea of discovery*,' how specially expressive would the words be at a time when there prevailed only the vaguest conceptions of the extent of the South Sea, and ever and anon were arriving fresh tales of its countless islets and its boundless expanses.   And it would be easy to illustrate much more fully how the Drakes and the Frobishers and the Davises captured the imagination of their age.   But even these famous mariners and their contemporaries did not wholly understand and appreciate—though the British merchants were becoming aware of it—the enormous alteration they had made in the relative position of the British isles as ascertained by their western expeditions—how they had, in fact, transferred England from a corner of the known world to a place in the middle of it, so that it became one of the chief links between the Old World and the New, *i.e.*, between the so-called hemispheres.[1]   In Shakespeare's *King Henry V.*, the French, speaking as our bitter enemies, heap contempt on our race, our habits, our climate, and

---

[1] ' By far the largest amount of land on the globe lies around London as a centre.   If we take London as the centre of a hemisphere, this hemisphere includes six-sevenths of all the land, and is hence called the Land Hemisphere.   The other half, a Water Hemisphere, which has New Zealand as its centre, contains only one-seventh of all the land on the globe' (Meiklejohn's *New Geography on the Comparative Method*, p. 9 of 1898 edition).

even on our poor island itself. The Duke of Bourbon is good enough to describe us as

'Normans, but bastard Normans, Norman bastards'!

and then swears he will even suffer such a frightful punishment as a residence in England, if King Henry is not at once encountered—of course encountered in this case, the chivalry of France taking part, being a synonym with defeated and routed:

> ' Mort de ma vie! If they march along
> Unfought withal, but I will sell my dukedom
> To buy a slobbery and a dirty farm
> In *that nook-shotten isle of Albion.*'

The epithet 'nook-shotten' has been interpreted variously, and we cannot discuss it at length; but we are ourselves very much of opinion that Knight, Staunton, Delius, and others are in the right, who maintain that it means 'an isle thrust or shot or spawned in a corner'—a castaway piece of land thrown down outside the area of civilization, a miserable patch on the remotest surface of the huge continent of Europe and Asia—God-forsaken, man-despised, a pariah of countries. Even were it so, the fervent patriotism of its natives would not have been damped or chilled, but might have rejoiced to quote from a well-known lyric:

> 'Ille terrarum mihi praeter omnes
> Angulus ridet';

but when Shakespeare wrote, that geographical definition had ceased to be applicable. England was no longer 'nook-shotten,' but found itself in the middle of the revised map, in the very heart of the world.

As to the beginnings of the glorious achievements of science in our present use of the term, we can only remind ourselves of the names of Gilbert and of Harvey—of William Gilbert, whose work *De Magnete*, on the Magnet and Magnetic Bodies, and the Earth as a Magnet, published in 1600, may be said to mark the birth-time of the study of electricity, which is now producing results beyond the wildest flights of the wildest fancy; and of William Harvey, some years Gilbert's junior, whose discovery of the circulation of the blood made a memorable epoch in physiology. The brilliant potentialities of the scientific movement had their eloquent and enthusiastic prophet in Francis Bacon.

We have not attempted more than a most general sketch of the conditions under which arose the great Elizabethan age of literature. We are well aware that all such general statements demand additions and qualifications, and cannot possibly be exhaustive. We point out only main aspects, not ignorant that there are many minor ones that might be advantageously presented. It was indeed a time of innumerable departures and activities; and all that can now be done is to emphasize the leading influences and motives. Nor do we forget that during Shakespeare's own life, and even during the best years of it, some of the conditions we have rapidly indicated were already ceasing to exist or act with their first intensity. Fresh problems of many kinds were slowly coming forward for solution, or at all events to be considered and so to distract. No order, social or other, can last for ever; and the arrangement of things about the year 1580 soon began to show that it was merely temporary. In the spheres of politics, religion, learning, literature, and literary style many innovations and developments exhibited themselves. The England of James I. steadily diverged from the England of Queen Elizabeth, as the England of Elizabeth's closing years had diverged from the England of her accession. The world of thought can no more stand still than the globe on which the thinkers dwell. But there are certain periods which a set of new forces make what are called epochs—literary solstices according to the original meaning of the word solstice. And what we have briefly essayed is to specify the paramount agencies that made the Elizabethan epoch what it was, and so in some degree to illustrate its absolute uniqueness in the history of English Literature.

THE AGE OF SHAKESPEARE.

BOOK I.

POETRY.

§ 1. *Introductory.*

THE year 1579 is a very memorable year in the history of English literature. It was the year of Lyly's *Euphues*, and of the version of Plutarch's Lives, by Sir Thomas North, which was to inspire Shakespeare. Above all, it was the year of *The Shepheardes Calendar* of Edmund Spenser, the earliest published poem of the first great English poet since Chaucer.

At the time *The Shepheardes Calendar* was published England can hardly be said to have been in possession of a native poetic literature. The old poets were dead or dying. Chaucer, to most people in the age of Elizabeth, was as unreadable as, unhappily, he is to most people in the twentieth century. His language was strange, his grammar and its inflections had been forgotten: no one could rightly read his verse. The latter fact alone suffices to explain neglect of him. Poets and cultivated men—a Surrey or a Spenser—might love him and partly perceive his greatness; but his consummate art was lost even upon them.

The nearer poets of the time just gone, the poets of *Tottel's Miscellany* (1557) and *The Mirrour for Magistrates* (1559-78)—Sir Thomas Wyatt, the Earl of Surrey, Lord Vaux, Nicholas Grimoald, Thomas Sackville, Earl Buckhurst—hardly yet superseded, were already old-fashioned. In various forms of experimental verse they had reflected the national and religious seriousness of the age just passed away; the tragedy of the Court of Henry VIII., the turmoil and doubt of the reigns of Edward and Mary. They were melancholy and even gloomy. They were no models for the generation growing up through the early years of the great Elizabeth with a deepening sense of national freedom and power.

Very little had yet been done towards the creation of a new poetic literature. George Gascoigne, who died in 1577, a writer of considerable cleverness and some originality, was a forerunner of the new age. He had written prose comedies and tales, had translated from the Greek, had published in the year before his death a serious satire in blank verse, entitled *The Steele Glas*, and reminiscent of *Piers Plowman*, and had left a number of lyrics written with freshness and force, and marked by a metrical handling easier and more graceful than that of Wyatt or Surrey. His work was to some extent an indication of what was coming, but none of it was strong enough to serve as a model.

George Gascoigne.

Quite recently, also, two writers, Barnaby Googe and George Turbervile, had been writing English pastoral poetry. It is a little difficult to say what is meant by 'pastoral' poetry. The scene of a sixteenth-century pastoral poem is laid in an

Googe and Turbervile.

imaginary land, peopled by shepherds and shepherdesses, who keep sheep only for the sake of appearances, and spend their time in moralizing, making love, and lamenting their misfortunes.   A pastoral poem may therefore be a love poem, or it may be primarily didactic or satirical or elegiac: so long as it conforms to the conventions of Arcadia we call it pastoral.   This form of poetry had been developed in England by Barclay [1] from Latin models, and had found a place in *Tottel's Miscellany.*

In 1563 Googe published a book of eclogues containing sundry reflections on love, religion, and the wickedness of the Pope and of Mary Tudor, put into the mouths of shepherds and shepherdesses with classical or Italian names. In 1567 Turbervile published a fluent and sometimes felicitous translation of the Latin eclogues of Mantuan (Battista Spagnoli Mantuanus; died 1516).   Googe was the more original of the two poetasters, but Turbervile furnished perhaps the better model.   The work of these men was certainly not wasted.[2]

In 1576 had appeared a remarkable collection of 124 poems by various authors, entitled *The Paradyse of Daynty Devices.*[3]   In spite of their collective title, these poems

[1] Alexander Barclay (1475-1552), author of the *Ship of Fools*, a paraphrase from the German *Narrenschiff* of Brandt.

[2] Turbervile also translated the 'heroical epistles' of Ovid, and in 1576 published ten 'tragical tales' from the Italian, chiefly from Boccaccio.   Googe published translations of the *Zodiacus Vitae* of Marcellus Palingenius, the *Regnum Papisticum* of Kirchmayer, and the *Proverbs* of Lopes de Mendoza, Marquis of Santillana.   Googe died in 1594, and Turbervile, apparently, still later.

[3] Edited by Richard Edwardes (d. 1566), musician and author of *Palamon and Arcite* and other plays, who contributed many of the pieces.   Other contributors were Lord Vaux, Edward De Vere, Earl of Oxford, Jasper Heywood, D.D. and Jesuit, and William Hunnis, who was a musician as well as a poet.

belonged rather to the period of *The Mirrour for Magistrates*
than to that which was now commencing.
The Paradyse The prevailing tone of them was didactic,
of Daynty solemn, and somewhat melancholy. In one
Devices. of the best of them Lord Vaux bewailed the
sinful and extravagant futility of youth : 'Pardon, I ask
for youth ten thousand times!' But the England of Drake
and Frobisher, Sidney and Raleigh, was renewing its youth
and was in no mood for any repentance.

Finally, in 1578, had been published another miscellaneous collection of poems, entitled *A Gorgious Gallery
of Gallant Inventions.*[1] It is a collection of trivialities ;
but it has considerable significance as illustrating some
evil tendencies of the moment. The poems are full of
alliteration for alliteration's sake. The ingenuity of the
authors is perverted to the base uses of letter-hunting and
the pursuit of far-fetched phrases. There was a strong
tendency at this time towards the publication of verse
which at worst was a kind of literary gymnastic exhibition
and at best was gracefully inane. Verse-making had become to some extent fashionable : it was a game often
played by men of literary culture.

Ever since the 'new learning' had begun to make way
in England, English poetry had been mainly experimental
and imitative. In the absence of any native literary tradition and of good and available English models, our writers
had turned with a commendable humility to the classics
and to the more recent Italian masters. Wyat+ and
Surrey had followed the Italians ; the more originai Sackville had been influenced chiefly by Virgil. The writers of
1579 found themselves in the presence of developed literatures, with the formal perfection and maturity of which

[1] Edited by Thomas Proctor. One of its poems—*The Willow
Song*—is quoted in *Othello.*

English literature could not bear comparison. They were oppressed by the superiority of the classics. It would not have been wonderful had the development of poetry in England been injured and retarded—as it was in France —by a too timid devotion to its models.[1]

It was actually a moot question in the year 1579 whether rhyme should not be altogether discarded and English poetry written for the future in metres consecrated by Greek or Latin usage. A modern English writer, in possession of a native poetic literature immeasurably superior to that of Rome, may be inclined to laugh at such a notion. We may say, with the shallow wisdom of posterity, that such men as Sidney, Dyer, and Thomas Campion ought to have known better. But they did not, and the fact should lead us to reflect.

The question of the adaptation of English to classical metres was first seriously raised in Roger Ascham's *Scholemaster* in 1570. The confused spelling and pronunciation of English at that time made the proposal far more plausible than it would now be. It must be remembered, too, that the spell of the classic literatures was as yet practically unbroken by any great English poet. Almost all the poetic literature produced since the collapse of the

[1] The popularity of the classics was evidenced and their influence strengthened by the work of a number of translators. As far back as 1513, Gavin Douglas had translated the *Aeneid* into couplets, and in 1557 appeared Books II. and IV. done into blank verse by Surrey. A complete translation into atrociously bad verse, begun by Thomas Phaer (d. 1560), and completed by Thomas Twyne (d. 1590), appeared between 1555 and 1562. Arthur Golding published (1565-7) a translation of Ovid's *Metamorphoses* into fluent rhymed couplets of fourteen-syllable lines. Several of the tragedies of Seneca had been translated before 1570. In 1566 Thomas Drant (d. 1578) published a translation into verse of Horace's *Satires*, and in 1567 a version of the *Ars Poetica*.

Roman Empire seemed barbarous in comparison with that of the ancients. No one had yet arisen to teach Englishmen the capacities of their own language. Because the ancients had not used rhyme—rhyme was condemned as barbarous and 'beggarly,' and the invention of it was naïvely ascribed to the Goths and Huns. Since Homer and Virgil had not rhymed, it was absurd, as Ascham put it, 'to follow the Goths in rhyming.'

Thomas Drant, Archdeacon of Lewes, a man of culture and some celebrity as a preacher, translator of the *Ars Poetica* and *Satires* of Horace, drew up rules whereby English might be tortured into pentameters and sapphics, and his rules were very seriously considered by Dyer and by Sidney.

In 1579 Gabriel Harvey, lecturer in rhetoric at Cambridge, author of various works in Latin, a man not only of learning but of shrewdness and humour, was endeavouring to persuade his friend Edmund Spenser to abandon 'rude, beggarly rhyming.' For a short time even Spenser hesitated. Sidney did more than hesitate; and there are many graceless specimens of English classicism in his *Arcadia*. Nor was the question absolutely settled for many years. In 1586 William Webbe, in his *Discourse of English Poetrie*, upheld the principles of Ascham and Harvey. Long poems were actually published in English hexameters.[1] Strangest of all, so late as 1602, Thomas Campion, writer of some of the most beautiful lyrics of the period, in his *Observations on the Art of English Poesie*, argued that 'the

---

[1] Abraham Fraunce published (1587-92) four volumes, each containing much hexameter verse, including translations into hexameter from Tasso, Virgil, and the Psalms. His hexameters seem to be better than those of his contemporaries. English hexameters are interspersed in John Dickenson's *Shepheardes Complaint*, and also in his *Arisbas*, a prose tale published in 1594.

vulgar and artificial custom of rhyming' should be discontinued.

There was more in all this than a misconceiving or over-humble admiration of the classics. Beneath the impracticable demand for English hexameters lay the real need of an unrhymed form of verse. For lyric poetry rhyme is always fitting; but for epic or for serious dramatic poetry rhyme is for many reasons unfitted. Though neither Sidney nor Harvey understood it so, the problem was how to provide for English an unrhymed measure strong and flexible enough for tragic drama or epic narrative. And that problem had already, in a sense, been solved by Henry Howard, Earl of Surrey. But while English 'blank verse' is fatally easy to write, it is exceedingly difficult to write well: so difficult that only a great poet can succeed with it. Until Marlowe arose no one realized the possibilities of Surrey's blank verse.

Almost all the men in whose hands immediately lay the making of English poetry in 1579 were quite young. Those of their elders who had done good work wrote little or had ceased to write. Thomas Sackville was a man of forty-three: he had unhappily entered the region of high politics, and was lost to literature. Judging by the power of the best of his work, the loss was serious. Edward De Vere, Earl of Oxford, was about thirty-five: he had written but little and wrote little more. Sir Edward Dyer, the author of the well-known lines beginning 'My mind to me a kingdom is,'[1] was near forty; he wrote nothing but occasional verse, and little of that. Thomas Churchyard, who had contributed to *Tottel's Miscellany* and to *The Mirrour for Magistrates*, was already a veteran near sixty years old. He continued writing till his death in 1604;

[1] Published in 1588 in Byrd's *Psalms, Sonets, and Songs of Sadness.*

but the length of his literary life is his sole claim to remembrance. There remained the young and untried or scarcely tried men. Of these, Nicholas Breton was about thirty-four and had published his first poems in 1577. He was a good deal the oldest of them. Spenser himself was twenty-seven; Lyly was about twenty-five; Thomas Lodge, whose first book, a prose essay in defence of 'poetry, music, and stage plays,' was published that year, was about twenty-one; Robert Greene had been born in 1560, and his first book appeared in 1580; George Chapman was about the same age as Greene; Thomas Watson, the sonneteer, was twenty-two; Philip Sidney, who began his *Arcadia* in 1580, was twenty-five. Fletcher, the dramatist, was born that year; Ben Jonson and Donne were then six years old; Marlowe and Shakespeare were boys of fifteen.

§ 2. *Sidney and the Sonneteers.*

The fashion in sonneteering was set for England by
Thomas Watson (1557-1592). Philip Sidney; but Thomas Watson, who preceded him in publication, has a claim to share the doubtful honour. In 1582 Watson published his first book of sonnets, under the title: *Hekatompathia or a Passionate Centurie of Love*. The second, *The Teares of Fancie or Love Disdained*, was published after his death, in 1593. Watson was a scholar [1] and excellently read in the Greek, Latin, French, and Italian poets, as his own poems testify. The sonnets of the *Passionate Centurie* are little more than a neatly put together mosaic of lines and phrases taken from his library.

---

[1] He translated the *Antigone* of Sophocles into Latin, wrote a Latin poem entitled *Amyntas* (based on Tasso's *Aminta*), translated songs from Italian, and wrote an elegy on the death of Sir Francis Walsingham. For his sonnets he translates largely from Theocritus, Mantuan, Serafino, and Ronsard.

Some of them are simply translations: nearly all of them are not quatorzains at all, but 18-line ' sonnets.' He left his readers in no doubt about his originality: his anxiety was to be regarded as a man of taste and learning. He appended explanatory notes to his sonnets, giving references to the authorities for his ideas and imagery. A good deal of trouble would have been saved, had later Elizabethan sonneteers followed his example in this respect.

Watson contributed nothing to English literature, but his work has a certain importance for its historian. His *Passionate Centurie* was the first published of a long series of sonnet-books. He was well thought of and must have had some influence in the formation of the taste for such productions. But the outbreak of sonneteering in England did not follow on the publication of the *Passionate Centurie*, but on that of Sidney's *Astrophel and Stella* in 1591.

Philip Sidney, son of Sir Henry Sidney and Mary Dudley, daughter of the Duke of North-
Philip Sidney (1554-1586). umberland, was born in 1554. Elizabeth's Earl of Leicester was his uncle. From his boyhood he is said to have been studious and of a precocious gravity. At Christ Church, Oxford, he was a fellow-student with Richard Hakluyt and William Camden, the antiquary, and with Fulke Greville, afterwards Lord Brooke, with whom he formed a permanent friendship.[1] In 1572 he began a grand tour on the Continent, was in Paris at the time of the massacre of St. Bartholomew, visited Vienna and Venice, and made acquaintance with the Courts of Protestant German princes. At Frankfort he met Hubert Languet, a learned Protestant of the school of Melanchthon, more than thirty years his elder, with whom he maintained a correspondence till Languet's

[1] Fulke Greville's finely written eulogy, miscalled his *Life of Sir Philip Sidney*, was not printed till 1652.

death in 1581. The influence of his elderly friend seems to have confirmed the naturally religious and serious habit of his mind. Soon after his return to England, in 1575, he made the acquaintance of Penelope Devereux, a girl of fourteen, daughter of the Earl of Essex, who was certainly the Stella of the sonnets. There was some talk of the arrangement of a marriage between them, Sidney as prospective heir of the Earl of Leicester being at that time a highly eligible person. However, in 1578 Penelope's mother herself married the Earl, and so had no further use for Sidney, and in 1581 Penelope was married to Lord Rich.[1] In 1577 Sidney was sent on a formal diplomatic mission to Vienna, and there he showed his enthusiasm for Protestantism and his ignorance of politics by haranguing the Emperor Rudolph on the danger threatening Germany from the combination of Spain and the Papacy. After his return from Vienna he lived about the Court or with his sister, Lady Pembroke, busying his idleness with literature and philosophic discussion, and interesting himself in exploration and projects of colonization. In 1583 he married Frances Walsingham, daughter of the great Secretary. His *Arcadia* was written in 1580-1; the *Astrophel and Stella* poems were probably completed in 1582-3. None of his writings were published in his own lifetime, but they were circulated freely in manuscript. The *Arcadia* appeared in print only in 1590, and *Astrophel and Stella* in 1591.[2] At the commencement of war with

[1] Later on she left her husband to become the mistress of Sir Charles Blount, afterwards Earl of Devonshire. Many years later Blount told King James that Penelope had been married ' against her will unto one against whom she did protest at the ceremony.'

[2] The first edition of *Astrophel and Stella* was pirated and was incomplete. Eight more of the sonnets were published only in 1592, along with Constable's *Diana*. The complete edition of Sidney's works in 1598 added a few others.

Spain, Sidney was sent to command at Flushing. He was mortally wounded at Zutphen, and died a few weeks later in October, 1586. Except for its heroic close it was an uneventful life: and there is nothing in Sidney's recorded actions or in his writings to justify the immense reputation he seems to have enjoyed in his lifetime.

As a poet Sidney had talent, but his talent was not strong enough to free him from constant affectation and imitation. It is difficult to understand how anyone with a poet's ear could have written the wretched sapphics and asclepiads of his *Arcadia*. He was essentially an imitator and never mastered his models.[1] With a real enthusiasm for letters, he did not often rise above the level of a clever and cultivated dilettante. Like De Vere and others of the earlier courtly poets, he played at making verses. For all his experiments in metre, he created nothing of value. The importance of Sidney's work is, however, considerable. It is just possible that without the *Astrophel and Stella* we should not have had Shakespeare's sonnets. But it is necessary to guard against the tendency to confuse historical importance with literary value. Sidney's reputation seems to have gained by such confusion. Yet it is true that in Sidney's poems as a whole there resides a subtle and delicate charm, which seems not to be due to the purely poetic power of their author. The high, chivalrous, enthusiastic mind of the writer, romantic rather than poetic, dwelling in the half realities of his Arcadia, has given them a tenderness, a chastity of colour, an unworldly nobility that is precious and rare.

The verse of the *Arcadia* is especially disappointing. Of poetic power there is hardly a trace. Sidney here

---

[1] He translated or adapted freely from Petrarch, Desportes, and Ronsard, Some of his best poems are adaptations from the French.

seems to aim chiefly at a display of dexterity; and his dexterity shows itself chiefly in ingenious contrivance or adaptation of ugly or unsuitable metrical forms. He manifests a childish love of quasi-comic rhyming: ' extortion — delightfulness — portion — rightfulness — superfluities—sightfulness — incongruities —lamentations—congruities—consolations.' He loves to keep a rhyme going as long as possible : it is a point in the game. He comes perilously near doggerel. He labours description, but rarely or never makes a picture.[1] A passionless extravagance, 'frigid and jejune,' as Hazlitt said, characterizes the love-songs. He is at his best, in the *Arcadia*, when he is moralizing. He is pithy then, sometimes, and even witty.[2]

All his best verse is in the *Astrophel and Stella*. This consists of a series of sonnets and lyric pieces or songs in various measures,[3] ideally connected in that they are all supposed to express some phase of the poet's feeling in relation to his mistress.[4] Critics have been much exercised as to how far these poems represent the real feelings of the poet towards a real person. Only the poet himself could accurately answer the question. A poet's love-song may be written out of his personal emotion at the moment; or it may be begotten by his imagination on

[1] See the long description of Philoclea (No. 17), minute without definition, and extravagant without warmth.

[2] See the passage in which Geron exhorts Histor to marry (71).

[3] Very few of Sidney's sonnets are constructed in the true Petrarchan manner, though he ordinarily uses the Petrarchan octave. But of the 108 sonnets, 85 have the closing rhymed couplet which had already appeared in *Tottel's Miscellany*. A good many are in a form distinctively French.

[4] It is probable that we have them in the order in which Sidney desired to present them; but the significance of the order is doubtful.

his experience. That experience, again, may be strictly personal, in that the poet may at one time have felt what he now expresses; or it may be the experience of observation only. A very true lover may write a very halting and unconvincing sonnet; but Shakespeare can write a sonnet of concentrated passion out of mere knowledge of his own mind and observation of the minds of others, without ever having felt any overwhelming devotion to any single woman.

Penelope Devereux (Stella) was married to Lord Rich, and Sidney, in the *Astrophel and Stella*, is in the position of a man who discovers the depth of his love for a woman only when he is bound in honour to fight against his desire.[1] If the poems are really a record of passion tragically thwarted and finally suppressed, it is somewhat strange that this passion should have needed so much help from Petrarch and Desportes in expressing itself.[2] Many of the sonnets seem touched by real feeling, but many others are more or less ingenious, cold, and tiresome conceits from the French or Italian. Love lurks in dark bush, which is Stella's eyes, and from thence shoots the poor poet unawares: he calls to his friends to fly the dangerous spot. Venus, angry with Cupid for not having sufficiently stimulated Mars, breaks his bow and arrows; but grandam Nature takes pity on the crying boy and makes him two nice new bows out of Stella's eyebrows, and finds any number of arrows for him in her eyes. In the first sonnet of the series Sidney represents himself as 'studying inventions fine her wits to entertain.' Then, while he bit his pen and beat himself for lack of ideas,

---

[1] Some of the sonnets may, however, have been written before Penelope's marriage.

[2] Strange also that he should have made the record of such a passion public property.

'Fool,' said my muse to me, 'look in thy heart and write.'
He might, perhaps, have done well to take her advice; but
instead of doing so he looked into Ronsard and Petrarch.

On the other hand, by comparison with the work of the
ordinary Elizabethan sonneteer, Sidney's sonnets are remarkably sincere.   A considerable number of them reflect
a genuine regret and tenderness, and a desire which, though
heightened by poetic licence, had nevertheless an actual
existence.   Many have a tender or pathetic gracefulness
quite distinctive and beautiful; his best verse, perhaps,
is to be found not in the sonnets, but in the songs of the
Astrophel and Stella.   Very charmingly imagined are the
verses beginning 'In a grove most rich of shade,' and the
song headed 'Love is Dead' is brilliantly conceived and
written.   And there is the insolence and audacity of true
love in the lines that follow :

> 'Who hath the eyes *that marry state with pleasure ?*
> Who keeps the key of Nature's chiefest treasure?
>   To you, to you, all song of praise is due—
> Only for you the Heav'n forgate all measure !
>
> 'Who hath the lips where wit in fairness reigneth ?
> Who womankind at once both decks and staineth ?
>   To you, to you, all song of praise is due—
> *Only by you Cupid his crown maintaineth !*' . . .
>   (Song after Sonnet 58.)

Contemporary admiration of Sidney was due partly to
the charm of his personality, and partly, perhaps, to his
social position.   It was natural that professional writers
should glorify a brother poet so highly connected.   But Sidney's sonnets were certainly very superior to any previously
written in English.   Admirers of the French sonneteers
could now read English sonnets which matched theirs:
for though Sidney never attained the melancholy beauty
of such a sonnet as Ronsard's *Quand vous serez bien vieille,*

his work was at least equal to that of the greatly admired
Desportes. His success was such that, for some years after
the publication of *Astrophel and Stella*, the production of
sonnet sequences of similar structure, addressed to a more
or less real mistress, was a dominant literary fashion.
Actual reading of these sonnet-books might incline one to
the opinion that Sidney's influence on English poetic
literature was chiefly malign. But in one respect it was
of real value. Like all romanticists, he had appealed to
nature. He had proclaimed love, love unadorned, a worthy
and sufficient theme for the poet. The success of poems
written on such a principle, at a time when Euphuism
threatened to make of lyric a scholastic exercise, must
have been really valuable.

Some of the most considerable poets and many of the
most inconsiderable poetasters of the time
followed the fashion of the years 1591-7,
and published sonnet-series constructed more
or less closely on the model of *Astrophel and Stella*. The
sonnet-books of Daniel, Constable, Lodge, Barnes, Drayton,
Spenser, and the poetasters resemble each other closely in
all points of structure. Some consist only of sonnets, some
of sonnets interspersed with lyric pieces in various measures.
All consist of a series of short poems supposed to be concerned with the same lady. None of them are constructed
so as to tell a story. The lady, if not an absolute fiction,
is always a mere name: in Spenser's *Amoretti* she is named
once, incidentally. Certain conventions are almost invariably followed. The lady is cold and 'cruel'; the lover
laments, implores, rages, and is frequently at the point
of death. All these sonnet-books, with the exception of
Spenser's, are essentially imitative and conventional. The
work of the mere poetasters is not worth comment. Giles
Fletcher, father of Giles and Phineas, William Percy,

The sonnet-
books.

Richard Linche, Bartholomew Griffin, William Smith, Robert Tofte, and others whose very names are unknown, all published sonnet-books, all alike feebly fantastic, extravagant and silly, affected and pretentious.[1] The sonnet-books of Daniel, Constable, Barnes, Lodge, and Drayton demand a little more attention.[2]

Samuel Daniel's sonnets to *Delia* were published early in 1592.[3] Their popularity was considerable, and they probably helped to fix the fashion set by Sidney as well as the form of the Elizabethan sonnet.[4] Daniel followed Desportes closely, in one case very literally translating a sonnet of his master without a word of acknowledgement. His best-known sonnet, that addressed to 'Care-charmer Sleep,'[5] is adapted from various

[side note: Daniel's *Delia.]*

[1] Fletcher's *Licia* was published in 1593; Percy's *Coelia* and a series called *Zepheria* in 1594; *Alcilia* by J. C. in 1595; Linche's *Diella*, Griffin's *Fidessa*, and Smith's *Chloris* in 1596; Tofte's *Laura* and Locke's *Sundrie Sonets* in 1597.

[2] The Elizabethans adopted various forms of sonnet, and the same writer often makes use of different forms. The true Petrarchan form, afterwards adopted by Milton, was very rarely used after Sidney. The Elizabethans broke the Petrarchan sonnet into three quatrains—generally quite disconnected in rhyme—and a final couplet. The final couplet is almost invariably present. The form most commonly used was that popularized by Daniel and used by Shakespeare. In Drayton's *Idea* we find the rhymes—excluding the final couplet—arranged in the following different ways: a b b a a c c a d b b d; a b b a c d d c e f f e (Daniel's form); a b b a a b b a c d d c; a b a b c c d d e f e f.

[3] Some of them had already appeared, affixed to the first edition of *Astrophel and Stella*. An augmented edition appeared in 1594. *Delia* was Daniel's first poetical work. His sonnets are praised by Spenser in *Colin Clout*.

[4] Daniel did not invent the form of sonnet which he adopted and popularized. It appears in *Tottel's Miscellany*.

[5] The 'Sommeil chasse-soin' of De Brach and De Baïf. Cf. the lines 'Care-charming Sleep' in Fletcher's *Valentinian*.

French sources. His pensiveness and the gravity and lucidity of his diction distinguish him from the ordinary sonneteer of his time. He thinks more seriously than Drayton or Lodge, and falls far less often into the puerile or the absurd. Now and again he writes singularly happy and beautiful lines, as when he invokes Apollo:

        ' O clear-eyed Rector of the holy hill '—

or:

    ' A modest maid, decked with a blush of honour,
    Whose feet do tread green paths of youth and love.'

But Daniel was not born to be a poet of love. He has no semblance of passion, and some of his addresses to his mistress are almost paternal in tone.[1]

Henry Constable (1562-1613) published a very typical sonnet-book, entitled *Diana*, also in 1592.[2] His model was Philippe Desportes, who was more imitated by English writers than any other French poet. Constable's sonnets are often ingenious, sometimes graceful, and always conventional. It is worth while to quote one of them, for its typical character and its resemblance to a sonnet of Shakespeare (No. 99):

Constable's Diana.

    ' My lady's presence makes the roses red,
    Because to see her lips they blush for shame:
    The lily's leaves for envy pale became ;
    And her white hands in them this envy bred.

---

[1] For Daniel see § 4, p. 51.

[2] Constable, a St. John's College, Cambridge, man, of good family, was a Roman Catholic, and on his returning from France without leave in 1603 or thereabouts, he was imprisoned for a time in the Tower. An augmented edition of his *Diana* appeared in 1594 ; others in 1597, 1604, and 1859. One of Desportes' heroines was a Diana. Constable wrote also religious sonnets which were not published in his lifetime, and a few lyrics by him were included in *England's Helicon*.

> The Marigold abroad the leaves doth spread,
> Because the sun's and her power is the same ;
> The Violet of purple colour came,
> Dyed with the blood she made my heart to shed.
> In brief : all flowers from her their virtue take ;
> From her sweet breath their sweet smells do proceed ;
> The living heat which her eye beams do make
> Warmeth the ground and quickeneth the seed.
> The rain, wherewith she watereth the flowers,
> Falls from mine eyes, which she dissolves in showers.'

This may be regarded as a fairly typical Elizabethan sonnet: typical in its conventionality, its confusion of thought, its trivial grace, its total lack of passion, and its occasional sweetness of phrasing. The declaration that the beauty of flowers, and indeed all the beauty of the world, is a reflection of that of the beloved, or otherwise, that the flowers have stolen from her, is a commonplace of the love-poetry of the time. This is no mere conceit, since it may be that the beauty of his mistress reveals to the lover for the first time the beauty of a flower. But the Elizabethan poet must needs illogically extend the thought with a puerile fancifulness: 'Because to see her lips they blush for shame'! The shame of the roses and the envy of the lilies seal the poem with the seal of unreality.

Barnaby Barnes, son of Richard Barnes, Bishop of Durham, published in 1593 a curious series of sonnets under the title *Partheno-phil and Parthenophe.*[1] This little book, besides regular sonnets, contains a number of 'madrigals' in various irregular and lifeless lyric measures. Barnes occasionally writes a melodious quatrain, and a few of his poems are really graceful; but the mass of his verse is a

Barnaby Barnes
(1569-1609).

---

[1] In 1595 Barnes published a collection of religious sonnets entitled *A Divine Centurie of Spirituall Sonnets.*

tissue of extravagances, absurdities, and affectations in the
very worst Elizabethan manner.   He would not be worthy
of being in any way distinguished from the crowd, but for
the fact that he may have been the rival referred to by
Shakespeare in some of his sonnets (Nos. 78-86).   Shakespeare writes of the 'proud full sail' of a rival's 'great
verse,' attributing to this rival a kind of inspiration, as
'by spirits taught to write above a mortal pitch.'   If
Barnes were the poet thus referred to, Shakespeare must
in mock modesty have been flattering his patron by such
references to the poet his patron favoured.   But whether
the rival poet were Barnes or Chapman or Drayton or
some other is a point of no importance to literature, and
one that cannot be determined on the evidence, which, in
fact, amounts to hardly anything.

In 1593, also, appeared Lodge's *Phillis*, on the whole
the most charming of the minor Elizabethan
Lodge's *Phillis*.   sonnet-series.   The charm of the forty
poems composing this little book lies not
in the sonnets proper, which, though pretty enough, are
distinguished only by the clever employment of metrical
devices for the sake of sound, and are inferior to Daniel's,
but in the pastoral lyrics numbered among them.[1]

In 1594 Michael Drayton published a sonnet-series
entitled *Ideas Mirrour, Amours in Quator-
Drayton's *Idea*.   zains*.[2]   His sonnets are neither more nor
less conventional and imitative than those
of Lodge or Daniel.   'My verse is the true image of my

---

[1] For Lodge cf. p. 59. In his sonnets he, like the rest, steals from
Desportes, borrowing both single conceits, retail, and complete
sonnets, wholesale.

[2] The title is significant of the imitative character of the poems.
The French sonnet-books were frequently called Amours : *Amours
de Méline*, and so on. In 1579 Claude de Pontoux had published
a book called *Sonnets de l'Idée*. Or Drayton's title might have

mind,' he declares : ' I am no pickpurse of another's wit.'
The second of these assertions is actually taken word for
word from Sidney. As a rule Drayton filches not from
Sidney, but from the fashionable Desportes. At their best
—one being excepted—his sonnets are as graceful as those
of Constable and a trifle stronger. But they are full of
the elaboration of pointless and puerile fancies, and of far-
fetched imagery that says nothing. Occasionally Drayton
writes fine lines, and sometimes he opens a sonnet well and
continues miserably.

> ' Love in a humour played the prodigal
> And bade my senses to a solemn feast '

is a fine opening. But we go on to read how his Heart
was, unfortunately, invited also, and how Love, having got
drunk on his tears and sighs, proceeded to murder his
poor Heart. His conceits are frequently of the lowest
degree of frigidity. His love has murdered his heart; her
lips are scarlet with its blood, the Boy who did the deed
lurks in her eye, her face is pale with the horror of it :
murder will out !

But there is one sonnet so magnificent in its restrained
passion, so true in tone, so perfect in the simplicity of its
beautifully balanced diction, that we find it with astonish-
ment among the crudities and trivialities of *Ideas Mirrour* :[1]

> ' Since ther's no help, come let us kiss and part :
> Nay, I have done, you get no more of me ;
> And I am glad—yea, glad with all my heart—
> That thus so cleanly I myself can free.

---

been suggested by Du Bellay's beautiful sonnet : *Si nostre vie est
moins qu'une journée.*

[1] According to Rossetti, one of the five or six greatest sonnets in
English. This sonnet, however, did not appear in any early
edition of the *Idea*, but was first printed in the 1619 Drayton
folio. Sonnets 37 and 44 approach it most nearly.

Shake hands for ever, cancel all our vows—
And when we meet at any time again,
Be it not seen in either of our brows
That we one jot of former love retain.
Now, at the last gasp of love's latest breath,
When, his pulse failing, passion speechless lies,
When faith is kneeling by his bed of death
And innocence is closing up his eyes,
    Now, if thou would'st, when all have given him over,
    From death to life thou might'st him yet recover.' [1]

Sir William Alexander's sonnet-series *Aurora*, though not published till 1604, probably belongs to this period, since he describes it as containing ' the first fancies of the author's youth.' Alexander (1567?-1640) was distinguished as a statesman and became Earl of Stirling. He published a large quantity of verse, chiefly on religious or scriptural subjects. His largest poem, *Doomes-day or the great day of the Lords Judgement,* is in eleven thousand lines. He translated the Psalms into verse and published several tragedies.

Fulke Greville's *Coelica,* published only in 1633, may probably have been written during the early years of sonneteering; but it is not a series of the same kind as the *Idea* or the *Diana.*

The publication of collections of religious sonnets was also fashionable in these years (1591-7). In addition to Constable's religious sonnets, circulated in manuscript, and the publication of Barnes, we have Chapman's *Coronet for his Mistress Philosophie* (1594) and Henry Lok or Locke's *Sundrie Sonets of Christian Passions* (1597).

In 1595 Sir John Davies circulated in manuscript *Nine Gullinge Sonnets,* caricature parodies of the prevailing fashion.

---

[1] Drayton's sonnets contain many parallels in subject or treatment with those of Shakespeare. Controversy has arisen as to which was the imitator. Both owe something to the strains of *Astrophel.* As a whole, however, the vintage of Drayton's early poetry is pre-eminently Spenserian. See p. 46; and Prof. Elton's *Introduction to Drayton,* 1895.

In 1595 Edmund Spenser published a set of eighty-
eight sonnets under the title *Amoretti*.[1] The
Spenser's
Amoretti.
series did not purport to be addressed to any
particular woman, and several of the sonnets
are not poems of love at all. A few are wholly expressive
of a religious aspiration (62 and 63), and in one (80)
Spenser represents himself as 'sporting' his Muse in an
interval of rest from serious work on *The Faerie Queene*.
As he was married a year after their publication, he was
inevitably thinking while he wrote them of the girl who
became his wife. In any case they are not such mere
play as the sonnets of Drayton and Lodge: they are
highly characteristic of his religious temperament and his
peculiar idealism. His mistress is to him, at times, more
than a mere woman. She becomes 'a glorious image of
the Maker's beauty' (61), an earthly manifestation of that
'heavenly ray' (87) which illumines the dull world, a type
of the eternal beauty, 'full of the living fire kindled
above' (8). There is hardly anything of sex in his love.
She raises him above passion:

> 'That being now with her huge brightness dazed
> Base thing I can no more endure to view' (3).

Beside the vision of the divine in her all is naught:

> 'All this world's glory seemeth vain to me
> And all their shows but shadows, saving she.'

Her eyes are likened to God himself:

> 'Whose light doth lighten all that here we see.'

But he is not always in this mood, and when he descends
from these platonic altitudes he generally becomes quite

---

[1] No mistress is invoked by name on the title as in the ordinary
sonnet-book, though the name is revealed in Sonnet 74. Cf. p. 40.

conventional in theme. Sometimes, indeed, he writes beautifully of the lady's wedded lowliness and loftiness (13 and 21) and of the pride of her purity (5 and 6) in a strain unknown to the ordinary sonneteer. With in- fallible instinct he avoids all base or gross mistakes, but a very large proportion of his sonnets are of the most con- ventional type. He represents his lady as a beautiful but carnivorous creature : in one sonnet she is a lion, in another a tiger, in a third a panther. Her cruelty is a constantly recurring theme. She is an angler who smiles on her dying victims so sweetly that they enjoy dying, a cruel dolphin who will not come to Arion, a new Pandora; her beauty is but a bait; she binds men in the golden net of her hair : again and again he begs her piteously not to slay him outright. Spenser's sonnets are a little disap- pointing, but they are beautiful pieces of workmanship, and very superior to any previously published in English. He had not sufficient power of concentration for the writing of perfect sonnets, nor did the sonnets afford him scope for the exercise of his greatest faculty, that of verbal painting. His thought is thin and he has no passion. The absence of earthly passion is a beauty in some of his sonnets : in most it is a felt want. But all of them are melodious, with a subtle, fine melody, not rich and deep and varied as Shakespeare's, and indeed distinctly mono- tonous, but rare and beautiful. However conventional his theme, he is always the exquisite artist in words. When he tells us (64) that his mistress is like ' a garden of sweet flowers,' he is dealing with a hackneyed fancy : but the names of the flowers stand like real posies in the sweet verse. The monotony of his effects may be partly due to the peculiar form of sonnet which he adopted.[1] He retains

[1] He rhymes his sonnets thus : a b a b b c b c c d c d - e e. He adheres to this form almost invariably. In one sonnet, but in

the ending couplet, but links his three quatrains by repetition of rhymes, producing a flowing stanza broken
abruptly at the close. He manages it exquisitely, but
finds it difficult to vary; and the closing couplet is something of a stumbling-block.

The sonnets of Shakespeare were given to the world
in 1609 by Thomas Thorpe,[1] a publishing
understrapper of piratical habits, who procured the 'copy' no one knows how, but
who almost certainly published the poems without their
author's consent. It is impossible to say precisely within
what years these sonnets were written. Meres, in 1598,
speaks of Shakespeare's 'sugred sonnets among his private
friends.' This proves that some considerable number of
them were at that time circulating in manuscript. The
line 'Lilies that fester smell far worse than weeds' occurs
in Sonnet 94, and in the play entitled *Edward III.*, written
about 1594. But there is nothing to show whether the
sonnet quoted the play, or the play the sonnet. In 1599
two of Shakespeare's sonnets (138 and 144) were published
in *The Passionate Pilgrim.* One of the series (107) has
been supposed to refer to the release from prison of the
Earl of Southampton in 1603. In spite, however, of the

The Sonnets of
Shakespeare.

only one, he adopts the common and Shakespearean form (No. 8).
In two others he varies his chosen form only by turning the last
line into a line of twelve syllables. In others he adopts double
rhymes—resounded, rebounded—and makes the final syllable an
eleventh. (See the beautiful No. 19.)

[1] Thomas Thorpe (fl. 1580-1624), a humble member of the
Stationers' Company, was apparently a kind of literary jackal,
who, in the absence of any regular copyright protection for authors,
hung about scriveners' shops, and from time to time, collusively,
'picked up' a manuscript in which he could 'deal.' This particular find was brought out by G. Eld 'for T. T.,' with the bald
title, *Shakespeare's Sonnets. Never before Imprinted. 1609.*

dearth of evidence, it may be regarded as probable that a very large proportion of Shakespeare's sonnets were written during the height of the sonnet craze, in the years 1593-7. Having regard to the character of the plays produced after 1599, it seems improbable that he wrote more than a very few sonnets after that year.

The order in which the sonnets were published by Thorpe is retained in the ordinary modern editions. That order involved a rough, and, to all appearance, a careless division of the sonnets into groups, according to apparent subject. As Shakespeare made no protest against the publication, and did not issue any corrected edition, it is a good inference that he did not positively object to the order which Thorpe gave to the sonnets; an inference that he approved of that order would obviously be unjustified. There is no evidence that Thorpe's order corresponds with anything in the actual chronology of the sonnets, or that the sonnets of each group formed by him were addressed to the same person. There is no proof that Thorpe knew who the persons addressed were, if indeed there were any such persons.

Many of the sonnets are formally addressed to a man, and others, as certainly, to a woman. But a large number might, so far as the language used goes, be addressed to either man or woman. In the case of these there can be no certainty. The first seventeen sonnets in Thorpe's order form a well-defined group. They are all exhortations to some person not to allow his or her beauty to perish utterly for lack of heirs. The language of No. 3 proves that sonnet to have been addressed to a man: no such inference can be drawn from the language of No. 2 or of No. 4. Not one of these seventeen sonnets, however, is manifestly addressed to a woman. There remains a probability, the degree of which cannot be accurately

estimated, that they are all addressed to a man. But the
fact that Thorpe placed them together scarcely heightens
this probability.

The most natural supposition would be that all the
adulatory sonnets addressed to a man were addressed to
the Earl of Southampton, a known patron of Shakespeare,
to whom he dedicated the *Venus and Adonis* and the
Lucrece. Elizabethan literature is full of such adulation
of patrons, extravagant and, as it were, candidly insincere.
In the supposition that these sonnets were addressed to
Southampton there is no inherent difficulty. It must be
remembered also that when we speak of a sonnet as
addressed to some one we do not necessarily mean that it
expresses either the poet's personal feeling or the poet's
desire to flatter. Shakespeare may have addressed to
Southampton sonnets without any personal reference,
purely ideal in theme, just as he addressed to him the
Venus and Adonis.

Unfortunately for everyone who cares for the sonnets,
Thorpe prefixed to his edition a dedication in the following
terms: ' To the onlie begetter of these insuing sonnets,
Mr. W. H., all happinesse and that eternitie promised by
our ever-living poet, wisheth the well-wishing adventurer
in setting forth.' This dedication throws doubt on the
natural hypothesis by introducing a mysterious W. H. as
the ' onlie begetter ' of the sonnets.

There is absolutely nothing to show who this W. H. was
or what is meant by ' onlie begetter.' Begetter may mean
inspirer or it may mean simply procurer. If it refers
simply to the person who got (begot) the sonnets for
Thorpe, then it is of no importance what that person's
name was. The question has no bearing whatever on the
sonnets. If ' begetter ' means inspirer, then, whoever
W. H. was, Thorpe is convicted of a gross inaccuracy

For the sonnets were certainly not all inspired by the same person, and the word 'only' is absurd. But, in this case, there is nothing to show whether W. H. was Southampton or some other patron, or simply some unknown young man whom Shakespeare loved. The theories on the subject are a mere mass of assumption and guessing. It almost seems as though writers on the sonnets considered themselves bound to come to some positive conclusion on the evidence. But there is no evidence worth considering. There is nothing to show whether (a) all the sonnets addressed to a man were addressed to Southampton, or (b) to some other hypothetical patron, or (c) whether some of them were addressed to a patron and some to an unknown friend; and, unless it be assumed that Thorpe possessed at least some accurate information, there is no evidence that any of these things were so.

The barren and hopeless controversy maintained upon these questions is the more singular because most of the questions raised have no sort of bearing on the sonnets. It would indeed be interesting to know that Shakespeare actually addressed sonnets of passionate endearment to a young man who was not his patron. And it would be interesting to know that he carried on a painful intrigue with a married woman. But even this knowledge would not throw much light on the sonnets themselves. And, as matters stand, there is simply no reason to suppose that any one of the sonnets was 'addressed' to anybody except in a merely complimentary manner, as *Venus and Adonis* was to Southampton. Mr. George Wyndham well says that critics have turned to the sonnets intent on finding in them the writer of the plays instead of caring for the sonnets themselves. They have only succeeded in heaping about the sonnets a mass of biographical speculation calculated to make any approach to them difficult.

The sonnets themselves are among the most splendid legacies left by Elizabethan England. They are unequal, and, to a certain extent, they are conventional. Such sonnets as Nos. 153-154 are poor examples of a thoroughly conventional style. If Shakespeare did not draw directly from the French, he yet drew largely on the common stock of fancies and affectations. He absorbed a good deal that was current and worthless, made sonnets on conventional themes, and possibly even in conscious rivalry or imitation. Certainly he gained nothing by so doing. Apart from comparative excellence of imagination and execution, there are certain marked differences between Shakespeare's sonnets and those of his contemporaries. That so many of Shakespeare's sonnets are addressed to a man is of itself remarkable, and widely differentiates his series from those of Daniel, Lodge, Drayton, and Spenser. Again, the ordinary Elizabethan sonneteer addresses his poems to a maiden, very fair and very cold. He pleads, weeps, despairs, rages or curses; he has little or no hope; he is dying of desire; he exalts her beauty and his own wretchedness with every extravagance he can devise. With Shakespeare all this is altered. He does not plead or despair, and his dark lady is his mistress in the fullest sense. If he rages, it is not against her coldness, but against himself and her irresistible charm. He does not exalt her beauty; he throws doubt on it. He is not sure that she is beautiful to anyone but himself. He cannot love her without dishonour, and she is not only false in loving him, but is false to him. His passion is tragic with the tragedy of real life, while his contemporaries deal with the fictitious tragedy of youthful inexperience.

Some of Shakespeare's sonnets are trivial literary exercises in the fashion of the day (as Nos. 153-154); most are the work of a consummate poetic artist, some may be the outcome of actual passionate experience (Nos. 129 or 141). Some are evidently written simply for the sake of their splendid imagery and melody. Others have the note of true personal feeling. Two poets—and only two—of the Elizabethan age produced love poetry in which the true note of absolute passion is struck—Shakespeare and Donne. But comparison of the two reveals the fact that, while Donne seems sometimes to set down his impressions hot and crude, in Shakespeare the passion is always mastered by the artist.

§ 3. *Spenser and the Pastoral.*

Edmund Spenser was born in London in 1552. Very little indeed is known of his parentage or early life. He was educated at Merchant Taylors' and at Pembroke Hall (now College), Cambridge, and probably spent considerable part of his early life in the then remote and wild county of Lancashire. Gabriel Harvey [1] became a Fellow of Pembroke the year after Spenser's entrance as a sizar, and the two formed a lasting friendship. Harvey's influence seems to have been somewhat dangerous for a time, since, so late as 1580, after the publication of *The Shepheardes Calendar*, Spenser was engaged upon English hexameters. But such genius as Spenser's could not have been permanently misled by theory, and Harvey did the poet good service if, as is probable, he introduced him to Philip Sidney about the year 1577. By Sidney he was introduced to Leicester, and he seems to have resided for some time both at Penshurst and at Leicester's house in the Strand. In 1579 *The Shepheardes Calendar* was published. In 1580, no doubt through Leicester's influence, Spenser obtained the position of private secretary to Lord Grey of

---

[1] See § 1, p. 6.

Wilton, recently appointed Lord-Lieutenant of Ireland.
From that time Spenser's home was in Ireland. Preferment in Ireland was, no doubt, not a very desirable form
of preferment; but Spenser, though he complained, seems
to have had little to complain of. For some ten years
after 1580 he held one official 'appointment or another,
and at an uncertain date between 1580 and 1590 he received a grant of Kilcolman Castle and 3,028 acres of land
in the county of Cork.[1] In 1589 he visited England,
taking with him to London the first three books of *The
Faerie Queene*; and in 1591 he was granted a pension of
£50 from the Crown.   Kilcolman was his home from that
time until the final catastrophe. In June, 1594, probably
at Youghal, he married Elizabeth Boyle, a cousin of the
'Great Earl' of Cork.   In 1595 he published, in a
single volume, *Colin Clout's come Home again*, the
Amoretti, and the *Epithalamium*.   Later that year he was
again in London with three more books of *The Faerie
Queene*. He remained in London till 1597, making a
friend of the Earl of Essex and writing the *Hymns to
Heavenly Love and Heavenly Beauty* and the *Prothalamium*.   In September, 1598, he was appointed Sheriff
of County Cork.   In October his house was plundered and
burnt by the wild Irish, he himself with his wife and
children barely escaping with their lives.   It is uncertain,
indeed, whether all of them did escape: according to a
statement made by Ben Jonson, a baby child perished.
Spenser reached London momentarily penniless and apparently physically broken. He died on January 16th, 1599, at
a tavern in King Street, Westminster, and was buried,
close to Chaucer, in Westminster Abbey.

It is remarkable that so little should be known of the

---

[1] Part of the forfeited property of the Earl of Desmond.

life of the greatest, putting aside Shakespeare, of the Elizabethan poets. This is probably due to the fact that so much of his life was passed in Ireland. It is certainly not due to any lack of appreciation of his work by his contemporaries. From the time of the publication of *The Shepheardes Calendar* (1579), Spenser seems to have been regarded as the greatest poet of the day, the successor to the throne of Chaucer. Drayton wrote that that poem was alone sufficient to immortalize the writer. Webbe, in 1586, pronounced Spenser the first of all English poets. Nash, on the publication of the first three books of *The Faerie Queene*, hailed him as the laureate of England.

The Shepheardes Calendar, the first poem by an Englishman of poetic genius since Chaucer, consists of twelve eclogues, each headed with the name of a month. There is some pretence of relating the content or tone of each eclogue to the character of the month under which it stands; and there is also some pretence that the poems as a whole are concerned with the unhappy love of a certain Colin Clout. Actually there is no connection between the different eclogues: they are separate poems, and Colin himself appears in only three of them.

Before the publication of *The Shepheardes Calendar*, Spenser had, of course, already written verses. As early as 1569 he had published a number of 'Sonets,'[1] and since that time he had written but not published a number of pieces, some of which are now lost.[2] He had been experimenting in rhyme and in classical metres, and he was still unsatisfied. But he was already in revolt against Harvey's classicism. Edward Kirke, who acted as sponsor and editor of the poem, adding 'arguments,' explanatory

[1] As letterpress to plates in a curious book 'devised by S. John van-der Noodt,' and known as *The Theatre of Voluptuous Worldlings*.

[2] *The Faerie Queene* had been begun by April, 1580.

notes, and a long letter of commendation addressed to
Harvey, states that Spenser, having 'long wandered in the
common labyrinth of love,' wrote his eclogues 'to warn
(as he saith) the young shepherds, his equals, and com-
panions of his unfortunate folly.' Spenser may have said
so, but it is obviously not true. He wrote the poems first
to please himself, and secondly, with the object of experimenting in metre and language. Chaucer had already
convinced him of the worthiness of English, and that
there was no need of borrowing from French, Italian, or
Latin. 'They have made our English tongue a galli-
maufry or hodge-podge of all other speeches,' he told
Kirke. He chose to write pastoral eclogues for this his
first great experiment, because the pastoral form enabled
him to write about anything or nothing, and to vary his
measures as much as he pleased. Naturally, he turned to
Virgil and Ovid, Theocritus and Bion and Mantuan, and
even to Googe and Turbervile; but his chief models
were Chaucer—the Tityrus of the *Calendar*—and Clement
Marot, the French Protestant poet, whose religiousness
attracted him. He set to work to make for himself and
for other English poets a language apart, a language
made out of Chaucer and Lancashire dialect and the
polite speech of his day; nor did he hesitate to coin
words if he wanted them for sense or sound. The result
was *The Shepheardes Calendar*.

An Elizabethan 'pastoral' poem is one in which the
poet speaks by the mouths of shepherds and shepherdesses
of Arcadia or of some land equally Arcadian. It may be
a love poem or it may be a moral or political or religious
disquisition. It may be dramatic in form, like Daniel's
Hymen's Triumph; but the personages are supposed to
be shepherds, and they have little or nothing to do except
talk and make love, and they live in a land where an ex-

treme simplicity of manner has, as a rule, just begun to be corrupted. Sidney's Arcadia is inhabited by knights and princesses, and its manners are fabulously chivalrous. William Browne's Arcadia is inhabited, not by the knights of literary chivalry, but by nymphs and river-gods. Spenser's Arcadia, like Daniel's, has none of these fabulous elements; but his shepherds and shepherdesses are as fabulous as any river-gods. They discourse of love and old age, the glory of Queen Elizabeth, the glory of poetry and its neglect by great personages, the 'loose living of Popish prelates,' the wiliness of the Roman Church, and, in fact, on any subject (usually a traditional one) that the poet desired to treat. One of the eclogues is a funeral tribute to a great lady, and two others contain allegoric fables, told with racy force and humour. If it had been Spenser's object to create a new language for the use of poets, his experiment was unsuccessful, as indeed it was bound to be. But the immediate popularity of poems so thoroughly English was of great value at a time when the chief danger lay in servile imitation of foreign models. In its general scheme *The Shepheardes Calendar* was quite conventional. Even in England the pastoral of Mantuan had already been written by Googe. Spenser had added nothing to the idea of the pastoral, and he had borrowed much. The eleventh eclogue was avowedly written 'in imitation of Marot his song, which he made upon the death of Loys, the French queen.' But he had followed no one model, and he had written eclogues in pure English matching anything written abroad. The experiment in versification was a triumphant success. No verse so musical had been written since Chaucer.[1]

After *The Shepheardes Calendar* is a gap of ten years,

[1] *The Shepheardes Calendar* was reprinted four times during Spenser's lifetime. Mainly employed was an accentual line of four beats, splendidly used in after time by Blake and Coleridge.

during which Spenser published nothing. The first three books of *The Faerie Queene* were published early in 1590. They were dedicated to the Queen, and were accompanied by seventeen sonnets addressed to eminent persons, by some commendatory poems by friends of the poet,[1] and by a letter to Raleigh explanatory of the character and purpose of the poem. The next three books appeared in 1596; and the first complete edition of Spenser's works (1609) included two additional cantos belonging to some later book, presumably never completed. The whole poem, as originally planned, was to have been complete in twelve books of twelve cantos each. In his letter to Raleigh, Spenser describes the poem, the greater part of which had

The Faerie Queene.

yet to be written, as 'a continued allegory or dark conceit.' He goes on to give some information apparently intended to guide one in the obscurity. 'The general end of all the book is to fashion a gentleman or noble person in virtuous and gentle discipline.' After this rather ambiguous declaration he adds: 'I labour to portray in Arthur, before he was king, the image of a brave knight, perfected in the twelve private moral virtues, as Aristotle hath devised; the which is the purpose of these first twelve books.' Arthur is to represent 'Magnificence' or the sum of the 'private' virtues, and each of the virtues is severally to be represented by a knight. By *The Faerie Queene*, he says, 'I mean glory in my general intention'; but in particular intention he means Queen Elizabeth. He is careful to add that, as Elizabeth is not only a 'most royal Queen or Empress,' but also a 'most virtuous and beautiful lady,' he represents her in the latter character in the person of Belphoebe. And that is all the light his preface throws on his 'allegory.'

[1] Two of these poems are by Raleigh.

It seems quite probable that Spenser's confused and inadequate explanation is in the main correct, and that he himself did not exactly know what was his intention as to the allegory. By his own account his conception was confused from the beginning : the Faerie Queene round whom all was to turn means two incongruous things. Again, if by 'glory' he meant the glory of God, why did he not say so ? Prince Arthur, who mysteriously appears as a sort of *deus ex machina* in all the six books, may mean Divine Grace throughout: but why, then, does Spenser say that he represents merely the perfected knight or 'Magnificence' ? Had the last book been written, it might conceivably have made matters clearer : but as it stands, the allegory, as a whole, is unintelligible. The Faerie Queene has no definite relation to the various stories, and the stories have no definite relation to each other. The different knights have little or no apparent relation to the virtues they are supposed to represent. To each virtue its own work : but the work of Spenser's knights is much the same in all cases. Britomart is not more chaste than Belphoebe, or than Amoret; Sir Calidore is not more courteous than another; Sir Guyon is not extraordinarily remarkable for temperance.

Take the first book. The Red Cross Knight sets forth with Una to establish her in her rights. He represents 'holiness,' and may conveniently be held to signify pure religion or primitive Christianity. He is armed, Spenser tells us, in 'the armour of a Christian man specified by St. Paul' (Ephesians, v. 1). Una is Truth, one and indivisible. Her Dwarf,

> 'That lazy seemed in being ever last,
> Or wearied with bearing of her bag
> Of needments on his back,'

is interpreted as the 'Flesh' or the lower nature, though one would have supposed this to be an appurtenance of the Knight rather than of Truth.[1] The 'covert nigh at hand,' with its lofty trees, 'not perceable by power of any star,' into which they enter, signifies the easy ways of the world, leading straight to Error. The Christian, backed by Truth, overcomes Error somewhat easily, and goes on to encounter a more formidable enemy in Archimago or Satan himself. Satan maligns Truth and succeeds in passing off on the Knight, as a substitute for her, the false Duessa (doubleness), who may here be taken for the Church of Rome.[2] Forsaken Una encounters a lion. A lion, according to ancient story, will not hurt a virgin;[3] but this explanation of the lion's conduct is clearly insufficient. The lion must be interpreted as pure, natural Reason, which, though devoid of faith, cannot injure Truth, and indeed cannot but defend her. A little later the lion kills Kirkrapine and a nice point arises: for this is hardly the action of pure Reason. But about the time when the Knight of the Red Cross (of St. George) is misled by Duessa, he may be taken to cease to represent mere primitive Christianity and to become the Church of England misled by the wiles of Rome. Therefore perhaps the lion, slayer of Kirkrapine, is for the moment no other than King Henry VIII.

Satan (Archimago) now proceeds to masquerade as the true Christian knight, and even Una is deceived. Then appears Sansloy. The lion is slain by him, for Reason is no defence against brutal lawlessness; and Truth is oppressed by violence. But no violence can stain immacu-

---

[1] The appearance of the Dwarf in Canto VII. has to be explained in a quite different manner!

[2] In Book V. 9 she appears as Mary Stuart.

[3] As in *The Seven Champions of Christendom.*

late Truth, and Una is rescued by the 'wood-born' people who represent the 'natural' man. Outcast and abandoned, Truth finds refuge and uncomprehending worship among the simple and unsophisticated.

The fortunes of the Red Cross Knight after his parting from Una are subject to similar interpretations, though of still more dubious character. If the 'House of Pride' must needs be Papistical, then the escape of the Knight from it and his subsequent recapture by Orgoglio may signify the events of the reigns of Edward VI. and Mary. And Divine Grace finally comes to unmask the false Duessa with the accession of Elizabeth.

Whether such interpretations heighten the beauty or increase the interest of the poem to the reader is a matter of temperament. But it may be pointed out that the interpretations here given reveal only quite commonplace ideas, and further, that the allegory is hopelessly confused and even obscure. The very fact that the meaning of an allegory is doubtful almost destroys the allegory, and it may certainly be held that an obscure allegory is worse than none. Yet it is in the first book of *The Faerie Queene* that the allegory is clearest. A full analysis would show that as he proceeded with the poem Spenser took less and less trouble to provide adventures susceptible of allegorical interpretations for his knights and maidens.

Regarded as an allegorical poem *The Faerie Queene* must be held to be a failure. It lacks any kind of real unity, and the 'allegories' of the different books are inconsistent, confused, and obscure. Spenser was a highly cultivated man, learned in literature, profoundly religious, and with a strong love of symbolism. But he was not a thinker, nor did his religion so dominate his mind as to enable him to produce, like Bunyan, a narrative in which the story and its allegorical import are absolutely at one.

He was simply a poet, and one of the most poetic. *The Faerie Queene* is not an allegory but a dream, full of symbolism, and touched here and there throughout with allegorical import more or less definite. From the point of view of the allegorist the lack of unity is a damning fault: but why demand unity of a series of dreams? On the other hand, though the allegory does constrain and even interrupt to some extent the narrative, yet, as Hazlitt said, it does not bite. The extreme beauty of the poem is hardly clouded by it.

This extreme beauty, testified to by poet after poet from that day to this, depends partly on style and verbal melody, partly on word-painting, partly on atmosphere, little, if at all, on thought. Leigh Hunt has very finely appreciated and illustrated Spenser's hardly matched power of word-painting.[1] It is almost always in dealing with still-life or allegoric figures or in broad effects that this power is displayed. In describing rapid action the poet generally fails through lack of realism and definition, and through diffuseness. His most elaborate combats would be ridiculous but for the never-failing charm of his diction. He seems hardly to realize that you cannot fight slowly, hand to hand. But in effects of richness or of gloom or of mystery, and in the projection of allegoric figures, perfect in beauty or in ugliness, he is unsurpassed if he be equalled.[2] The stanza in which the poem is written, and which he invented, is a metrical creation of the first order, and he handles it with the most consummate art, never falling below a very high level.[3] But what gives the poem

---

[1] In *Imagination and Fancy.*

[2] Compare the procession of Counsellours in Book I. 4 with the procession of the months in what is called Book VII. 7.

[3] Lowell has admirably described what Spenser did with the *ottava rima*: ' He found the *ottava rima* too monotonously itera-

as a whole its most distinctive, and perhaps its highest, beauty is its atmosphere: an atmosphere of dreamland, silvery and pure and faint and mysterious as moonlight, in which the figures of the noble knights and maidens shine with an unearthly beauty.

The allegory apart, the faults and weaknesses of this wonderful poem are obvious; but they are almost reducible to one—a certain monotony. This monotony is due partly to the fact that the adventures recorded in the six books are very similar in character. Spenser shows extraordinary imaginative power in the invention of symbolic figures; but he shows little power of inventing a story. Moreover, he totally fails to differentiate character distinctly, otherwise than as angelic or heroic, or, on the other hand, diabolical. There is a sameness about his knights and his ladies. Spenser has created a world as ideal as, and even more beautiful because less tormented than, that of Shelley. The magical atmosphere and unearthly music of that world we find in all his poems and most perfectly of all in *The Faerie Queene*, the *Epithalamium* and *Prothalamium*, and the *Hymns*. The world of Spenser, in spite of its symbolism and its chivalry, is not a world of the Middle Ages or of the Renaissance, or of pure romance. It is serious and a little melancholy; it is

tive; so by changing the order of his rhymes, he shifted the couplet from the end of the stave, where it always seems to put on the brakes with a jar, to the middle, where it may serve at will as a brace or a bridge; he found it not roomy enough, so first ran it over into another line, and then ran that added line into an Alexandrine, in which the melody of one stanza seems for ever longing and feeling forward after that which is to follow.' Spenser varies the cadence of his stanza chiefly by variety of pause, and makes but too little use of the variety in weight and length of actual words. Hence the variety of his cadence, though extraordinarily great, is subtle rather than obvious.

touched with Puritanism and troubled by religious controversy. In *The Faerie Queene*, that which was dead and that which was dying are blended with that which was to come. And the whole is distinctively Elizabethan and still more distinctively Spenserian.[1]

The poems of Spenser were written and published, so far as can be ascertained, in the following order:

1. 'Epigrams' and sonnets published in *The Theatre of Voluptuous Worldlings* in 1569. These are all translations or imitations.

2. *The Shepheardes Calendar*: published 1579.

3. First three books of *The Faerie Queene*: published 1590.

4. *The Complaints*: published 1591. This is a collection of poems of various dates. *The Ruines of Time*, *The Teares of the Muses*, and *Muiopotmos, or The Tale of the Butterflie*, had apparently been written shortly before publication. *Mother Hubberd's Tale* was an early work, retouched, in which the poet had closely imitated Chaucer. The remaining poems of this volume—*Virgil's Gnat*, *The Ruines of Rome*, *The Visions of the World's Vanitie*, and the *Visions* of Bellay and Petrarch—are all early works more or less recast, and either translations or adaptations —the *Visions* of Bellay and Petrarch being versions of the poems that had appeared in 1569.

5. *Daphnaïda*, an elegy: published 1591.

6. *Colin Clout's come Home again*, the *Amoretti*, and the *Epithalamium*: published together in 1595. Of these the *Colin Clout* had been written as early as 1591. The sonnets were probably mostly written in 1593, and the *Epithalamium* in the year of Spenser's marriage, 1594.

---

[1] There can be little doubt that the idea of *The Faerie Queene* was first suggested to Spenser by a reading of Ariosto's *Orlando Furioso*. Spenser, like Ariosto, makes use of giants, enchanters, and so on; and both *The Faerie Queene* and the *Orlando* are a medley of stories and adventures. There the real resemblance ends. Nothing could be more unlike the atmosphere of Spenser than that of Ariosto.

7. The fourth, fifth, and sixth books of *The Faerie Queene*: published 1596.

8. The *Foure Hymns* to Love and Beauty, the *Prothalamium*, and the *Astrophel*, an elegy on the death of Sidney: published in 1596.

Spenser's only work in prose, *A View of the Present State of Ireland*, 'discoursed by way of a dialogue between Eudoxus and Irenaeus,' was registered in 1598, but did not appear till 1633.

Of the immediate disciples and imitators of Spenser two are, above all, noteworthy: Giles and Phineas Fletcher. They were sons of Dr. Giles Fletcher and first cousins of John Fletcher, the dramatist.[1] Giles Fletcher the younger was born about 1585 and died in 1623. He took orders at

Giles Fletcher (1585-1623).

Cambridge, became famous there as a preacher, and latterly held the living of Alderton, in Suffolk, where he died. His only literary work of importance was a poem entitled *Christ's Victorie and Triumph in Heaven and Earth, over and after Death*, which was published at Cambridge in 1610.

The *Christ's Victorie* is an epic poem of more than 2,000 lines, divided into four parts, written in a modified form of the Spenserian stanza, but bestrewn with passages in purely lyrical measures. Fletcher spoils his master's stanza by dropping its seventh line; but he adopts his allegorical method of presenting abstractions and many of his mannerisms. His style is extremely antithetical, and he shows a marked fondness for such words as debellishèd

---

[1] Dr. Giles Fletcher (LL.D.) was a man of some learning, the poetaster of *Licia* (1593), and author of some poems in Latin, and a work on Russia (1591), to which country he was sent on an embassy. His brother, Richard Fletcher, Bishop of Bristol, of Worcester, and finally of London, was the father of John Fletcher.

and besilverèd. He writes 'belgards' for *belles regardes*, and calls soap bubbles 'watry orbicles.' But he treats his difficult subject with discretion and a real and manifest reverence, and his pedantries and affectations do not affect the sincerity of his work. The poem is not a literary exercise, but a long labour of love by a man of marked literary talent, ingenious and cultivated and of some imagination. In spite of laborious antithesis and meretricious adornment, the poem retains much of the simplicity and charm that come of sincerity. The following stanza perhaps shows the poet at his best:

> 'When I remember Christ our burden bears,
> I look for glory, but find misery;
> I look for joy, but find a sea of tears;
> I look that we should live and find Him die;
> I look for angels' songs and hear Him cry:
> Thus what I look I cannot find so well;
> Or rather what I find I cannot tell,
> These banks so narrow are, those streams so highly swell.'

Milton studied this poem carefully and with profit, and it has fallen into a somewhat undeserved neglect, chiefly owing, probably, to its length and diffuseness.

Phineas Fletcher, the elder of the two brothers, also took orders, and died rector of Hilgay, Norfolk, in 1650. As a poet he was much the more prolific of the two. By far his most important poem is *The Purple Island*, a poem still well known by name, though not by perusal.[1] *The Purple Island* is an allegorical and religious poem of twelve cantos and over 4,800 lines, written in a debased

Phineas Fletcher (1582-1650).

---

[1] The subject of the poem was evidently suggested by the house of Alma in Book II. 9 of *The Faerie Queene*. In Canto V. 1 Phineas announces that his two masters are Virgil and Spenser: 'To lackey one of these is all my pride's aspiring.'

Spenserian stanza of seven lines.[1] The first canto is intro-
ductory. Spenser, 'whom all the graces and all the muses
nurst,' is glorified and his fate lamented, and there follows
a compendious account of the creation of the world and of
man, with reflections on man's fall and redemption. In
Canto II. we begin the description of the Purple Island,
that is, of the body of man—a description prolonged
through the next three cantos with considerable minute-
ness of anatomical detail. The poet shows considerable
knowledge of anatomy: his physiology is less good! The
island has three metropolitan cities: the Brain, the Heart
and 'fair Hepar,' the Liver, in which 'rise' the great
'rivers' of blood. Numerous other cities are described, as
Koilia, the stomach, and 'merrie Diazome,' the diaphragm.
Fletcher appended to his poem a number of explanatory
notes from which strange things might have been learned,
as that 'flesh' is 'made of blood indifferently dried.' In
Canto VI. the inhabitants of the island are described:
fancy, understanding, will, conscience, and so on. Then
in Canto VII. we have elaborate descriptions of the enemies
by whom the 'isle of man' is encompassed, all personified
and allegorized in Spenser's fashion, as Idolatros, Haeret-
icus, 'a wrangling carle,' Murder, Adultery, 'owl-eyed Superstition,' and 'proud Dichostasis—a mitre trebly crowned
the impostor wore.' In Canto VIII. the forces of Satan
are marshalled for attack, and there is much more allegorical personification. In the next two cantos the heavenly
defenders of the island—as faith, humility, fortitude—are
similarly dealt with; and in the last two we have a grand
battle, ending with the thrusting of the Dragon into hell
and the marriage of the fair Eclecta (the Church) with
her Lord.

[1] It was not published before 1633, but was written many years
earlier.

The pedantry and affectation of this astonishing poem obscure considerable merits. Its style is vigorous and antithetical, its phrasing frequently happy and strong. If not imaginative, it is highly ingenious. But there is little or no beauty either of diction or fancy, and in this respect Phineas is inferior to his brother. A total lack of humour, leading to unabashed elaboration of the commonplace, marks the work of both the Fletchers.

Of the Elizabethan writers of 'pastoral' poetry otherwise than in lyrical snatches, the best, after Spenser, is William Browne. He was a Devonshire man, born at Tavistock, a man of some property, and after 1616 seems to have lived a retired life in the country. He published the first book of his *Britannia's Pastoralls* in 1613, and the second in 1616.[1] In 1614 appeared his *Shepheards Pipe*, consisting of seven eclogues, the fourth of which is perhaps his most perfect work. The third and last book of *Britannia's Pastoralls* was not published till more than two hundred years after Browne's death.

William Browne (1591-1643).

He commences *Britannia's Pastoralls* by asserting that he is not going to write of Arcadia :

> 'My Muse for lofty pitches shall not roam,
> But homely pipen of her native home.'

He would have us believe that his Marina and Remond are Devonshire country folk. But the manners of his people are quite Arcadian, and his Devonshire has a large population of river-gods, well-gods, and nymphs. His

[1] The third book of the *Pastorals* remained in manuscript in the Salisbury Cathedral Library until 1852, when it was printed by the Percy Society ; the genuineness of this book has been questioned on no fully sufficient grounds. It is very inferior to the first two books.

lovers are truly 'pastoral,' and express their sentiments chiefly by weeping and moaning and endless talk about torments and flames. Yet his assertion that he writes not of Arcadia, but of his native home, is not a mere affectation, for the value of his poem consists just in this, that with an easy and simple charm of manner he sets before us the pleasant things of real country life. He gathers for us posies of flowers and introduces us to a 'Musical Consort of Birds':

> ' The lofty treble sung the little wren;
> Robin the mean, that best of all loves men;
> The nightingale the tenor; and the thrush
> The counter-tenor sweetly in a bush:
> And that the music might be full of parts,
> Birds from the groves flew with right willing hearts.
> But, as it seem'd, they thought as do the swains
> Which tune their pipes on sack'd Hibernia's plains;
> There should some droning part be, therefore will'd
> Some bird to fly into a neighbouring field,
> In embassy unto the king of bees,
> To aid his partners on the flowers and trees:
> Who condescending gladly flew along
> To bear the base to his well-tunèd song.
> The crow was willing they should be beholding
> To his deep voice, but being hoarse with scolding
> He thus lends aid; upon an oak doth climb,
> And nodding with his head, so keepeth time.'
>
> (*Pastorals*, bk. i., song iii.)

An obscure pastoral writer who has been confused with William Browne was William Basse (1583-1653), a native of Northampton, who knew many Oxford men, lived at Thame Park and died there, a belated Elizabethan, in 1653. His *Pastoral Elegies* (or Eclogues in the manner of *The Shepheardes Calendar*) and his *Polyhymnia* (written

about 1622) remained in MS. until 1893, when a sumptuous edition was brought out by Mr. R. Warwick Bond.
To Basse is attributed with tolerable certainty the interesting *Elegy on Shakespeare* subscribed ' W. B.' in the 1640
edition of the *Poems*, and written, it would appear, before
1623.[1]   Basse's ' choice ' song, *As Inward Love breeds
Outward Talk*, had the honour of being introduced into
The Compleat Angler (1653) of Izaak Walton.

A curious and original poem, entitled *The Secrets of
Angling*, published posthumously in 1613, may fitly be
mentioned here. It was written by John Dennys, a country
gentleman of Pucklechurch, Gloucestershire, who died in
1609, and it was translated into prose by Gervase Markham
in 1614. Simply and unaffectedly written, in a slightly
moralizing tone, it is pleasant reading. It gives detailed
instructions to the angler concerning his fishing tackle
and concerning different kinds of fish. It has no poetic
power, but there is in it a sincere and quiet delight in the
various beauty of things rural. Some of its best verses
are quoted by Izaak Walton.

§ 4. *The Metrical Historians : Drayton and Daniel.*

The intense patriotism of Elizabethan times expressed
itself in literature through chronicle plays, historical epics,
and patriotic song as strongly and splendidly as on the
Spanish Main. Of the poets who drew inspiration from
English history the most important is
Michael Drayton, the friend of Ben Jonson, and of Drummond of Hawthornden.
Drayton was a voluminous writer, and the great mass of
his verse is devoted to the glorification of England or

Michael Drayton
(1563-1631).

---

[1] It first appeared in Donne's *Poems*, but Basse's name is appended to it in several MS. copies.

the illustration of English history. He wrote every sort
of poetry, epic, religious, amatory, pastoral, lyrical, satiric,
dramatic; but he was pre-eminently the poet of the
chronicles and of the land he loved. There have been
few poets more industrious. When he was not engaged
upon some new work he appears to have been occupied
in collecting and editing the poems he had already
written.[1] He began in 1591 with a volume of religious
poetry, *The Harmonie of the Church,* and his next production
was *Idea. The Shepheards Garland, Fashioned in nine Eglogs,*[2]
followed in 1594 by *Ideas Mirrour. Amours in Quatorzains,*
fifty-three sonnets. In 1593 came the first of his 'legends'
from the chronicles: *The Legend of Peirs Gaveston.* The
legends of *Matilda the Fair* (1594) and of *Robert of Normandy* (1596) followed; though that of Robert of Normandy is not really an historical poem, but a poem on the
freaks of fame and fortune. In 1596 appeared the first
version of his historical epic, *The Barrons Wars,* which was
finally completed and published in 1603 in over 3,600

---

[1] Drayton, a fellow-countryman of Shakespeare, was born at
Hartshill, Warwickshire, and began to write about the same time
as the dramatist, and also as his compeer Daniel. He was, perhaps,
assisted at Oxford by Sir Henry Goodyer (1571-1627), the friend of
Jonson and Donne, himself the author of a few courtly fragments of
verse (*e.g.*, *Shall I like a Hermit dwell,* which has often been ascribed
to Raleigh). Drayton addressed his *Odes* in 1606 to Goodyer,
whose cousin, Anne Goodyer, of Polesworth, is now held to have
been the original of his *Idea.* He issued four different collected
editions of his own works: in 1605, 1619, 1627, and 1630. The
edition of 1605 was three times reprinted down to 1613. The
edition of 1619 was definitive for the moment, and contained
everything, except the *Polyolbion,* which Drayton desired to
live. See Prof. Elton, *Michael Drayton,* 1895.

[2] The eclogues of *The Garland* were subsequently refashioned in
Poems Lyrick and Pastorall, 1606. The sonnets, too, were constantly being changed by their fastidious composer (1599, 1600, 1619).

lines.[1] In 1597 appeared *England's Heroicall Epistles*,[2] consisting of a series of long love-letters, supposed to pass between historical personages, as Henry II. and Rosamund, the Black Prince and Alice of Salisbury, Edward IV. and Jane Shore. All these 'letters' are written in heroic couplets, and such interest as they have does not now lie in the historical reality of the personages supposed to write them, though possibly it was otherwise with Drayton's contemporaries. Some attempt at historical realism seems to appear in the boastful audacity of a letter from Owen Tudor to Katherine of France; but it is hard to suppose that Drayton imagined that anything like the letters ascribed to King John or the Black Prince could have been written by those worthies. In 1607 Drayton added *The Legend of Thomas Cromwell*[3] to his historical series, and in 1627 he completed it with two long and dull romantic poems, entitled *The Battaile of Agincourt*[4] and *The Miseries of Queen Margarite*. All these poems are founded on the chronicles; but the *Heroicall Epistles* are essentially love poems, and the *Robert of Normandy* is a morality. They are, for the most part, well wrought and resonant, but dull and without conspicuous merit. *The Barrons Wars* is an epic narrative (in stanzas of octave rhyme) of the events of the reign of Edward II., ending with the retributive overthrow of Mortimer and Isabella by Edward III. As in all these poems, the style is rhetorical and conventional, frequently turgid, and rarely

[1] In its first form it was entitled *Mortimeriados : The Lamentable Civell Wars of Edward II.* . . . 'written in rime royal' (changed subsequently into octave stanzas).

[2] Taking a hint from Ovid's *Heroycall Epistles* in Turbervile's version of 1567.

[3] This was included in the 1610 edition of *The Mirrour for Magistrates*.

[4] Not to be confounded with the famous ballad.

if ever poetical. Of vivid or picturesque narrative there
is hardly a trace, and Drayton had not Daniel's gift either
for moralizing or for plain speech. The story of the
ill-treatment and murder of Edward II. is very badly told.
After describing how the murderers wash the wretched
king with puddle water, Drayton continues:

> ' His tears increased the water with their fall,
> Like a pool rising with a sudden rain,
> Which wrestled with the puddle and withal
> A troubled circle made it to retain;
> His endless griefs which to his mind did call,
> His sighs made billows like a little main.'

The required impression is completely ruined by this non-
sense.[1]

Drayton's ever-to-be-admired *Polyolbion*[2] is a kind of
metrical megatherium inspired by the
The *Polyolbion*. poet's love for his native land. It was
described by its author as: ' A Choro-
graphical description of all the Tracts, Rivers, Mountains,
Forests, and other Parts of the Renowned Isle of Great
Britain, with intermixture of the most Remarkable Stories,
Antiquities, Wonders, Rarities, Pleasures, and Commodities
of the same.' It is in thirty parts and nearly 15,000
lines. Drayton was apparently at work on it in 1598: the
the first eighteen cantos or ' songs ' appeared in 1613, and
the complete poem in 1622. It is written in twelve-
syllable rhymed couplets. Mountains and rivers and
other ' parts ' tell their own tales. The Muse begins with
the Channel Isles, and goes thence to ' the utmost end of

[1] The poem is written throughout in a rather featureless eight-
lined stanza, not featureless in other hands, however, for it is the
popular *ottava rima* of Tasso, Ariosto, Fairfax, and Spenser
(*Muiopotmos*): a b a b a b c c.

[2] Polyolbion = Greatly-blessed, or Land of many blessings.

Cornwall's furrowing beak,' listens to remarks from St. Michael's Mount and certain rivers, notices the Devonian wrestlers, hears from the river Dart the story of Brutus the Trojan, and so comes to Exeter. In the second song she moves eastward to Salisbury, and so on. The poem shows that Drayton knew well the England he loved. The style is more natural, more frankly prosaic, than in the historical poems, and there are pretty passages. But as a whole it can only interest the antiquary.

Though Drayton devoted most of his time to the production of rhetorical narrative and 'chorographical description,' it is in occasional lyrical outbreaks that he really shines. Everyone knows the ballad of Agincourt: a triumph of inspiration and direct phrasing, and metrically the prototype of Tennyson's *Charge of the Light Brigade*. It was originally printed in the volume of 1606 under the title 'To my Frinds the Camber-Britans and theyr Harp.' His 'pastoral' lyrics are always pretty. There is some delightful verse in *The Muses Elizium*, the last poems of his life, published in 1630, and divided not into cantos but into 'Nimphals,' of which the eighth, describing the preparations for a 'Fays Bridal,' is perhaps the best. In one of Drayton's 'Eclogues' (the ninth) there is an especially pretty lyric:[1]

> 'Gorbo, as thou cam'st this way
> By yonder little hill,
> Or as thou through the fields did'st stray
> Saw'st thou my daffodil?'

Very daintily imagined, dexterous and quaintly comic is the *Nimphidia*,[2] the famous tale of how Oberon, King of

---

[1] The nine eclogues are included in a volume of 1606, entitled *Poems Lyrick and Pastorall.* It contains much of the best of Drayton's work.

[2] First printed in 1627.

Fairies, and the valiant Pigwiggen, mounted on earwigs, helmeted with beetle heads, sworded with hornet's stings, with cockle-shell shields and armour of fish scales—dear to painters!—fought for love of Queen Mab, and were cured by the waters of Lethe. The song in *The Shepherd's Sirena* (1627) is equally dainty, extravagant, and charming, and is still prettier. These things are astonishing after the heavy commonplaces of *The Barrons Wars*. They prepare us, to some extent at any rate, for the Shakespearean depth and fervour that breathes through that noble sonnet:

'Since ther's no help, come let us kiss and part,'

undoubtedly one of the finest in the English language, which first appeared in the folio of 1619.

The remaining chief works of Drayton are: (1) *The Owle* (1604) and *The Moone-Calf* (1627), dull and pointless satires; (2) *Moyses in a Map of his Miracles*, a dull poem on the life of Moses; and (3) two long poetical addresses to King James on his accession (1603-4). Between 1597 and 1602 he was writing for the stage in collaboration with Dekker, Chettle, and Munday. In October, 1599, he shared with Munday, Wilson, and Hathway the sum of £10 paid for a poor play called *The First Parte of Sir John Oldcastle*, attributed by a fraudulent bookseller to Shakespeare. He may possibly have had some share in *The Merry Devil of Edmonton*. Drayton died on 23rd December, 1631, and was buried in Westminster Abbey.

The most ambitious work of Samuel Daniel was also an

Samuel Daniel
(1562-1619).

historical epic. His first published verse [1] consisted of twenty-seven sonnets attached to the first edition of *Astrophel and Stella* (1591). Next year he published the whole series of his

---

[1] He was born near Taunton; studied at Magdalen Hall, Oxford, and in Italy; became tutor in the Herbert and Clifford families;

sonnets to *Delia*, together with an 'historical' narrative poem, *The Complaint of Rosamond*, who is made to tell her own story in a pleasant and unexciting manner, with much rather commonplace moralizing, in the metre of Shakespeare's *Lucrece*.   In 1594 appeared his rhymed Senecan tragedy *Cleopatra*, the first act of which consists of a chorus and an immense soliloquy, in which the Egyptian enchantress moralizes on her own fall through 196 lines. In 1595 appeared the first four books of his huge historical epic, *The Civile Wars between the two houses of Lancaster and Yorke*, which was not completed till 1609, when it numbered seven thousand lines.   In 1599 he published a long *Letter from Octavia to Marcus Antoninus*, written in the same eight-line stanza he used for *The Civile Wars*, truer in tone and less conventional than his *Rosamond*.   In the same year appeared *Musophilus*, 'a general defence of learning,' one of the best and most characteristic of Daniel's works, admirable for sense, lucidity, and grave eloquence. On the accession of James I. he published (1603) a long *Panegyrique congratulatorie* of that monarch.   From that time he was a good deal at Court, was now and then called upon to produce masques or semi-dramatic entertainments for performance there, and was given an official post in connection with the licensing of plays.   At Court he came into unhappy competition with Ben Jonson.   In the years 1601-3 he produced a number of 'epistles' addressed to eminent persons, including Shakespeare's Southampton and Lucy Russell, Countess of Bedford, a friend of Donne.   These contain much of his best work.   In 1605 he published his second Senecan tragedy, *Philotas*, and in 1606 *The Queene's Ar-*

---

and was perhaps introduced into the group of which Sidney was the centre before he began writing. His father and brother were both musicians. His earliest work (1585) was in prose.

cadia, in which some scenes were borrowed from Guarini's *Pastor Fido.* In 1615 was published his last, and on the whole his most perfect work, *Hymen's Triumph.* Both this and *The Queene's Arcadia* he described as 'pastorall trage-comedies.' Soon after this, being comfortably off, he retired, a successful man, into Somerset, where he seems to have occupied himself with farming at Beckington till his death on October 14th, 1619.[1]

Daniel seems to have been more deeply influenced by the Latin moralists and pastoralists than any of his con-temporaries. The motive of almost all his work is ethical. He was the only considerable disciple of Seneca in England: his two tragedies are moral dialogues. The *Rosamond, Octavia,* and *The Civile Wars* are moralized narrative or romance; the Epistles are moral discourses on the uses of adversity, on equity, on the serenity of the virtuous and philosophic mind; *Hymen's Triumph* celebrates the beauty and the reward of faithfulness in love. Daniel has an easy, natural style, unadorned but untormented, with little imagery, singularly lucid and supple, eminently graceful in *Hymen's Triumph,* weighty and antithetical in the Epistles. He has no rapture and little emotion of any kind: at times he drops into diction that is completely prosaic; at times he rises to a grave eloquence that is almost majestic. There is nothing in Elizabethan litera-ture finer in its way than a passage in his epistle to Margaret, Countess of Cumberland. He is speaking of the serenity of the wise and virtuous man—a favourite Elizabethan theme:

[1] Daniel also published in prose (1) *A Defence of Ryme* (1602), in answer to Campion's treatise (cf. p. 100), and (2) *The Historie of England.* Part I. of the *Historie* was published in 1612, and reached the end of the reign of Stephen; Part II. appeared in 1617-18, and continued the history to the end of Edward III. Cf. p. 194.

'He looks upon the mightiest monarch's wars
But only as on stately robberies,
Where evermore the fortune that prevails
Must be the right; the ill-succeeding mars
The fairest and the best-faced enterprise:
Great pirate Pompey lesser pirates quails;
Justice, he sees, as if seduced, still
Conspires with power, whose cause must not be ill.

*   *   *   *   *

And whilst distraught Ambition compasses
And is encompassed; whilst as craft deceives
And is deceived; whilst man doth ransack man
And builds on blood and rises by distress;
And the inheritance of desolation leaves
To great expecting hopes; he looks thereon
As from the shore of peace with unwet eye
And bears no venture in impiety.'

This is Daniel at his best; but he is equally at his best in
that very graceful and truly Arcadian poem *Hymen's
Triumph*, in which he uses alike blank verse and rhyme
with charm and distinction. Though his verse has little
colour, it has great beauty of line, and though his imagination is not profound, few poets match him in sanity and
lucidity, and in a plain gracefulness. The weakest of all
his productions is the most ambitious of them in appearance, *The Civile Wars*. This is little more than a matter-
of-fact versification of the chronicle.[1]

---

[1] 'Well-languaged' Daniel was admired both by Coleridge—
who spoke of him as 'the admirable Daniel'—and by Hazlitt.
His lucidity, his common sense, his unadorned graces, his simplicity of phrasing, his respect for the unities, and his ethical tone
remind one of the 'classical' French poets of the seventeenth
century. A collected edition of his poems was published in 1601,
and a complete edition in 1623: Selected Poems in 1605, 1607, 1611.

Another chronicle poet was William Warner, who published the first part of a long rhyming
William Warner   history entitled *Albions England* in 1586,
(1558-1609).   the second part in 1589.[1]
The most interesting point about this poem, which was
written in fourteen-syllable couplets, is its comparative
popularity in the eighteenth century, when a pastoral
episode, that of Argentile and Curan, was much admired.
It was, however, keenly appreciated in its own day, probably on account of its patriotic character. It was written
when 'Chronicles' were all the fashion, and it must to
some extent have inspired both Daniel and Drayton. Meres
in 1598 classes Warner with Spenser as the chief English
'heroic poets.'

The 'saurians of English Poetry' Lowell wittily calls
Drayton, Daniel, and Warner. Their interminable poems,
book after book, canto after canto, extend ' like far-stretch-
ing vertebrae that at first sight would seem to have
rendered earth unfit for the habitation of man. They
most of them sleep well now, as once they made their
readers sleep, and their huge remains lie embedded in the
deep morasses of Chalmers and Anderson '

§ 5. *Song-Books and Lyrists.*

Sonneteering was a fashion the force of which was
soon spent; but the publication of light lyrical verse,
generally in song form, and in an immense variety of
measures, of course continued throughout the period.
Next to Elizabethan drama, Elizabethan song is perhaps
the most characteristic literary product of the age. Yet
the Elizabethan poets comparatively rarely published

---

[1] Finally 'Revised and newly enlarged a little before his Death,'
1612.

volumes containing lyric poems only. Such poems were frequently published in volumes containing poems of a different order, as in Drayton's *Poems Lyrick and Pastorall.*

The Lyrical Miscellanies.

Lyric verse is also found scattered through the romances of Greene, Lodge, and others, and in the plays of Shakespeare, Fletcher, Webster, and Jonson, and in the sonnet-books. But the principal collections of purely lyrical verse published in the age of Elizabeth are the miscellanies and the song-books. The number of miscellanies published is significant of the popular taste. In 1584 appeared *A Handefull of Pleasant Delites*, a collection of, up to that time, unpublished lyrics. In 1592 appeared a similar publication, entitled *Breton's Bower of Delites*, the attribution of which to Breton was fraudulent. In 1593 was published *The Phoenix Nest*, a collection containing unpublished verse by Lodge, Peele, De Vere, and Sir Walter Raleigh; and in 1599 *The Passionate Pilgrim*, falsely attributed to Shakespeare, but containing two of his sonnets. In 1600 appeared *England's Helicon* [1] and *England's Parnassus.* *England's Helicon*, though it contained some previously unpublished verse, was in the main an anthology and a very admirable one, containing poems by Sidney, Spenser, Drayton, Lodge, Greene, Peele, Shakespeare, Breton, and Barnfield. Finally, in 1602 was published Francis Davison's

---

[1] The editing of *England's Helicon* has been commonly but very dubiously attributed to John Bodenham, who appears also to have published in the same year a very inferior poetical scrap-book entitled *Belvedere*. Whoever did the selection did it very well. A second edition of *England's Helicon* (with nine additional pieces) appeared in 1614. Bodenham had previously been concerned in the publication of two collections of sententious extracts, *Wits Commonwealth*, 1597, and *Wits Theater*, 1598; but he seems rather to have planned the series of compilations than actually to have edited them.

Poetical Rapsody, a miscellany of published and unpublished verse.[1]

Still more significant of popular taste are the song-books—little books in which words and music were printed together—a very large number of which were issued. The most important of these are the song-books of William Byrd, John Dowland, Thomas Morley, and Thomas Campion. In many cases the nominal author of such books was responsible both for music and verse.[2]

Most Elizabethan poets, of course, wrote lyrical verse, and the work of two at least of the greatest of Elizabethan lyrists, Donne and Ben Jonson, is markedly unlike that of their contemporaries.[3] Elizabethan lyric in its most characteristic forms, the lyric of Greene, Lodge, Drayton, Breton, and Campion, the lyric of the miscellanies and the song-books, is marked by extreme lightness and dexterity of touch, by a melody various but generally slight, by lack of intensity and passion, by brilliant fancy, conventionality of theme, and unfailing vivacity. But the most essential of its characteristic qualities is its objective idealism, its impersonal character. The lover is commonly represented as a shepherd, a device which effectually separates lover and poet. The poet loves love—'sweet

---

[1] *The Poetical Rapsody* was republished with additions or alterations in 1608, 1611, and 1621.

[2] Byrd (1543-1623) published his first song-book in 1588, and his last in 1611. He was at one time organist of Lincoln Cathedral, then of the Chapel Royal, and died in 1623. Dowland was a celebrated lute-player, and published song-books in 1597, 1600, 1603, and 1612. He died in 1626. For Campion see p. 61. John Daniel, brother of Samuel Daniel, published a song-book in 1606. Another pretty book is Robert Jones's *Muses Gardin for Delights*, printed in 1610.

[3] For Donne, Drummond, and Wither, see § 6, pp. 65, 75, 80. For Jonson see Book III.

desire '—but no single woman. He does not write from
his own but from common experience. He generalizes on
the folly or the pain or the idolatry of love; whether in
the first person or no matters nothing. You may search
Lodge or Greene in vain for any note of personal passion
or distinct individual experience. It is the same when the
poet is moralizing. Whether, like Dyer, he write, ' *My*
mind to me a kingdom is,' or, like Greene, '*A* mind content
both crown and kingdom is,' the meaning is exactly the
same. This last theme in one form or another—the happiness of lowly desires, the superiority of a shepherd's life to
that of a king, the tranquil self-possession of the virtuous
mind—is a very favourite one with the Elizabethans. They
ring the changes on it just as they do with love.

Of the Elizabethan poets whose work as poets was
primarily lyrical, the most characteristic are
Greene, Lodge, Breton, and Campion.[1] Greene's
lyric work is admirable, though it hardly attains
the perfect lightness and wantonness of that of Lodge.
He is even more fond than most Elizabethan lyrists
of fantastic measures and classical allusion. His work
is to some extent marred by euphuistic affectation, and
his execution is frequently careless. But he is brilliantly fantastic and rich in pretty phrases.[2] He has, also,
a pretty turn of moralizing:

Robert
Greene.

> ' In time we see the silver drops
> The craggy stones make soft,

---

[1] Drayton's talent was perhaps primarily lyrical, but his work
was not. Peele was primarily a dramatist, and Barnfield is not
typical. For Drayton see § 4, p. 46.

[2] Among his best poems may be mentioned the cradle-song, *Weep
not, my wanton, smile upon my knee*, and the shepherd's wife's song,
Ah, what is love? It is a pretty thing. See *Poems of Greene, Marlowe, and Ben Jonson*, ed. Robert Bell. See Bk. III., vol. ii., p. 22.

The slowest snail in time we see
Doth creep and climb aloft.

' With feeble puffs the tallest pine,
In tract of time doth fall;
The hardest heart in time doth yield
To Venus' loving call.'

The prettily put commonplace of these verses, together
with the blank inadequacy of the personal note with which
the little poem ends—

' In time I loathed that now I love,
In both content and pleased,'—

is typically Elizabethan.

Thomas Lodge was a son of Sir Thomas Lodge, at one
time Lord Mayor of London. Apparently
his respectable but prosaic father disin-
herited him for his Bohemian habits and
unseemly scribbling. He travelled in Italy, visited the
Canaries, and even went as far as Magellan Straits. His
first work, a prose pamphlet—*A Defence of Poetry, Music,
and Stage Plays*—was published in 1579; his first poem, ten
years later. His literary work includes lyric and satirical
verse, prose romance, moral and religious tracts, translations of the works of Josephus and Seneca, and a treatise
on the Plague. He also wrote for the stage in collaboration
with Greene and probably with others. He finally abandoned
literature for medicine and became a Roman Catholic.[1]

Lodge was a poet of rare and delicate talent, wholly
lacking in seriousness or passion. He was a more de-

Thomas Lodge
(1558?-1625).

---

[1] He published *Scillaes Metamorphosis*, the first English mythological poem, in 1589; *Euphues Golden Legacy* in 1590; *Phillis* in
1593; and *A Fig for Momus*, epistles and satires in verse, in 1595.
Poems by him were printed for the first time in *The Phoenix Nest*
and in *England's Helicon*.

liberate artist than Greene, and was more influenced by
the French.[1]   He delights in ingenious verbal effects, has
the deftest touch and a fine ear.   No poet is more wan-
tonly and delicately playful.   He has the daintiness of
Ronsard, though not his seriousness.   The well-known
madrigal of Rosalynde, in which love appears as a kind of
tickling, is perfect for absolute harmony between form and
content, and as an example of his style :

> ' Love in my bosom like a bee
>   Doth suck his sweet ;
> Now with his wings he plays with me,
>   Now with his feet.
> Within mine eyes he makes his nest,
> His bed amidst my tender breast ;
> My kisses are his daily feast,
> And yet he robs me of my rest.
>   Ah, wanton, will ye ?

> ' And if I sleep then percheth he,
>   With pretty flight,
> And makes his pillow of my knee,
>   The livelong night.
> Strike I my lute, he tunes the string ;
> He music plays if so I sing ;
> He lends me every lovely thing ;
> Yet cruel he my heart doth sting.
>   Whist, wanton, still ye ! '

Nicholas Breton lived by his wits in literature for some
fifty years, and died in harness at about
eighty, vivacious and *naïf* to the last.
He published his earliest work in 1577,
and his last in the year of his death.   He was a literary

Nicholas Breton
(1545 ?-1626).

---

[1] Lodge adapts and translates freely from Desportes, immensely
improving on his original.   His longest poem, the *Scillaes Metamorphosis*, is a euphuistic production of a rather sickly grace.

man of all work, facile and versatile, adaptable and generally competent. He wrote lyric, elegiac, pastoral, satirical, and religious verse, as well as much prose—essays, dialogues, romances—and a model letter-writer. He scribbles carelessly, plays with words, defies grammar and logic, worries conceits to death, and is wonderfully seldom dull considering how little he has to say. He is far less of an idealist than Greene or Lodge, and his writings, both in prose and verse, are perhaps fuller of the actual life of his time than those of any of his contemporaries save Dekker and Ben Jonson.[1] Much of his verse is very charming, owing its charm partly to freshness and gaiety, partly to Breton's genuine pleasure in country sights and sounds. At his best he has a deft touch and a rippling movement, and he phrases neatly:

> ' In the merry month of May,
> In a morn by break of day,
> Forth I walk'd by the wood side,
> Whenas May was in his pride:
> There I spied, all alone,
> Phyllida and Corydon.
> Much ado there was, God wot!
> He would love and she would not.'

Thomas Campion (buried March 1st, 1620) was a man of very different type from that of Greene or Breton. A doctor of medicine, an accomplished musician, a scholar, author of a treatise (1602) in which he gravely argued against the use of rhyme, he seems to have given to poetry only hours spared from what

Thomas Campion.

---

[1] In 1580 Humphrey Gifford published a volume, half verse, half prose, entitled *A Posie of Gilloflowers, eche differing from other in colour and odour yet all sweete.* These are among the earliest lyrics of the Elizabethan period, and they remind us of the work of Breton by their facility, their tinkle and ripple, their prettiness and triviality.

appeared to him as more serious occupations. It is fortunate that his practice was somewhat better than his theories. Between 1601 and 1619 he published three song-books, to two of which he contributed both verse and music, and to the third all the verse and half the music.[1] His poetry had until recently been curiously neglected. If his verse is less brilliantly fantastic than Greene's and less dainty than Lodge's, it is far more intellectual than that of either, and attains at times a beauty of diction which they never approach:

> ' When thou must home to shades of underground
> And there arrived, a new, admired guest,
> The beauteous spirits do engirt thee round,
> White Iope, blithe Helen, and the rest,
> To hear the stories of thy finished love
> From that smooth tongue whose music hell can move.

> ' Then wilt thou speak of banqueting delights,
> Of masques and revels which sweet youth did make,
> Of tourneys and great challenges of knights
> And all these triumphs for thy beauty's sake:
> When thou hast told these honours done to thee,
> Then tell, O tell, how thou did'st murder me ! '

It is highly characteristic of Elizabethan lyric that this poem with its solemnly musical verse is a pure fantasia and the close of it patently false. As a rule Campion wrote more lightly, as in his best-known song: *There is a garden in her face.*

A striking feature of Elizabethan literature is the

---

[1] *A Booke of Ayres* (1601), words by Campion, music by Campion and Ph. Rosseter ; *Two Bookes of Ayres,* and *The Third and Fourth Booke of Ayres,* published between 1613 and 1619. Campion also published a collection called *Songs of Mourning* (1613) on the death of Prince Henry, and poems in Latin in 1595 and 1619. He wrote several masques, which were performed at Court.

quantity of admirable lyric verse written and published
by men who were in no sense professional men of letters.
Much of this was published anonymously ; a considerable
amount of it was written by courtiers like Dyer and
Sidney, men of affairs like Raleigh [1] or Sir William
Alexander, professional men or men of learning like
Campion or Edmund Bolton.[2] Even Drummond, like
Gray, was primarily a student; while Donne was a man of
the world, who published hardly anything.

Among the amateur poets few were so talented as
Richard Barnfield, who amused himself
with verse-writing only while quite a
young man, and at about twenty-five
withdrew from literature altogether to live on his estate in
the country. In 1594 he published *The Affectionate Shep-
heard,* in which he set forth the love of a shepherd, not for
a shepherdess but for a youth (cf. Virgil's Alexis), written
partly in the metre of *Venus and Adonis* and partly in that
of *Lucrece.* In the following year he published his second
volume of verse, which contains a love poem of ordinary
type, twenty sonnets and a number of short 'odes' addressed to a young man, and a narrative poem on the
legend of Cassandra.[3] In 1598 appeared his last volume.[4]

Richard Barnfield (1574-1627).

---

[1] Raleigh's well-known poem, *The Lie,* written before 1593, was
first printed in *The Poetical Rapsody* (ed. 1608). His most ambitious poem, *Cynthia,* only exists as a fragment. His reply to
Marlowe's *Come live with me*—if it be his, as Izaak Walton
declares—appeared first in *England's Helicon.* Dr. Hannah has
collected his poems (1885).

[2] Author of a learned treatise, *Elements of Armories* (1610), and
various historical works. A fine poem by him appears in *England's Helicon.* See Book II., p. 217.

[3] *Cynthia. With certaine Sonnets and the Legend of Cassandra.*

[4] *The Encomion of Lady Pecunia.* This contains poems on
various subjects, so thin and artificial in character as to suggest

Barnfield has been compared with Keats; and with the
Keats of *Endymion* comparison is justified by the cloying
sweetness and occasional richness of his diction, by his
sentimentality, his affected prettiness, and his sensuous
feeling for natural beauty.

The *Venus and Adonis* (1593) and the *Lucrece* (1594)
of Shakespeare fall to be considered here as being essentially lyrical poems in spite of their narrative form.
The product of two successive years both alike betray im-
maturity. The euphuistic passion of Venus is really
hardly more youthful than the didactic descants on time
and opportunity in the *Lucrece*. Both poems are thoroughly
undramatic ; which would be singular if it were not obvious that in each case Shakespeare had deliberately set
himself to write a form of narrative poetry in which action
is nothing and decoration everything. The *Venus and
Adonis* is, however, by far the more minutely ornamented.
It is extraordinarily full of colour, rich in fancy, sensuous
—and extravagant to the verge of silliness and even beyond.[1] The *Lucrece* is far graver, more restrained, and
written in a nobler measure.[2] On the moral side the contrast is more apparent than real : it is, in the main, a
contrast of subject. Both poems are somewhat imitative.
In the *Venus and Adonis* the influence of Ovid and of

that Barnfield's poetic faculty was already exhausted. Poor
as it is, it was imitated in a piece called *The Massacre of Money*,
by 'T. A.,' 1602. Two poems by Barnfield appeared in *The Passionate Pilgrim* (1599).

[1] As when Venus speaks of the boar as killing Adonis in trying
to kiss him. Henry Constable's *Shepherds Song of Venus and
Adonis*, a short poem in a curious trochaic measure, reprinted in
England's Helicon, may possibly have suggested the particular
theme. Cf. also Spenser's description of the hangings in the Lady
of Delight's Castle.

[2] a b a b b c c : the rhyme-royal of Chaucer. Cf. Daniel's *Rosamond*.

Lodge [1] is apparent; in the *Lucrece*, the influence of Ovid and of Daniel. [2]

§ 6. *John Donne.*

John Donne was the elder son of a London merchant of

John Donne
(1573-1631).

Welsh extraction by Elizabeth, daughter of John Heywood the epigrammatist. His mother was a Catholic, to whom all Protestantism was hateful. [3] His father died when he was but three, and John inherited a considerable fortune, which he spent rapidly in travel and the pleasures of the town. As a quite young man his restless disposition and insatiable intellectual curiosity led him to travel and adventure. He was with Essex at Cadiz in 1596, travelled in Italy and Spain, and visited the Azores. As a young man he seems to have been dominated by two things, the desire of knowledge and the desire of amorous adventure. He studied law and theology, and all strange or new branches of learning had an especial fascination for him. His love poems were probably all written before he was thirty. They circulated in manuscript, but he published none of them, either then or later. Gradually he worked out his sensuality: the intense intellectuality of his temperament gained the mastery. He had been brought up a Roman Catholic, but had certainly ceased quite early to be in communion with

---

[1] Shakespeare may well have taken his subject from the first part of Lodge's *Scillaes Metamorphosis* (1589). The two poems are also in the same common and obvious metrical form : a b a b c c. But Shakespeare's verse is very unlike Lodge's.

[2] Shakespeare greatly improves on Daniel's moralizing *Rosamond*.

[3] Mr. Gosse traces his descent on the mother's side from Sir Thomas More. Donne went to Hart Hall, Oxford, and entered Lincoln's Inn in May, 1592.

that Church. Philosophic speculation had, however, always attracted him strongly. He became more and more interested in religion on its intellectual side, and plunged into the controversy between the Roman and Anglican Churches. At the age of twenty-eight he had married clandestinely Anne, daughter of Sir George More; and for many years after the marriage he was in difficulties for money. His mind was more and more occupied with religious subjects, and, all efforts to obtain secular preferment having failed, while ecclesiastical preferment was assured to him, he took orders in 1615. He was made a royal chaplain, then appointed preacher at Lincoln's Inn, and in 1621 was made Dean of St. Paul's. He became the most admired preacher of his day, and died on March 31st, 1631, with the reputation of a saint. With the exception of the two *Anniversaries* (1611-12) he had published no verse; but his poems were collected and published by his son.[1]

To turn from the love lyrics of Drayton or Spenser or Greene to the love lyrics of Donne is to receive a shock, pleasant or unpleasant. If unpleasant it is probably very unpleasant. Almost all Elizabethan love poetry is impersonal, ideal. Compared with Donne's it may be called cold. Fantastic as he is, Donne writes of his own experience. Not that his lyrics are poems of pure passion. It is improbable that he ever loved simply. He had a passion for passionate experience, and at bottom is always more intellectual than emotional. His lyrics are poems of transcendental sensuality, highly intellectualized.

To demand of love poetry that it shall be pretty and graceful is to demand that it shall not be personal and passionate. Shakespeare's sonnets, though in them all

---

[1] *Poems by J. D. with Elegies on the Author's Death,* London, 1633. Reprinted 1635 (with substantial additions), 1639, 1649, and again enlarged, 1669.

passion is mastered, are not pretty or graceful: they are splendid and melancholy. Passion is neither graceful nor pretty: it is tender at one moment, cruel at another; it may be brutal and ugly; it is egotistic always. If it weeps there is rage in the weeping; if it pleads it is with an undertone of fierceness. It may go with scorn or bitterness, or even with hatred; but it is not pretty and it knows nothing of taste. So with Donne. His love poetry is sometimes positively ugly. It is abrupt, scandalous, ecstatic, fantastic, mocking, actual.

> ' Love 's not so pure and abstract as they use
> To say, who have no mistress but their Muse ! '

Drayton and Lodge and the rest keep saying the same things over and over again: Donne runs through mood after mood. Sometimes, but rarely, he expresses a universal feeling :

> ' I wonder, by my troth, what thou and I
> Did till we loved.'

Ordinarily he is more intimate. He declares boldly his passion for experience. He will not be held; he appeals to Nature, to birds and beasts, against the claim to constancy.

> ' Now thou hast loved me one whole day ;'

but even to-morrow we two shall not be ' just those persons which we were.' He can love any woman ' so she be not true '; and the worst torture of love he finds, is to love ' one that loves me.'

> ' Rob me but bind me not and let me go.
> Must I, who came to travel thorough you,
> Grow your fixed subject because you are true ?'

He expresses contempt for the women he loves.

> ' But they are ours as fruits are ours ;
> He that but tastes, he that devours
> And he that leaves all, doth as well ;
> Changed loves are but changed sorts of meat ;
> And when he hath the kernel eat,
> Who doth not fling away the shell ? '
>
> (*Community*.)

Yet he knows the idolatry of love, and would have passion perfect and eternal if he might.   He insists on the idea that lovers make their own world, a very fragile world, but the only real one while it lasts.   Sometimes he rails against his love for a woman who cannot understand him. 'Well then,' he says to his heart :

> 'Well then, stay here ; but know,
> When thou hast stay'd and done thy most,
> *A naked, thinking heart that makes no show,*
> *Is to a woman but a kind of ghost.*
> How shall she know my heart ; or, having none,
>   Know thee for one ?
> Practice may make her know some other part ;
> But, take my word, she doth not know a heart.'
>
> (*The Blossome.*)

All through he knows that he is seeking for something he does not know.

> ' I never stoop'd so low as they
> Which on an eye, cheek, lip can prey ;
>   Seldom to them which soar no higher
>   Than virtue or the mind to admire.
> For sense and understanding may
>   Know what gives fuel to their fire ;
> My love, though silly, is more brave ;
> For may I miss whene'er I crave,
> If I know yet what I would have !'[1]

[1] Donne, *Complete Poems*, ed. Grosart, 1873, vol. ii., p. 230.

The following poem (*The Relique*), which the blending of irony, sadness, worship and aspiration makes one of the most extraordinary in English, is highly characteristic of Donne.

> ' When my grave is broke up again,
> Some second guest to entertain,—
>
> . . . .
> . . . .
>
>   And he that digs it spies
> *A bracelet of bright hair about the bone,*
>   Will he not let us alone
> And think that there a loving couple lies,
> Who thought that this device might be same way
> To make their souls at the last busy day
> Meet at this grave, and make a little stay?
>
> ' If this fall in a time or land
> Where mass devotion doth command,
> Then he that digs us up will bring
> Us to the bishop or the king,
> To make us relics ; then
> Thou shalt be a Mary Magdalen, and **I**
>   A something else thereby ;
> *All women shall adore us and some men.*
> And since at such times miracles are sought,
> I would have that age by this paper taught
> What miracles we harmless lovers wrought.
>
> ' First we loved well and faithfully,
> Yet knew not what we loved nor why ;
> Difference of sex we never knew,
> No more than guardian angels do ;
>   Coming and going we
> Perchance might kiss but not betwixt those meals ;
> Our hands ne'er touched the seals
> Which nature, injured by late law, sets free.

> These miracles we did ; but now, alas !
> All measure and all language I should pass,
> Should I tell what a miracle she was.'

This perhaps represents, among other things, what was possibly the last stage of an exhausted and intellectual sensualism: the desire for a love essentially sexual, in which sex should be almost forgotten.

That Donne plays with words to excruciation, that he rejoices in the mere ingenuity of conceit, that he tortures his fancies to death and delights in the display of his curious lore, does not affect the originality or the essential sincerity of his love poems. In these respects he seems deliberately to exaggerate the mannerisms and affectations of Elizabethan literature. Yet it is in his later rather than in his love poetry that frigid conceits, learned flourishes, and the 'monstrous and disgusting hyperboles' which roused the wrath of Dr. Johnson, especially abound.[1]

In his later phase Donne's poetry was for the most part religious in character. He was certainly not insincere, but there is no sign that his religious sentiment was ever very profound. To compare him with George Herbert as a religious poet seems absurd: they are poles apart. Herbert indulged in vapid conceits, and even wrote shaped verses; but at his worst he is always tender and spiritual. Donne's religious poetry is, as a rule, cold, tortured, and artificial. He became more and more 'metaphysical': more and more he intellectualized among abstractions. Sometimes the thought of his 'divine poems' is deep and striking: far more often it is merely ingenious. Of these poems perhaps the best is *The Litany*, composed in 1609.

> 'From being anxious or secure,
> Dead clods of sadness or light squibs of mirth,

---

[1] It is significant that he wrote very few love sonnets.

From thinking that great courts immure
All or no happiness, or that this earth
    Is only for our prison framed,
    Or that Thou 'rt covetous
To them whom Thou lovest, or that they are maim'd
From reaching this world's sweet who seek Thee thus,
With all their might—good Lord, deliver us.

'From needing danger to be good,
From owing Thee yesterday's tears to-day,
    From trusting so much to Thy blood
That in that hope we wound our soul away,
      From bribing Thee with alms, to excuse
      Some sin more burdenous,
From light affecting, in religion, news,
From thinking us all soul, neglecting thus
Our mutual duties—Lord, deliver us.

'Hear us, O hear us, Lord; to Thee
A sinner is more music when he prays
    Than spheres' or angels' praises be
In panegyric alleluias;
      Hear us, for till Thou hear us, Lord,
      We know not what to say;
Thine ear to our sighs, tears, thoughts, gives voice and word;
O Thou, who Satan heard'st in Job's sick day,
Hear Thyself now, for Thou in us dost pray.

'That learning, Thine ambassador,
From Thine allegiance we never tempt;
    That beauty, paradise's flower,
For physic made, from poison be exempt;
      That wit—born apt high good to do—
      By dwelling lazily
On nature's nothing, be not nothing too;
That our affections kill us not, nor die;
Hear us, weak echoes, O, Thou Ear and Eye.'

Putting the love poems aside, this is Donne at his best.

But the emotional fire has almost gone out, and little but the subtle intelligence remains. The crowding of the thought would remind us of Shakespeare but for the almost complete absence of imagery. Strange as it may seem in a writer so fond of verbal quip and fantastic conceit, this absence of imagery is characteristic.

In the year 1610 died Elizabeth Drury, a girl of fourteen, daughter of Sir Robert Drury, a gentleman of Suffolk and one of the richest in England. In 1611 there was published Donne's *Anatomy of the World*, 'wherein by occasion of the untimely death of Mistress Elizabeth Drury, the frailty and decay of this whole world is represented.' In the following year this was republished along with a new poem for the second anniversary of Elizabeth's death. These extraordinary poems look almost like a caricature of Elizabethan extravagance: it is as if Donne had deliberately set himself to outdo the world in hyperbole. On the death of this child of fourteen, whom the writer had never even seen, 'the world,' Donne declares, 'had fits': it could 'have better spared the sun *or man*': only the memory of Elizabeth Drury keeps things alive at all. He told Ben Jonson (who said that such eulogies might be appropriate if addressed to the Virgin Mary) that in writing these poems he had not thought of Elizabeth, but of the 'Idea of a Woman.' This does not make things much better. The truth seems to be that the Elizabethans enjoyed the extravagant, and that Donne set his ingenuity to work to produce something sublimely and preposterously extravagant. Yet these outrageous poems are full of weighty and subtle reflection, and in parts—especially of the *Second Anniversary*—are splendidly written. There are passages of intense imagination and profound philosophy. He has been saying that his hymns to her memory may so far, as it were, 'embalm

and spice' the world as, though they cannot revive it, to
preserve it from actual putrefaction. And after this declaration he goes on:

> 'These hymns thy issue may increase so long
> *As till God's great Venite change the song.*
> Thirst for that time, O my insatiate soul,
> And serve thy thirst with God's safe-sealing bowl;
> Be thirsty still and drink still till thou go
> To th' only health; to be hydroptic so,
> Forget this rotten world; and unto thee
> Let thine own times as an old story be.
> Be not concerned: study not why nor when;
> Do not so much as not believe a man,
> For though to err be worst, to try truths forth
> Is far more business than this world is worth.'

Again:

> 'Dost thou love
> Beauty—and beauty worthiest is to move?
> Poor cozened cozener! that she and that thou
> Which did begin to love are neither now;
> You are both fluid, changed since yesterday;
> Next day repairs—but ill—last day's decay.
> *Nor are, although the river keep the name,*
> *Yesterday's waters and to-day's the same.*'

In this *Second Anniversary* Donne is at his best and at his
worst.

Donne founded no school, though he of course had
imitators. That which was valuable in him was quite
inimitable. He certainly did not found the school of
religious poetry which produced Herbert, Crashaw, and
Vaughan. Elizabethan religious poetry did not begin
with Donne, nor did he give it anything permanent save
his own poems, though his popularity no doubt stimulated
this kind of poetic expression. As to his versification, it is

hard to say whether he was the more careless or perverse.
He has a fine ear, as he shows constantly, yet he is capable
of verse so harsh and crabbed as to be a positive offence.
He deliberately breaks up the natural sequence of accent
and trusts to his ear to restore the broken cadence by a
nice balance of emphasis. No poet's cadence depends
more absolutely on his meaning, and therefore it is, indeed,
that his cadence is often tortured and crabbed. Yet at his
best his verse has a depth of often broken music rarely
equalled by more regular craftsmen.[1]

In his later years Donne was immensely admired and
praised alike as preacher and saint, controversialist and
poet. Carew's celebrated epitaph hailed him as a king:

> ' Who ruled, as he thought fit,
> The universal monarchy of wit.'

Izaak Walton, his biographer, was especially anxious to
show forth his saintliness and his repentance for the sins
of his youth. In his own lifetime Drummond of Hawthornden had written of him: ' Donne, among the Ana-
creontic lyrics, is second to none and far from all second.'
But the justest judgement pronounced upon him by his
contemporaries was that of Ben Jonson. ' The first poet
in the world in some things ' Jonson declared him, and
added acutely that ' Donne, for not being understood,
would perish.' This prophecy concerning the most perverse and the most intellectual of all Elizabethan lyrists
has almost been fulfilled.

---

[1] Mr. Gosse calls him a ' metrical iconoclast '; but it does not
appear that he had any theory or distinct intention. Coleridge
speaks of his ' wreathing iron pokers into true love-knots.'

§ 7. *Drummond and Wither: Religious Poetry.*

William Drummond, son of Sir John Drummond, a
Scottish landowner of considerable property,
was educated at Edinburgh and in France—
where he studied law a little and poetry a
good deal—and succeeded to the domains of
Hawthornden in 1610. At Hawthornden he lived for the
rest of his life—a life of study and meditation, among the
books of which in 1627 he gave 500 to the young University
of Edinburgh. He read Latin, Greek, French, Italian,
Spanish, and Hebrew. He cared nothing for preferment and
never sought it. He seems to have lived almost as a recluse,
caring only for the company of learned or accomplished
men. He was a close friend of Sir William Alexander,
maintained a correspondence with Drayton, and towards
the end of 1618 received a famous visit from Ben Jonson.
'When his spirits were too much bended by severe studies,
he unbended them by playing on his lute.' Yet this gentle
and retiring student, late in his life, plunged valiantly,
with his pen, into the struggle against the Covenanters.
His first poems, *Tears on the Death of Mœliades* (Prince
Henry), appeared in 1613, and showed his tastes rather
than his qualities.   Soon after this he was betrothed to a
lady named Cunningham; but in 1615, after the date for
the marriage had been fixed, she died.

William Drummond (1585-1649).

In 1616 Drummond published a volume of poems[1] in
three parts, consisting of (1) sonnets and lyric pieces in
honour of his love; (2) others in lamentation for her
death; and (3) *Urania*, 'spiritual' poems, chiefly on the
vanity of earthly hopes and ambitions.   In 1617 James I.

---

[1] *Poems, amorous, funerall, divine, pastorall, in sonnets, songs, sextains and madrigals,* Edinburgh, 4to.

visited Edinburgh, and Drummond then published an elaborate panegyric entitled *Forth-Feasting*, finely written but grossly adulatory, though the poet had nothing either to hope or to fear from the monarch. In 1623 Drummond published his finest work, *Flowres of Sion*,[1] a volume of sonnets and lyric or heroic verse, entirely philosophic or religious in character. His later literary work was chiefly in prose, and his epigrams and satires were mostly political and are of no literary value.

All Drummond's valuable work is in the two publications of 1616 and 1623; and the best of it is extremely good. As a sonnet-writer Drummond stands easily above all his contemporaries save Shakespeare; as a writer of religious poetry in any strict sense, he is rivalled only by Spenser. His imagery too is often Spenserian, but many phrases are 'lifted' by Drummond directly from Shakespeare. Ben Jonson told him that his verse 'smelled too much of the schools'; and it was true. Thorough artist as he was, he was certainly something of a pedant. He is absurdly fond of decorating his verse with classical names, and though he sometimes gets good sound-effects with them he often uses them pedantically.[2] He is imitative, and sometimes absolutely translates from Petrarch, Marino, or Sannazzaro. He disfigures his poems with far-fetched conceits and silly ingenuities: but perhaps to a less extent than almost any other poet of his age. His

---

[1] Appended to the *Flowres of Sion* was his stately and sonorous meditation on death, entitled *A Cypresse Grove*, one of the finest pieces of prose-writing of the period. Drummond was one of the first of Scottish prose-writers to use English as his mother-tongue.

[2] As:

> 'Look on the woefull shipwreck of my youth,
> And let my ruins for a Phare thee serve
> To shun this rock Capharean of untruth.'

feminine sensitiveness sometimes betrays him into the mawkish. But frequently he frees himself from all these faults.

Drummond is not a poet of love or even a poet of sorrow. Though there is real melancholy in them, few would have supposed that the poems of 1616 refer to the recent and actual loss of a bride. Evidently their careful composition relieved him considerably:

> ' What doth it serve to see Sun's burning face
> And skies enamell'd with both the Indies gold,
> Or moon at night in jetty chariot roll'd,
> And all the glory of that starry place ?
> What doth it serve earth's beauty to behold,
> The mountains' pride, the meadows' flow'ry grace,
> The stately comeliness of forests old,
> The sport of floods which would themselves embrace ?
> What doth it serve to hear the Sylvans' songs,
> The wanton merle, the nightingale's sad strains,
> Which in dark shade seem to deplore my wrongs ?
> For what doth serve all that this world contains,
> Sith she for whom these once to me were dear,
> No part of them can now have with me here ? '

This beautiful sonnet comes as near to a perfect expression of grief as Drummond ever gets. Very fine also is the second song in the *Poems* of 1616: that of the vision of his dead mistress, with its appeal to God's law and its vision of heaven.

But Drummond is at his best in his religious poems, and when, in a mood of pensive and contented melancholy, he reflects, with conviction born of religion and the aversion from action of a natural recluse and student, on the vanity of human endeavour and worldly prizes. His religion was deeply influenced by Plato, and frequently, like Wordsworth, he uses almost pantheistic language. His

God is a God of beauty and love, and he is ecstatic rather than philosophic in his contemplations. He has not the subtlety or the strange strength of Donne, but he has far more religious feeling. The most exalted, the most profound and beautiful of his distinctively religious poems is *The Hymn of the Fairest Fair* (written in heroic couplets of a dignified regularity) in the *Flowres of Sion*: there is nothing to match it in Elizabethan 'divine' poetry save Spenser's *Hymns*. Of his reflective sonnets the following is one of the most beautiful and characteristic:

> 'A good that never satisfies the mind,
> A beauty fading like the April flowers,
> A sweet with floods of gall that runs combine'd,
> A pleasure passing ere in thought made ours,
> An honour that more fickle is than wind,
> A glory at opinion's frown that lowers,
> A treasury which bankrupt time devours,
> A knowledge than grave ignorance more blin ',
> A vain delight our equals to command,
> A style of greatness, in effect a dream,
> A fabulous thought of holding sea and land,
> A servile lot decked with a pompous name,
>   Are the strange ends we toil for here below,
>   Till wisest death make us our errors know.'

Among writers of verse of religious or philosophic import, Sir John Davies, politician and successful lawyer, Attorney-General for Ireland in 1603, knighted in 1607, a judge in 1620, and Lord Chief Justice in 1626, demands brief mention. He is interesting as an example of the way in which, at this period, ambitious and successful men of affairs, with no poetic talent whatever, took the trouble to elaborate long poems. His first poem was *The Orchestra*,

Sir John Davies
(1567-1626).

a poem in seven-line stanzas and nearly a thousand lines long, published in 1596.   It is a curious production, turning on the conception of the musical motion of all things in a dance of love.   Fancifully extravagant and far more ingenious than poetical, it yet shows some command of verse, and at times its diction has distinction and dignity. In 1599 he published the *Hymnes of Astraea*, and his most ambitious work, the *Nosce Teipsum*.   The *Hymnes* are a series of thirty-six acrostics on the words Elizabetha Regina: clever as acrostics.   The *Nosce Teipsum* is a long and dull poem on the soul and its immortality, of which the argumentation is poor and the diction generally prosaic.[1]

A poet of far greater talent was Robert Southwell, the
Jesuit martyr.   After a long residence
Robert Southwell   abroad Southwell returned to England
(1561-1595).
in 1587, along with Father Henry Garnet, and became chaplain to the Countess of Arundel. Most of his poems seem to have been written between that time and his arrest in 1592.   Two volumes of verse by him, *Saint Peter's Complaint with other Poemes* and *Maeoniae*, were published in 1595.   As a religious poet he stands high, his verse being marked by strong individuality, great vigour of diction, and fervent faith.   He wrote also a number of devotional tracts in prose.

The most profound and original of all the religious poets who wrote in this period, George Herbert (1593-1632), 'who sang on earth,' wrote Walton, 'such hymns and anthems as he and the angels and Mr. Ferrar now

---

[1] He wrote a number of *Epigrammes*, and several poems (two of them in dramatic form) by him appear in the 1608 edition of *The Poetical Rapsody*.   He wrote also on legal subjects, and published a pamphlet on the condition of Ireland in 1612.   His chief poems were collected in 1622.

sing in heaven,' does not come within our ken, since *The Temple* was only published posthumously in 1633.[1]

George Wither may naturally be placed last among Eliza-
bethan lyric (and religious) poets. Not
only was his life prolonged into the days of
Charles II., but his poetry is to some ex-
tent a link between the song-books and the more colloquial
and less ideal lyric of Carew and Suckling and Waller.
Almost all his good work is contained in the volume called
Juvenilia, published in 1622. This contains *Abuses Stript,
Prince Henries Obsequies, Epithalamia, The Shepheards
Hunting, Wither's Motto, Fidelia*, and *Faire-Virtue, the
Mistresse of Phil'Arete*, in octosyllabic verse. After 1622
he abandoned secular for religious poetry, of which he
wrote a large quantity, extremely unequal in quality.
His secular lyric is marked by facility and spontaneity,
frequent felicity in expression, a tendency to bathos, a
colloquial ease and directness, and charmingly high spirits.
On the intellectual side he is neither very original nor very
strong; on the moral side he is one of the most original of
poets. He is full of joy and confidence, of high and
happy thoughts, and the cheerful spirit (of his early verse,
at least) gives to his lines 'an elasticity like a dancing
measure.' No one writes more spontaneously. He is a
natural warbler, garrulous and now and then inspired. His
'native wood-notes' offer an extreme contrast with the
scholarly sweetness of Drummond or the subtleties and
perversities of Donne.[2]

George Wither
(1588-1667).

[1] See *The Age of Milton*, where Herrick also is treated at
length.

[2] *Abuses Stript and Whipt*, a thin, moral 'satire' in decasyllabic verse, totally lacking in positiveness or sting, first appeared
in 1611, the *Obsequies* in 1612. In 1615 he published a volume of
pastoral eclogues, *The Shepheards Hunting*. The fourth of these
contains the famous laudation of the poetic gift. *Fidelia*, an

§ 8. *Chapman: the Verse Translators.*

At the head of the list of Elizabethan translators stands

George Chapman (1559-1634).

George Chapman, whose great translation of the works of Homer has placed him among the immortals. The first instalment of his translation of the *Iliad* (in fourteeners) appeared in 1598; other instalments followed in the same year and in 1609; the whole work appeared in 1611.[1] His translation of the *Odyssey* in heroic couplets was published in 1614-15.

Chapman's was not the first attempt to render the *Iliad* into English verse. In 1581 a certain Arthur Hall (1540?-1604) had published a verse translation of ten of the books. But Chapman's version is not only immensely superior to Hall's, it is superior to any later version, in that it is more Homeric. The extreme liberties which he took with his

elegiacal epistle in heroic couplets, enshrining the famous song, *Shall I, Wasting in Despair?* was issued privately in 1615 (Bodleian), and reprinted 1617 and 1619. In 1621 he published the long and curious poem called *Wither's Motto*, an extreme expression of fluency and *naïveté*. Like Wordsworth he wrote for a short while admirably, and for a long period indifferently. But Wither seems to have feared the secular Muse as much as Gresset. His first original religious verse, *Hymnes and Songs of the Church*, appeared in 1623. Of both heptasyllabic and octosyllabic verse he had a special command, while in his songs he shows considerable power of metrical invention. For his religious poetry see *The Age of Milton*. (Bibliographical notes kindly given by Mr. F. Sidgwick; and see his *Poetry of G. Wither*, 2 vols., 1903.)

[1] *Seaven Bookes of the Iliades* (bks. i.-ii., vii.-xi.), 1598; *Achilles Shield* (from bk. xviii.), 1598. Five more books in 1609. *The Iliads of Homer, Prince of Poets*, 1611 (complete; the whole in 'fourteeners,' *i.e.*, heptameters, or seven-stress lines). In 1616 he issued the *Iliad* and *Odyssey* together. Chapman also published translations of Hesiod's *Georgics* (1618) and of the fifth Satire of Juvenal (1629).

I.   G

original may offend the technical scholar; but as compared with more scholarly versions Chapman's has the advantage of being the version of a poet.   Yet it must be admitted that, while Chapman finely renders a good deal of the spirit of the Homeric poems, he catches little or nothing of the Homeric art.   His translation is a barbarization; a rendering of Homer into the *Nibelungenlied*.   Above all he fails in rendering the stern, delightful brevities of the Greek.

But Chapman was far more than a translator; he was an original poet and dramatist of great power.   A learned, laborious, and high-minded man, of great force and independence of character, he lacked taste and judgement, seems to have been generally overworked, and entertained a studious contempt for popular opinion.   'The profane multitude I hate,' he wrote, 'and only consecrate my strange poems to those searching spirits whom learning hath made noble and nobility sacred.'   Again: 'That which being with a little endeavour searched adds a kind of majesty to poesy is better than that which every cobbler may sing to his patch.'

His poems are certainly 'strange' and more than a little endeavour is necessary to understand them.[1]   Of all Elizabethan poets he is the most obscure.   To read Chapman lightly is to think him an obscure and intolerable pedant; but he who reads him with care may think him a great poet who never in any single piece realized his powers.   For the most part he is either inarticulate or he is labouring pedantically, often with execrable taste, at heavy and meretricious embroidery.[2]

---

[1] Cf. esp. *Ovid's Banquet of Sence.*
[2] His first poem was *The Shadow of Night*, published in 1594. In 1595 appeared *Ovid's Banquet of Sence, A Coronet for his Mistress Philosophie* (ten sonnets), and *The Amorous Zodiacke.*

One of the pioneers among metrical translators from the Latin, after Phaer and Surrey, was Arthur Golding, who lived until 1605, but whose best-known translation, that of Ovid's *Metamorphoses*, written in a ballad-metre and full of life, was published in 1567 and was well known to Marlowe and Shakespeare. G. Sandys (see p. 209) rendered the *Metamorphoses* into heroic couplets, 1621-6.

In 1582 Richard Stanyhurst (1547-1618), a native of Dublin, a Roman Catholic and an excellent Latinist, who spent his later years in the Low Countries, issued at Leyden his *First Foure Bookes of Virgil his Aeneis*, published in London, with additions, 1583. The version is a literary curiosity, being the only attempt ever made to put Gabriel Harvey's prosody into practice on a large scale. It is written neither in rhyme nor in blank verse, but in English hexameters of 'incomparable oddity,' extraordinary words being invented to supply the necessary dactyls, while recourse is likewise had to the most grotesque inversions.

Minor Translations in verse.

Of translations from the Italian one of the most important was a rendering of Ariosto's *Orlando Furioso* by Sir John Harington (1561-1612), a great wit and virtuoso of Elizabeth's Court, who scandalized even his godmother (the Queen) by his saucy sallies. Ostracized from the Court, he prepared his free translation of Ariosto, issued in folio in 1591. It keeps to the *ottava rima* of the original. But the composite style of Ariosto owes its charm to the skill with which the delicate tints of the poet's irony and gay humour are blended with the more sober colouring of the narrative. Harington (like Smollett rendering Cervantes) overcharges the picture with farce and caricatures his original into burlesque.[1]

His first published play appeared in 1598, in which year he also published his completion of *Hero and Leander*. In completing that splendid fragment Chapman was stirred to unusual directness and lucidity; but his work cannot be compared with Marlowe's. For some years he was mainly occupied with drama (see Book III.). In 1609 appeared *The Teares of Peace*, and in 1614 *Andromeda Liberata*.

[1] Harington prefaced his *Orlando* by his *Apologie for Poetrie* (see Book II., p. 105).

The first translator of Tasso was Richard Carew (1555-1620), a Cornish gentleman and scholar, who took a prominent part in the proceedings of the Society of Antiquaries established by Archbishop Parker in 1572 (reorganized by Cotton, Camden, Sir John Davies and others in 1614). His *Godfrey of Bvlloigne or the recoverie of Hierusalem*, from Tasso, was issued in 1594 and is noted more for accuracy than for spirit. It was indeed entirely eclipsed by the version from the *Gerusalemme Liberata* in 'English heroicall verse' by Edward Fairfax (d. 1635), a Yorkshire scholar and recluse, who refines upon the literal method of his predecessor, though he retains the octave measure of the original. In musical and poetical qualities this translation of 1600 has scarcely ever been surpassed. The elaboration of its stanzas frequently bespeaks *The Faerie Queene*, the vocabulary of which it is clear that Fairfax appreciatively studied. Another translator of Ariosto was Robert Tofte (d. 1620), who gave a version of the *Satyres* in 1608, but is better known as the translator of Boiardo's *Orlando Innamorato*, 1598.

The favourite subjects for metrical translation from the French were the Scriptural epics of the Huguenot Guillaume de Saluste, Seigneur du Bartas (1544-1590), whose fame was thus kept alive in England long after it had been totally eclipsed in France. Thomas Hudson, one of James VI.'s Edinburgh musicians, translated Du Bartas's *Historie of Judith* in 1584; Sir Philip Sidney and William Lisle essayed various fragments; but the great bulk of Du Bartas's *magnum opus*, *La Semaine*, the Week or Birth of the World, originally issued in two instalments, 1579, 1584, was first seriously taken in hand by Josuah Sylvester (1563-1618), an indefatigable rhymester, who surpassed even his original in quaint phraseology and religious enthusiasm. Begun in 1592, the work was issued collectively as *Du Bartas his Devine Weekes* in 1605-6. Sylvester was mistaken by his contemporaries for a rival of Spenser; and his pastoral style was undoubtedly imitated to some extent by Browne and even by Milton. But he went out of fashion with Lyly (before 1660), and the fame of his voluminous works is condensed into a name, which lingers in the text-books alongside of Munday and Churchyard.

Bacon's experiments with Psalmody in English metre (of which he himself formed a high opinion) are noticed later (p. 176).

§ 9. *Hall and the Verse Satirists.*

The misanthropy, the cynicism, bitter or gay, the humorous tolerance of or profound revolt against evil, one or other of which must go to the making of great satire, are not to be found in any high degree among Elizabethan writers. The Elizabethans were too much in love with life to satirize it effectively. Their genius was lyrical and dramatic, and with such genius satire is commonly inconsistent. Elizabethan satire is artificial: it is a literary pose and one so uncongenial that few of the greatest Elizabethan writers concern themselves with it at all. The only Elizabethan poets of remarkable talent who wrote formal satire were Lodge, Drayton, Wither, and Donne (these are all noticed elsewhere); and all these failed with it completely.

Elizabethan satire is more or less imitative and feeble. It rarely has vigour except when it ceases to be satire and becomes mere denunciation, in which case it shows a strong tendency to degenerate into mere abuse, as in Marston. Sometimes it is modelled formally on the Latin; sometimes it takes the form of 'epigrams'; sometimes, as in Drayton's *Owle*, it assumes allegorical dress.

The more notable of the verse satirists (excluding Donne) are Joseph Hall, John Davies of Hereford, and John Marston. Joseph Hall (1574-1656) published six books of satires entitled *Virgidemiarum Libri Sex* in 1597-8.[1] He styled the first

---

[1] See p. 135. In claiming the title of first English satirist, Hall conveniently ignored the satires of Wyatt and Lodge. In Lodge's *Fig for Momus* (1595), with Horatian epistles to private friends are joined several satires in the Latin manner. The heroic couplets of these served as models to all later English satirists. Lodge had already in *A Looking Glasse for London* shown himself a master of the couplet. Three of Donne's *Satires* go back to 1593-4.

three books (1597) 'toothlesse' and the last three (1598) 'byting' satires; but the difference is not so great as he apparently supposed. His satires are written in heroic couplets and show a decided though immature literary talent. They are written with vigour, wit, and scurrility. His satire of social manners is shallow and insincere; but his literary satire shows appreciative criticism. The diction is rough and crabbed, and the allusions frequently obscure.[1]

The satire of John Davies of Hereford (1565-1618) is at least as forcible as that of Hall and is less academic. His *Scourge of Folly*, distinguished by a very quaint title-page, was published in 1611. At its best it is coarsely vigorous, with a realism rare among the satirists of the time.[2]

John Marston (1575-1634), the dramatist, published his *Scourge of Villanie* in 1598. In these satires Marston, one of the most abusive and obscene of Elizabethan writers, attempted with entire lack of success to assume the tone of a Juvenal. They are full of scurrilous personalities and empty declamation, and the diction is coarse and obscure; a rough vigour is their sole merit.

[1] For Hall's life and prose work see Book II., and for Marston Book III.

[2] Davies was by profession a teacher of penmanship; but he was also a voluminous writer of verse. Most of his poems are philosophical or religious in character, and of no value whatever. The epigrams in the *Scourge* have much interest for the literary antiquary: one refers in somewhat ambiguous terms to the 'rayning wit' of 'our English Terence,' Mr. Will. Shakespeare. In 1602 he published a long philosophical poem entitled *Mirum in Modum*, and 1603 another, still longer, which he called *Microcosmos*. In 1605 appeared *Humours Heav'n on Earth* and *The Triumph of Death, or the Picture of the Plague*; in 1606 *Bien Venu* (welcoming Danes to English Court); and in 1610 or 1611 *Wittes Pilgrimage*, a poetical miscellany. His satire, though poor enough, is distinctly better than his philosophy and religion.

Among the less known satirists of the period may be mentioned Samuel Rowlands (1570 ?-1630 ?), who is chiefly remarkable for his pictures of low life in London. In 1600 he published
two volumes of satire and epigram, *The Letting of Humours
Blood in the Head-Vaine* and *A Mery Meetinge, or 'tis Mery when
Knaves mete*, which had the honour of being publicly burnt.
Tis Merrie when Gossips meete (1602), a four-part tavern dialogue in the favourite six-line stanza, though pale beside Dunbar, is a remarkable piece of Elizabethan genre. His later
satires include *Diogines Lanthorne* (1607), *Doctor Merrie-man*,
rich in illustrations for *Measure for Measure*, *The Melancholie
Knight* (1615), showing some acquaintance with *Don Quixote*,
and *Good News and Bad News* (1622). The verse of Rowlands
varies from doggrel to decasyllabic couplets wellnigh as smooth
as those of Pope. He seems to have been a man of considerable
wit and power of picturing.

William Rankins (d. 1601), author of *The Mirrour of Monsters*
(1587), directed against the spotted enormities of the players,
and *The English Ape* (1588), wrote *Satires* (1598) in a seven-line
stanza, in a similar strain to his previous work, ridiculing the
follies of fashion. Robert Anton published in 1616 satires on
literary subjects, a long way after Ariosto, entitled *Vice's
Anatomy Scourged*.

Among the epigrammatists the most important are Bastard
and Harington. Thomas Bastard (1566-1618), a clergyman,
published in 1598 a book containing 290 epigrams on various
subjects, entitled *Chrestoleros*. Sir John Harington, the courtier
and wit and translator of Ariosto (§ 8), produced *Epigrams both
pleasant and serious*, 1615, published complete in 1618.

John Weever (1576-1632) published in 1599 a volume of
Epigrammes in the oldest Cut and newest Fashion, which contains
a sonnet to Shakespeare, and epigrammatic praises of Drayton,
Daniel, and Ben Jonson. The *Epigrammes* of Sir John Davies
appended to Marlowe's *Elegies* were a little earlier.

The more frequently cited Epigrams of Campion's friend,
Charles Fitzgeffrey (*Affaniae*, 1601), and of John Owen (d. 1622),
the witty disciple of Martial, were written in Latin, though many
of Owen's were 'Englished' in 1628, by Hayman, and by

others. These things have a 'curious' value for the literary detective.

Edward Guilpin, a friend of Gervase Markham, produced in 1598 his *Skialetheia*, or *A Shadow of Truth in Certain Epigrams and Satyres*. Both epigrams and satires are coarser than is ordinary among Guilpin's contemporaries, and the satirist remarks apologetically:

> 'Excuse me, reader, though I now and than
> In some light lines doe show myself a man.'

But the references to well-known contemporaries give the book a certain interest, second in its kind only to that of Davies's *Scourge of Folly*.

A slenderer interest of a similar description attaches to Thomas Freeman, whose queerly entitled *Rubbe and a Great Cast* contains two 'bowles' or sets, of a hundred epigrams each, in various rhyming measures. No. 192 is consecrated to 'Master W. Shakespeare,' and commences:

> 'Shakespeare, that nimble Mercury thy brain.'

Another more riotous minor humorist, who sought to express a ripe knowledge of and mature contempt for the world through the medium of crude and juvenile verse, was Richard Brathwaite (1588?-1673), the compiler many years later of the still unforgotten *Barnabee's Journal* (1638), who brought out in 1615 his *Strappado for the Devil*, a miscellany of epigrams, satires, and occasional pieces, in pretended emulation of Wither's essays at 'stripping' and 'whipping' abuses. In this he quotes *Tamburlaine*, *Richard III.*, and *Don Quixote*, and, he would have us believe, confirmed his right to be pointed at in the streets as an author and a wit. But less wit would seem to have gone to the making of an Elizabethan satirist than to that of any other specimen of the large literary confraternity of those days.

§ 10. *Hero and Leander.*

In 1598 was published an incomplete poem by Christopher Marlowe, entitled *Hero and Leander.* In the same year the poem was completed and published in its complete form by Chapman, who divided Marlowe's work into two sestiads and added four more of his own.[1] Written at least as early as 1592-3,[2] Marlowe's poem should, perhaps, have been considered earlier in this brief survey; but it stands in such strong contrast to the mass of Elizabethan poetry that its chronological position is of small importance.

The mass of Elizabethan lyrical and narrative poetry, beautifully ornamented, graceful, dainty, even exquisite as it often is, is in a high degree conventional. The lyric of Greene and Lodge, Breton and Drayton can, in general, only be acquitted on the charge of conventionality and insincerity, on the ground of its freshness of handling. The light, glad, nervous touch of these writers vitalized the conventional themes and thoughts they borrowed from a common stock. Among the narrative poets Drayton and Daniel are conventionally moral or sentimental. Drummond's verse, in spite of its peculiar individuality, has the air of a scholarly and academic exercise. Even the *Venus and Adonis* and the *Lucrece* are conventionally planned and academically written: their whole merit consists in their abundance of delicious imagery and mastery of delicate verse. It is this conventionality in theme and

---

[1] In the third sestiad there is an obscure passage which appears to indicate that Chapman completed the poem at Marlowe's request.

[2] Marlowe died in June, 1593 (see Book III.), and *Hero and Leander*, 'an amorous poem,' was entered upon the Stationers' Registers on September 28th following.

in thought that perhaps most deeply distinguishes the romantic poetry of the Elizabethans from the romantic poetry of the nineteenth century. The creative genius of Spenser and the extraordinary intellectuality of Donne raised them to a different plane; and though not comparable with the work of Spenser for beauty or with that of Donne for sheer cleverness, this poem of Marlowe's must rank with theirs on the score of originality.[1]

It is written in heroic couplets, and if we compare Marlowe's use of this form of verse with that of Drayton in the *Heroicall Epistles*, the immense superiority of the earlier poet's work is immediately manifest. No other Elizabethan writer used heroic verse with this energy and fervency, or inspired it with this fire and strength.[2] It is doubtful, indeed, whether the heroic couplet has ever been more finely handled. The matter of the poem is not less rich than the manner. It is disfigured by singularly few of those tedious ingenuities and affected extravagances which disfigure so much Elizabethan verse.

> ' As she spake
> Forth from those two tralucent cisterns brake
> A stream of liquid pearl, which down her face
> Made milk-white paths.' . . .

---

[1] Marlowe's fragment contains some eight hundred lines. It is said to be founded on a poem attributed to the legendary Greek poet Musaeus. But Marlowe appears to have taken from the pseudo-Musaeus nothing but his story.

[2] There are some fine and also some very free couplets in the early *Elegies* (from Ovid's *Amores*), but these are schoolboy exercises compared with the verse of *Hero and Leander*. The three books of *Elegies* were followed by *XLVIII. Epigrammes* by Sir J[ohn] D[avies]. The volume was printed unobtrusively ' at Middleborugh,' without date, about 1597-8. Marlowe's lyric, *Come live with me*, appeared in *The Passionate Pilgrim* of 1599.

This, indeed, is execrable;[1] but there is very little of this
kind. As a rule the expression has a simplicity and
nervous force rarely matched in Elizabethan poetry. The
diction of the poem is more typically illustrated by such
lines as these:

> ' But love, resisted once, grows passionate,
> And nothing more than counsel lovers hate;
> For as a hot proud horse highly disdains
> To have his head controlled, but breaks the reins,
> Spits forth the ringled bit and with his hoves
> Checks the submissive ground; so he that loves,
> The more he is restrained, the worse he fares:
> What is it now that mad Leander dares?
> "Oh, Hero, Hero!" thus he cried full oft;
> And then he got him to a rock aloft
> Where having spied her tower, long stared he on't
> And prayed the narrow, toiling Hellespont
> To part in twain, that he might come and go;
> But still the rising billows answered: "No."
> With that, he stripped him to the ivory skin,
> And crying, "Love, I come," leaped lively in.'

In the story of Hero and Leander Marlowe sees first of
all the beauty of the two lovers and then the beauty of
their mutual passion. The poem is a glorification of
sensuous beauty and of the loveliness of sensuous love.
It is one of the very few poems in English which glories
in the bodily beauty of a man. It is curiously pagan and
almost Greek in sentiment.[2] The licentious sensuousness

---

[1] Eyes are not in the least like 'cisterns,' and neither eyes nor
'cisterns' are tralucent; tears have no resemblance to pearls, and
neither pearls nor tears are milk-white.

[2] ' *Hero and Leander* stands out alone amid all the wide and
wild poetic wealth of its teeming and turbulent age as might a
small shrine of Parian sculpture,' says Mr. Swinburne. But for
sheer felicity the encomium passed upon the 'dead shepherd' by

of *Venus and Adonis* is all in its ornamentation : in *Hero and Leander* it is essential. The poem may even be called pure in the sense that it is utterly without shame or mis-giving. Leander's pleading against Hero's worship of 'this idol which you call virginity' is as heartfelt as it is fervent in expression.

But the poem does not merely celebrate the loveliness of passion and of physical beauty : through it all there runs a sense of the wantonness and cruelty of the gods, of the supremacy of the 'adamantine fates.' 'It lies not in our power to love or hate ': and Marlowe's lovers are the sport of the Destinies. His narrative, like all the tales of the greatest tale-tellers in prose or verse, opens up glimpses of the widest issues. Whether, had he lived to complete the poem, its ending would have been more worthy of its commencement than is that supplied by Chapman may be doubted. The fragment remains splendid and unique ; and there is perhaps nothing in Marlowe's plays which makes us feel so strongly how much we may have lost by his early death.

Drayton in his *Epistle to Henry Reynolds* of 1627 has never been surpassed :

> 'Marlowe, bathèd in the Thespian springs,
> Had in him those brave translunary things
> That the first poets had ; his raptures were
> All air and fire.' . . .

BOOK II.

PROSE.

§ 1. *Introductory.*

EVEN the development of poetical drama between 1579 and 1629 is hardly more extraordinary than the sudden expansion of English prose and its adaptation to every kind of literary requirement. Up to the commencement of Elizabeth's reign an occasional chronicle, theological or educational treatise had virtually absorbed English talent for expression through the medium of vernacular prose. Before the end of the reign twenty or thirty presses are active in London alone and classification becomes a problem. Book-making rapidly becomes a regular trade, and the process begins which leads us to the *English Catalogue* with its thousands of entries per annum. Practically almost every class of book that is produced now from year to year began to be produced when Elizabeth was Queen. There were Novelists, headed by Lyly and Sidney, Lodge and Nash, whose works were eagerly bought up by country pedlars. There were character-writers, precursors of Boz, such as Hall and Overbury, Breton and Earle. The Essayists could claim Bacon and Felltham; the Critics,

Sidney and Jonson; and one of these names at least has dominated his department from that day to this. In every literary census the Divines occupy a conspicuous place, but in the harmonious eloquence of their periphrases those of the Shakespearean era, as represented by Donne and Hooker, are not likely ever to be surpassed. The historians include Raleigh and 'well-languaged' Daniel, respectable names. Bacon's *Henry VII.* is a vital book which deserves to rank with Tacitus. Then there is a group of writers who compile wisdom from the ancients with an infusion of satire and simples of their own, and their great exemplar is Robert Burton. This brings us to a large and very miscellaneous group of compilers and pamphleteers, the 'general servants' of literature; nor does this by any means exhaust even a rough survey of the distinct types that may be discerned among the prose-writers of our period. There is already a small but powerful confederation of antiquaries and scholars (including Spelman, Camden, and Ussher) to be reckoned with. Then there are the geographers, topographers, and travellers (it is enough to mention Coryate, Sandys, Hakluyt, and Purchas); and last, but far from least, an unrivalled band of translators—not drudges, but with scarcely an exception enthusiasts—including such names as North, Florio, Shelton, and Philemon Holland.

For a good prose currency in modern times two things would seem to be requisite—the existence and recognition of good models and plenty of high-class periodical writing. The Elizabethans had neither of these things. There were indeed examples of good prose, but the examples were bewildering in their diversity. There was the prose of the pulpit and Prayer Book, and of Tyndale's Bible, the prose of the Court, generally affected and subject to passing caprices, the prose of the lawyers, and the prose of the compilers. That this last should be good, as it became with Dryden, Swift, Arbuthnot, Steele and Defoe, is a great point gained. In Elizabeth's time it was for the most part a very loose homespun, much subject to experiments.

In the generation before 1579, Fox, Hall, Ascham and Latimer had written clearly and well. But their prose had been adapted only to straightforward exhortation, exposition or narrative. The last twenty years of Elizabeth were marked, as we have seen, by the development of every variety of writing. A notion of the extent of this variety can best be obtained by an attentive survey of the selected publications enumerated in our chronological table. Many of those who aspired to cater for the omnivorous reading public of the day were avowed experimenters, and the aberrations of writers such as Greene and Nash, Harvey and Lyly, tended greatly to retard the development of a lucid and generally intelligible prose. Most of our authors were drenched with classical idioms and Italian refinements. They coined expressions and phrases with a freedom and originality which is often singular and seldom advantageous. Bacon himself, somewhat later, is often strangely tentative in these respects. Both he and Shakespeare represent a spoken language differing considerably, as we can hardly fail to recognize, from that of the present time. Shakespeare's prose, however, is stronger and richer, more colloquial and yet more individual, than the frequently curious amalgam with which Bacon welds together his aphorisms.

A greater simplicity and beauty of structure in ambitious prose is seen in Sidney's *Apologie*, in *The New Atlantis*, in Ben Jonson, in Spenser's prose tract, in Earle, Felltham, and some others. Prose especially adapted in the one case for witty epigram, and in the other for copious classical illustration, is shown in Overbury and Burton. The prose of the

divines is generally over-weighted with illustration; and
though, as in Hooker, it contain passages of beautiful inter-
laced music and majesty, yet it is rendered laborious and
obscure by the excess of circumlocution and parenthesis.
The travellers are affected in the same way. Many of the
translators are delightfully vigorous; to accuracy they lay
little claim, but there is a healthy vernacular strength about
them, of which the grandest expression is found in the
Authorized Version of the Bible. The compilers, as is apt
to be the case, aped the mannerisms rather than the merits
of their betters.

The prose as a whole is experimental. Scattered here and
there are notable melodies, and there is much isolated music.
In some of the prayers that have reached us there is an
echo of those in the Liturgy, and a cadence that is as
exquisite as a chime of bells at sunset. But, as in Ariel's
song in *The Tempest*, the burthen of the music is ' dispersed.'
More uneasy experiment was needed before a standard prose,
which should blend the ease and plasticity of colloquy with
the solidity and dignity of rhetoric, could be definitely
heralded by Dryden and his successors.

§ 2. *Critics.*

The English as a people first became conscious of form
and style in their native literature about the middle of the
sixteenth century. In 1531 Sir Thomas Elyot ' devised '
his famous *Boke named the Governour*, which was followed
by a notable series of translations from his pen. In 1545
Ascham produced his discursive and admirable dialogue
Toxophilus, and in the late sixties he composed the *Scholemaster*, which was brought out after his death by his widow
in 1570. In all these books the idea of ' style ' appears for
the first time to be definitely articulated in English. In

1553 Thomas Wilson, who had two years previously given the world his *Rule of Reason*, or ' Arte of Logique,' utilized a vacation spent quietly in the country with his friend Sir Edward Dymoke, to produce his better remembered *Arte of Rhetorique*,[1] to which is probably due the distinction of being the first systematic contribution to literary criticism written in the English language.

Such works as *The Arte of Rhetorique* and George Gascoigne's *Notes of Instruction concerning the Making of Verse* (1575) may best perhaps be described as explaining the terms and otherwise preparing the ground for the works of classification and exposition which appeared in the eighties from the pens of Puttenham, Harvey, and Webbe. It was rather before this, probably in 1581, that, required to defend poetry by an ephemeral attack, Sir Philip Sidney essayed his permanent and immortal *Defense*, not indeed upon local or temporary, but upon universal and fundamental grounds. This was followed by the less memorable ' Defences ' of Lodge and Harington. In 1598 comes the accidentally famous discourse of Francis Meres and the critical period ends with the more sophisticated and Italianate treatises of Bacon and Ben Jonson.

Thomas Wilson's *Arte of Rhetorique*, for the use of all such as are studious of eloquence, was published not later than 1553, and was to a large extent a judicious compilation from Quintilian's *Institutes of Oratory*. But it is remarkable not only for its strong academic tinge, but also for its weighty good sense. He vindicates the use of the vernacular in the treatment of scholastic subjects, and advocates simplicity of language, condemning those who sought ' to catch ink-horn terms by the tail ' and to ' powder their talk with exotic conceits.' Literary criticism during our period was chiefly concerned either with the general question whether poetry and drama is worth writ-

---

[1] Warton says it may justly be considered as the ' first system of criticism in our language.' Dr. Johnson used it in preparing his *Dictionary* and gave his copy (now in the British Museum) to George Steevens.

ing at all, or with technical questions relating to the structure of verse.

In 1575 George Gascoigne, at the request of 'Master Edward Donati,' published his *Notes of Instruction concerning the Making of Verse*, in which he notes the use of the caesura and the predominance of the iambus among English feet.[1] It is clear from his remarks that the principle of Chaucer's versification had been entirely lost.   Four years after this, from letters passing between Spenser and his senior at Pembroke Hall, Cambridge, Gabriel Harvey (1545-1630), a pedantic classicist and rhetorician of considerable learning and great proselytizing activity, we gather that a literary party was forming having for its programme strict observance of classical forms, divisions, and unities; but above all the foundation of a new metrical standard for English verse, based not upon rhyme and accent, but upon quantity. Its object was, in Harvey's own words, to 'pull down rhyming and set up versifying,' after Latin models.   Harvey had a gift of persuasion and a lordly contempt for fustian English rhyming. Ascham had said that rhyming was an invention of the Goths and Huns of the rudest ages, and the dictum had, no doubt, lingered on at Cambridge. Many courtiers were dazzled by Harvey's specious rhetoric, and it is not surprising that he found a number of converts, whose 'spavin'd dactylls' have come down to us as a solemn warning and an awful example.[2]

Harvey maintained that the normal accent of English

Gabriel Harvey and his theories.

[1] He was on a wrong tack in talking about 'feet' at all.

[2] Of these fabricators of sham antiques (hexameters and sapphics and the like) it will be sufficient merely to mention here Richard Stanyhurst, the translator of the *Aeneid* into hexameters, and Abraham Fraunce, so frankly described to Drummond by Ben Jonson as a 'big fool.' See Book I., pp. 6, 83.

words must be preserved in scansion, though subordinated
to classical metres. Thus he would scan 'carpenter' as a
dactyl, and would not lengthen the first *e* as in accordance
with strict rules of Latin prosody it should be lengthened.
Thomas Drant, however, went further and sought to bring
the rules of English prosody into strict conformity with
those of Latin. A coterie was formed, having among its
members Sidney, Dyer, Greville and Spenser, and named
the Areopagus, in order to deliberate and to give judgement. It should be noted that about ten years previously
Baïf had attempted a similar revolution in France. Stanyhurst, in his translation of the *Aeneid*, availed himself of
the latitude granted by Harvey; but most of the courtiers
and scholars, in an exalted bigotry of youthful enthusiasm,
were strongly inclined to the stricter course. The results,
however, were far from encouraging. Staggered by the
absurdities of these doctrinaires and Della Cruscans (*pace*
Mr. Swinburne), Thomas Campion, staunch classicist
though he was, suggested that the hexameter should be
given a rest and that recourse should be had to new
forms of verse of trochaic or iambic measure. Campion's
Observations on the Art of English Poesie (1602) was one
of the most stringent in the claim that it made to the
strict observance of a classical prosody.

On natures such as those of Spenser and Sidney, to
which poetry made so much stronger appeal than prosody, it was not likely that the pedantries of such men
as Harvey or Drant would produce any profound effect.
In his *Defense* Sidney is more occupied with the value
of poetry as a whole than with metrical detail. In what
he does say on the subject, he appears as a reconciler
between the ancient and the modern style of versifying.
'There being in either,' he says, 'sweetness, and wanting
in neither majesty. Truly the English, before any other

vulgar language I know, is fit for both sorts.' About the same time that he wrote, the famous schoolmaster, Richard Mulcaster, was giving expression with even greater force to somewhat similar sentiments. ' I love Rome, but London better; I favour Italy, but England more; I honour the Latin, but worship the English.' Daniel, in his *Defense of Ryme* (1602), gave the *coup-de-grâce* to the academic theory of English verse, to which Cambridge had given a kind of sanction for nearly half a century. He pleads, in the vigorous prose which he knew so well how to employ, that the use of rhyme was sanctioned in England both by custom and by nature. In such matters, he adds with justice that ' custom must stand above law and Nature above all Art.' The passage in which he concludes his treatise, expatiating upon the hatefulness of innovation and the futility of seeking perfection by the sole avenue of change, is justly deemed a *locus classicus* in English prose.

The largest piece of poetical criticism in Elizabeth's reign —*The Art of English Poesie*—was published anonymously, with a dedication to Lord Burghley, in 1589, though it was probably written three or four years earlier. The author wrote, firstly, for the personal information and pleasure of the Queen, of whose poetical efforts one or two examples are given. Secondly, he wrote for the Court and its pretty mistresses; and, lastly, he wrote to make the art vulgar for all Englishmen's use. He treats first of the theory of the origin of various kinds of poetry; he discusses classical poetry and the application of quantity to English verse; and then proceeds to deal with punctuation, language, rhetorical terms, and further, taking a leaf out of Castiglione's *Courtier*, with the seemingly foreign subject of decorum. The book is attributed on no very certain grounds to George Puttenham, the brother of one of the

Puttenham's *English Poesie*.

Queen's Yeomen of the Guard; but it is clearly the work of a scholar and a gentleman, if not of a great critical genius. He dwells on the importance of accent, and he gives the first place among our native poets to Chaucer; on the other hand, he dwells with evident fondness upon geometrical figures in verse, such as the pilaster, the taper, the egg, the turbot, and that most beautiful figure the lozenge. The third book, 'Of Ornament,' is almost entirely devoted to the figures of speech, the treatment of which is beyond measure tedious, and may well have in-spired the famous lines :

> 'And when he happened to break off
> I' th' middle of his speech or cough,
> He'd hard words ready to show why,
> And tell what rules he did it by.'

The Discourse of English Poetrie, by William Webbe, a
William Webbe
(fl. 1568-1591).
tutor of St. John's College, Cambridge, was written about the same time as *The Art of English Poesie,* and published, it would seem, in 1586. Webbe wrote under the strong influence of three works: Ascham's *Scholemaster, The Paradyse of Dainty Devices,* and Spenser's *Shepheardes Calendar.* It is greatly to his credit, as a judge of poetry, that he instinctively fixes upon this last production as the revelation of a great poet.

There are many interesting references to contemporary poets and high commendation for the more scholarly among them. Of the old masters, Chaucer, Gower, Lydgate and Piers Plowman are put first ; while among the moderns he praises, among others, the Earl of Surrey, Skelton, Wyl Hunnis, George Gascoigne, ' the very cheese of our late rhymers,' Masters Phaer, Twyne, Golding, Googe, Whetstone, Munday, and lastly ' the rightest English poet that ever I read, Master Sp.' Unfortunately Webbe was at pains to belittle our ' tinkering English rhyme,' and entreats his fellow-countrymen to attempt to versify in imitation of Greeks and Latins, and within the compass of their rules.   He seeks to illustrate what may be done in that direction by a number of rickety hexameters, apologizing not unduly for an occasional 'great misse.'

> ' Tityrus, happilie thou lyste tumbling under a beech tree,
> All in a fine Oate pipe these sweet songs lustilie chaunting.'

The distinction of writing the first philippic against the evil influence of the English drama would appear to belong to John Northbrooke, whose *Treatise*, wherein ' dicing, dauncing, vain plays or interludes ' are reproved, was licensed for the press in 1577.   Two years later, with a dedication to Philip Sidney, appeared *The School of Abuse*, containing ' a pleasant invective against poets, pipers, players, jesters, and such like caterpillars of a commonwealth,' by Stephen Gosson, a youthful Cato, who had only left Oxford, and that without taking a degree, about five years previously.

Gosson's is a quaint puritanical attack upon a form of diversion which he denounces as heathen, effeminate, and demoralizing.   Theatres, he maintained, were contrivances of the devil to wound the conscience : ' there set they abroach strange conceits of melody to tickle the ear, costly apparel to flatter the sight, effeminate gesture to ravish the sense, and wanton speech to whet desire to inordinate lust.'   These views he supports with much perverted learning from the Scriptures and the classics.

A champion for the maligned players was promptly discovered in Thomas Lodge, who wrote in *Defence of Plays*, and incidentally in defence of music and of poetry, within a month or two of Gosson's original diatribe.   The bitterness of this last is partially explained, perhaps, by the revelation that Gosson himself was a renegade actor.   Gosson now produced his *Plays Confuted in Five Actions*, and this was followed by chapters in censure of plays by Philip Stubbes in his *Anatomie of*

Abuses and by Whetstone in his *Touchstone for the Time.* More convinced even than Gosson of the wickedness and immorality of poets and players were the anonymous author of *The Second and Third Blast of Retreat from Plays and Theatres* and William Rankins, author in 1587 of the abusive *Mirrour of Monsters.* Later on, in 1599, appeared the drastic *Overthrow of Stage-Playes* by that profound scholar, Dr. Rainolds, and in 1610 the violent and abusive *Histriomastix,* which sought to hoist the stage with its own petard, for it was itself thrown into the form of a play, the title of which was adopted by Prynne some twenty-three years later.[1]

In the meantime several competent critics had rallied in defence of poetry and the drama. Prominent among them, in addition to Lodge, were Sidney, Harington, Samuel Daniel, and Thomas Heywood. By far the most important of these apologetic treatises is Sidney's noble *Defense of Poesie,* written at some time between 1580 and 1585, though not published until 1595. It was then issued by two different printers, Olney and Ponsonby. The first gave it the title *An Apologie for Poetrie*; the second, *The Defense of Poesie.* Sidney begins by maintaining that the purpose of poetry is moral and didactic. He shows the high estimation in which poets have ever been held, defines the various orders of poetry, and takes pains carefully to distinguish between poetry on the one hand, and divinity, philosophy, law and history on the other. Philosophy deals with the abstract, the historian is bound to reproduce particular instances, only the poet can present to the imagination a picture at once ideal and concrete.

Sidney's Apologie.

By a negative process we are thus brought to understand the true nature of poetry; the subdivisions or

[1] For a succinct account of this fray se' Introduction to *Much Ado* in Bankside Shakespeare.

species of creative poetry are then explained; while the various objections commonly brought against the art are enumerated, examined, and refuted.

From his method of handling his subject, it is apparent that Sidney's theory of poetry is an epitome of the criticism of the Italian Renaissance. For the general theory he drew upon the treatises of Minturno *De Poeta* and Scaliger's *Poetics*. His definitions are commonly in accordance with the light of Renaissance Aristotelianism. Sidney himself, of course, knew the classical authors familiarly—especially Aristotle, Plato, Cicero, and Horace. But it is clear that he saw the first two at least mainly through Italian spectacles. And so to express the aim of poetry in a word he went to Scaliger's *Docere cum Delectatione*, while for aid in discriminating between the various literary *genres* he went to Trissino, and for the theory of the unities to Castelvetro.

But perhaps the most interesting portion of Sidney's treatise is that which he devotes at the end to an examination of the contemporary state of poetry in England. Why, he inquires, is England, the mother of excellent minds, such a hard stepmother to poets? He admits greatness to Chaucer, and poetical beauties to *The Mirrour for Magistrates*, to Surrey, and to *The Shepheardes Calendar*; but he deplores the defects of the English drama; while he strongly deprecates the tendency to affectations euphuistic and other. This state of things, he concludes, should not be; England ought to be the reverse of sterile in regard to poetry, for the English language is specially favourable to poets. Our language is equal to all demands upon it; its composite nature, its facile grammar, its richness in compound words, are so many advantages, contributing to various and melodious expression. Finally, for the purposes of modern versification, the English language is specially adapted. 'Fie, then, on the Englishman who scorns the sacred mysteries of poetry! On all such earth-creeping minds,' says Sidney, in his humorous peroration, 'I ought to invoke some terrible curse such as that you be rhymed to death: I will not do that, but thus much curse I must send you in the behalf of all poets—"that while you live, you live in love and never get favour for lacking skill of a sonnet; and when you die your memory die from the earth for want of an epitaph."'

The extent to which his views had expanded in connection with versification indicates that if Sidney had seen the romantic drama in its prime instead of in its rude and chaotic infancy he would have readjusted his theories to embrace the masterpieces of Marlowe and of Marlowe's greater successor. For the anachronisms and absurdities of the popular stage in his own day he entertained the scorn of the high-bred university scholar; and it was in order to lash it with the greater effect that he applied to it the academic test of the unities, which the ingenuity of Italian critics had elaborated from the suggestions of Aristotle. In this part of his *Defense*, and in his inclusion of prose fiction in his definition of poetry, he showed the weakness of applying a rigid deductive process to the subject-matter of literary criticism. Upon the whole, however, his essay is distinguished by its soundness of judgement and its clearness of expression, no less than by the modesty and charm of its language. We can obtain from it not a few glimpses of the urbanity, the persuasiveness, and the magnanimity which caused Sidney to be regarded as the type of the scholar-gentleman of his time.

Of Sir John Harington's *Apologie for Poetrie*, prefixed to his paraphrase of the *Orlando Furioso*, which appeared in 1591, it is enough to say that, although it follows a set pattern, it is, as might be expected from its author, witty.

Sir John Harington (1561-1612).

It defends the poet from the ancient imputation of being a liar, a fribble, and a corrupter of youth; and it defends the translator of Ariosto in particular from such objectors as his old tutor, who said, 'Here have I grounded you for years in Aristotle and Plato, and these frivolous Italianate toys are the result!' The objection to all these formal answers to the Philistines, Huns, Tartars and other barbarians, is that it is quite useless trying to convince such people by set arguments. The man who wants to know what poetry proves will not be overcome, nor will the Puritan, who says that all fiction is a pack of lies, be converted by a set of metaphors and illustrations, however brilliant. It is no use telling the purblind that the stars are in the heavens; that their position is relatively a very lofty one; that they have been there for a considerable time, and will probably there remain. They cannot realize these circumstances. Those who can, need no such elaborate confirmation of the faith that is in them. Such general propositions are not now seriously argued by men of the intellectual calibre of Harington and Sidney.

Heywood's Apologie.

Thomas Heywood's *Apologie for Actors*, published in three parts, dealing with the antiquity, the dignity, and the quality of stage-players, in 1612, was another contribution to the defence of poetry, and more particularly the drama, against the advancing tide of Puritanism. Its literary interest is small, though in its frank appeal to antiquity to decide the question, it is characteristic. The enemy relied greatly upon Plato, upon Holy Scripture, and upon the Fathers. Heywood, with the relentless pedantry of a Prynne, searches the whole field of classical antiquity and bestrews his pages with extracts and references from Ammianus, Dion Cassius, Pliny, Origen and the like. It took his opponent

'J. G.' three whole years to ballast a minute and systematic *Refutation* (1613). As to the moral effect of the theatre Heywood tries to show how most of the follies and faults of mankind were brought to shame upon the contemporary stage.

A passing notice is due to a little thesaurus (a prototype of *Who's Who?*) of contemporary wits, entitled Francis Meres *Palladis Tamia* (1598), by Francis Meres, a (1565-1647). graduate of Pembroke College, Cambridge, who took orders and kept a school at Wing in Rutland. This worthy schoolmaster was a mere compiler, of no great learning and less critical judgement. But it is no paradox to say that it is this circumstance which gives to his discourse its chief interest. Except where he is borrowing from Puttenham, Meres' little book represents simply current opinion in literary circles at the time. And it is impossible not to be struck with the general fairness of these opinions and their conformity with the sentence of posterity. No injustice is done to Shakespeare, who is placed at the head of the dramatists ; full justice is done to Spenser, who is called divine; to Sidney, both as a prose-writer and a poet; also to Lodge, Drayton, and Daniel. For giving us a rough glance at the reputations that had sprung up since the appearance of 'Puttenham' in 1589, with some idea of their relative value in the eyes of contemporaries, Meres is thus invaluable, as he is unique.

The last critical treatise of the period with which we shall have to deal here, though by no means Ben Jonson's one of the least important, is Ben Jonson's *Timber*. *Timber, or Discoveries made upon Men and Matter,* a species of commonplace book of aphorisms flowing out of the poet's daily reading, first published in the posthumous Jonson folio of 1641, but jotted down at intervals between 1620 and the end of our period. By that time the controversy raised by the pedants who wished to latinize English verse was dead. That question, at least, was settled; and if the Puritan attack on the stage was increasing in strength, to Jonson, at all events, the drama needed no defence. The title of the work is characteristically pedantic, indicating the dense and promiscuous growth of diverse timber-trees (notions) in a wood—' Silva, the raw material of facts and thoughts,' ὕλη, wood, as it were, so called from the multiplicity and variety of the matter contained therein. The book resembles somewhat the commonplace books of Southey, the entries varying from a mere note, or aphorism, to a respectable essay. In force and condensation the utterances resemble Bacon rather than Southey. They exhibit naturally the variety and extent of Jonson's reading, his insatiable curiosity, and his unslakable thirst for knowledge.

There is little or no arrangement of *The Discoveries*, but the most interesting consecutive passages form short essays on such subjects as Kingcraft, Oratory, Style, Poetry, and the Drama; the treatment of these themes is modern as compared with that of a thesis so general and academic as that of Sidney. As was the case with most political thinkers of the day, Jonson's views of all state problems were saturated with Macchiavelli. His critical theories also were filtered through an Italian medium. But for all his preoccupation with literary classicism there is a substratum of sanity, moderation, and native good sense about every one of Jonson's opinions which separate him by a wide gulf from pedants such as Drant, Harvey, and Webbe. He is over-profuse in classical tags and quotations, but that was the universal fashion in Jacobean times amongst all who wrote the higher prose. He recognizes Aristotle as the first of critics, but he recognizes that Aristotelian rules are useless without natural talent, and that a poet's liberty cannot be bound within the narrow limits prescribed by grammarians and philosophers. While recognizing a certain validity in the rules in regard to the dramatic unities, he is by no means prepared to accept

them *au pied de la lettre*, as Sidney was apparently anxious
to do. In regard to language and style, his ultimate
conclusions derive from his basic wit and shrewd sense:
'Custom is the most certain mistress of language.' 'Pure
and neat language I love, yet plain and customary.' 'The
eldest of the present and newest of the past language is
the best.' 'Writings need sunshine.' 'The chief virtue
of a style is perspicuity.'

The best and especially the clearest authors should be read
first—Livy before Sallust, Sidney before Donne. Chaucer and
Gower may pervert the unformed taste; thus Spenser, affecting
the ancients, wrote no language. For epistolary style he notes
four necessary qualifications—Brevity, Clearness, Life (plenty
of happy illustrations), and Discretion, that is conformity to
the style and manner that best suits the writer. 'Virgil's
felicity left him in prose, as Tully's in verse.' Nothing in our
age, he says, 'is more preposterous than the running judgements upon poetry and poets.' He gibes bitterly at Heath's
Epigrams and the poem of the Sculler (*i.e.*, Taylor, the Water
Poet). These fellows are preferred to Spenser, as Cestius was
to Cicero. People praise poets for the wrong things.[1] This
introduces his remarks about Shakespeare. And of all the
good things which make Jonson's *Timber* so eminently readable and instructive, there are none which surpass in interest
these personal matters. For of the truly great Jonson speaks
nobly and with magnanimity. Of Shakespeare, *our countryman*, as he adds with a touch of pride, 'I loved the man and
do honour his memory on this side idolatry as much as any.
He was indeed honest and of an open and free nature; had an
excellent fancy, brave notions, and gentle expressions, wherein
he flowed with that facility that sometimes it was necessary he
should be stopped.' Herein is one of the soundest criticisms
on Shakespeare ever passed. Shakespeare's fondness for in-
opportune flourishes, sometimes an euphuistic conceit in the

---

[1] A notable exception was the fine criticism of Drayton, *Epistle
to Reynolds*, 1627.

middle of a serious speech, occasionally even the insertion of a bravura passage when the situation clamours for rapidity of movement—these are faults which every reader has at one time or another perceived, though few have had the courage or the critical aplomb to declare. The players boasted of Shakespeare that he never blotted out a line. Would he had blotted a thousand, said Jonson, with a perhaps pardonable exaggeration, adding with a measure of real justice, in the words of Augustus, 'Sufflaminandus erat': he ought now and again to have been clogged. Fortunately for us, Shakespeare's plays never were edited either by Shakespeare himself or by his executors in accordance with the strictures of the censorious Ben ; for obvious as certain defects may be, there is no man who ever lived to whose taste we should care to submit them for amendment—least of all to Jonson's. For great as was his admiration of Shakespeare, it is plain that Jonson could not understand him, and that a large tract of Shakespeare's mind and art was utterly beyond his ken.[1] Jonson had, in fact, an uneasy sense of Shakespeare's superiority, but he was at a loss to comprehend it. He regarded Shakespeare as one of that class of incoherent dramatists, possessing no real classical acquirement, and unable to distinguish properly between a comedy and a tragedy—a class including such men as Fletcher, Rowley, Marston and Dekker, for whom he had a profound contempt ; and this made it more difficult for him to square Shakespeare's superiority with his own theories, sharply defined as these were. Such a play as *The Tempest* must indeed have little less than outraged Jonson's sense of dramatic propriety.

With Bacon's genius Jonson's mind was much more sympathetic. Both men alike were interested in classical studies and in out-of-the-way book-learning. Both had an aptitude for generalizing and for the elaboration of theoretical systems. Both normally took an erudite point of view both of things in general and pre-eminently of what was meant by literary excellence. To Jonson, too, as a professional playwright,

---

[1] It is characteristic that he can see nothing in Marlowe's *Tamburlaine* but ' scenical strutting and furious vociferation.

Bacon, who was not only a great philosopher, essayist and historian, but also a great statesman and courtier, a chancellor learned in the law, and the most brilliant orator of the day, must have appeared as the type of accomplished versatility. We are not surprised, therefore, at his placing Bacon easily first among the minds of his generation and paying not merely to his intellect, but also to his character (of which he can have known very little), one of the finest eulogies ever uttered.[1] When he could dispense with jesting, of which he was perhaps overfond, Bacon's language was, in Jonson's estimation, 'nobly censorious,' his speaking full of gravity. 'No man ever spoke more neatly, more presly [succinctly], more weightily, or suffered less emptiness, less idleness in what he uttered. No member of his speech but consisted of his own graces. His hearer could not cough, or look aside from him without loss. He commanded where he spoke, and had his judges angry and pleased at his devotion. No man had their affections more in his power. The fear of every man that heard him was lest he should make an end.' It was a great age for wits, said Jonson truly, of the century that had just passed. He instances More, Wyatt, Surrey, Sir Thos. Smith, Sidney, Hooker, Raleigh, Savile, Sandys, Sir Nich. Bacon, and Lord Egerton, the chancellor, 'a grave and a great orator, and best when he was provoked; but his learned and able, though unfortunate successor [Bacon] is he who hath filled up all numbers [a Latinism for attained perfection] and performed that in our tongue which may be compared or preferred either to insolent Greece or haughty Rome. In short, within his view, and about his times, were all the wits born that could honour a language or help study. Now things daily fall, wits grow downward, and eloquence grows backward; so that he may be named and stand as the mark and ἀκμή of our language. . . .

'My conceit of his person was never increased toward him

---

[1] A good deal of his language about Bacon is adapted directly from the Latin (Seneca's eulogy of Severus Cassius), but this fact would have rendered it certainly not less acceptable to its addressee.

by his place or honours.   But I have, and do reverence him for
the greatness that was only proper to himself, in that he seemed
to me ever, by his work, one of the greatest men, and most
worthy of admiration, that had been in many ages.   In his
adversity I ever prayed that God would give him strength ; for
greatness he could not want.'

§ 3. *Novelists.*

Elizabethan novels are of small intrinsic interest to
modern readers.   It is unnecessary to warn people against
them.   They are practically inaccessible—a fact which
speaks for itself.   The sudden development of a taste for
idle luxurious reading would not be difficult to explain.
In mediaeval times reading must have been rather a
chilly business in the cold cloisters of our English climate.
The introduction of glass made for sunny nooks, where in
all houses of any pretensions great ladies, their ladies and
pages, and their imitators in the upper middle class could
devour light literature *ad libitum.*   The development of
education and of the renaissance spirit contributed surely
to the same result.   The Elizabethan novel was a hasty
attempt, very largely imitative, to supply this new demand.
The vigour of the demand was a great boon to the
struggling confraternity of professional authors.   The
abundance of the supply, in its turn, artificially stimulated
it.   The stories themselves were mainly designed after an
Italian pattern, but ingenious affectations were borrowed
from the Spanish, and additional properties were drawn
from the classics, from the *Gesta Romanorum*, and from
every kind of out-of-the-way source.   Clever verbal embroidery, which, though it seems to us often inane, must
have cost its producers an infinite amount of patient ingenuity, seems to have constituted one of the chief attrac-
tions of the new *genre*.   The taste faded, the novel-reading

mania declined (at least among the better classes in London and the larger towns) as soon as a healthy native product came to the front with the Elizabethan drama.

Yet the novels are not by any means unimportant in a survey of the period. The dramatists themselves read the novels, and drew from them materials which they used extensively in their plays. During the fifteen years that heralded the opening of our period—from 1566 at least—the Italian stories of Boccaccio, Bandello, Ser Giovanni, Straparola, and their foreign (chiefly French) imitators had been freely imported into England. Roughly and for the most part very inaccurately translated, they were garnered in numerous collections or treasuries, such as those of Painter, Fenton, Fortescue, Pettie, Whetstone, Gascoigne, Rich, and others. The collections had a large sale, while many of the stories were also sold separately at a cheap rate. From these operations our native compilers of fiction received a great stimulus. The result was the outpouring of a vast amount of English novels and romances, which attained to their height of popularity between 1580 and 1590.

The great ancestor of the new fiction was John Lyly or Lilly (the founder of a 'school,' though he must not be confused with the once celebrated schoolmaster, William Lilly), who wrote on a topic which has always exercised a curious fascination for English readers—Court life.

For a short fifteen years Lyly was *arbiter elegantiarum* in all matters pertaining to literature at the Court of the great Queen. Recognized as the high priest of a polished and witty fashion, he not only encroached upon the attention paid by fashionable dames to the sit of a ruff or the health of a pet dog, and imposed his very phrases and sentiments upon their obedient lips, but he was even paid the sincerer homage of imitation by the greatest wits of the

age, including not only Greene and Lodge, but William
Shakespeare himself. A strange caprice of fortune overtook this strangely exalted reputation. A generation passed
away, and Lyly was already a semi-obscure and ridiculous
figure. After the Restoration his name was forgotten as
utterly as if he had never existed, until the scholars at
the close of the eighteenth century disinterred that quaint
novel of *Euphues* by ' one John Lilly.' A somewhat analogous fate overtook the once famous Court painter Jervas,
of Queen Anne's day, who is with difficulty identified as the
'Jarvis' on the title-page of a popular edition of *Don Quixote*.

John Lyly or Lilly (a descendant of the grammarian,
Wm. Lilly) was born in Kent in the last
months of 1553, or possibly early in 1554,
went up to Magdalen, Oxford, in 1569, graduated M.A. in 1575, and about 1577-8 settled in London,
having a lodging in the Savoy, where he got to know
Gabriel Harvey. He seems to have had some post about
the Court, and his chief employment between 1578 and
1598 would appear to have been the supervision and man-
agement of the Court entertainments. He trained the
children of St. Paul's, managed the stage and its ac-
cessories, and even discharged some of the duties of a
dramatic censor. He won the complete confidence of the
Court. All the ladies of the time, we are told, were Lyly's
scholars, she who spoke not Euphuism being as little regarded at Court as she who now spoke not French. Poor
Lily failed to obtain the object of his ambition, the Mastership of the Revels, but he sat in the four last Parliaments
of Elizabeth, and took a share in defending the Prelates
in the Martin Marprelate controversy. In 1595 and again
in 1598 he petitioned Elizabeth for protection against his
creditors and payment of arrears—instancing the case of a
poor courtier who, having served his Queen for ten years

*John Lyly
(1553?-1606).*

without salary, committed a robbery and took it out in a pardon. He withdrew from Court towards the end of the reign, not, it may be hoped, without a pension, outlived the Queen and the first popularity of his remarkable novel *Euphues*, and was buried in St. Bartholomew's the Less, November 30th, 1606. We can picture him not unlike the old Lord Lafeu in Shakespeare's *All's Well*, a familiar figure at Whitehall, Greenwich, Hampton Court, Richmond, wherever the Court was, 'stepping daintily about the ante-chambers, shrewd and humorous, with a keen eye for the follies, fashions, swagger, and pretensions of the courtiers.'

The first part of *Euphues* is called 'The Anatomie of Wit wherein are contained the delights that Wit followed in his youth.' It was 'hatched' in December, 1578, having been written at the university where Lyly was waiting in search of an opening at Court. Writing to please himself, he is outspoken upon the abuses of the time. The supplementary volume, known as *Euphues and his England*, was written later (it appeared in 1580) and in a more courtierly vein. 'Euphues' had been explained by Ascham in his *Scholemaster* (1571) : 'Euphues' is he that is apt by goodness of wit and appliable by readiness of will to learning. In the novel, Euphues, an Athenian gentleman of good estate travels to Naples, where he is warned by Eubulus against the pitfalls of the place. He disdains his counsels and makes a friend of a Neapolitan gentleman, Philautus. He supplants Philautus in the love of the beautiful Lucilla, but is himself supplanted by Curio, and leaves Naples a wiser and a sadder man. The plot is nothing; the bulk of the book consists of quaint moralizing, and its popularity was due to its style. The framework is a very slender pipe, from which are blown clouds of words, arranged in quaint and not inelegant patterns. The later part of the book is devoted to a dis-

quisition on education, drawn mainly from a Latin version
of Plutarch's *Moralia*, and the second part of *Euphues and
his England* describes an educational tour in England. Like
the writers of the previous generation, Lyly had picked
over the Italian authors from Plutarch downwards for conceits and allegories : he drew similes largely from Pliny's
Natural History, and he made free with Pettie's *Palace
of Pleasure* (1566), a collection of classical and modern
Italian tales, and with North's *Dial of Princes*,[1] 1557, a
version of a Spanish book by the popular but affected
writer, Antonio de Guevara, something after the pattern
of the well-known *Cortegiano* or 'Courtier' of Castiglione.
Upon the whole, however, Lyly's book, with its slender but
never wholly suppressed thread of narrative, its feminine interest, and its clearly marked style, is notable for its originality. From it perhaps more than any other single work,
the English novel can be traced back as from a source.

With Lyly for the first time among original story-tellers,
as opposed to translators from the Italian, we leave epic
and mediaeval tales of chivalry, and approach the novel of
manners. There is no longer question of Arthur and his
marvellous knights, but rather of contemporary men, who
in spite of excessive oratorical finery, possess some resemblance to reality. There is some attempt, at any rate,
to depict contemporary manners, and conversations are
reported in which the tone of well-born persons of the
period may often be detected.

The special points of the style of *Euphues* are mainly, it
must be confessed, what we should call faults. Take a
fairly typical passage : 'But as the cypress-tree the more

---

[1] Guevara's *Dial of the Princes* was one of Lyly's chief models,
but Guevara had already been imitated in England by North,
Fenton and other translators, even to the extent of transverse alliteration.

it is watered the more it withereth, and the oftener it is
lopped the sooner it dieth, so unbridled youth the more it
is also by grave advice counselled or due correction controlled, the sooner it falleth to confusion, hating all reasons
that would bring it from folly, as that tree doth all
remedies, that should make it fertile.' The unvarying
formula of his sentences is that used above: 'For as the
A is B, so the C is D, and the more E is F, the more G
is H.' 'The antitheses,' says Mr. Hannay, 'work with the
regularity of pistons; there is a steady march past of
similes, drawn as often as not from a natural history
worthy of Sir John Mandeville, and arranged in twos and
threes.' But it is only after reading a dozen or so pages
of Lyly consecutively that the reader can form any idea
of the monotony of *Euphues*. Through page after page
the antitheses are laboured by the balancing, sentence
after sentence, of substantive against substantive, adjective
against adjective. And if the style is tedious in its
mechanical elaboration, the ornamentation is not one whit
less monotonous. The constant recurrence of trivial play
on words, of alliterations, of allusions and similes drawn
from the *Natural History* of Pliny, the mythology of the
ancients, and the bestiaries of the Middle Ages to the
taste of the present unsympathetic and unclassical age
soon becomes positively nauseating. Yet with all their
faults it is plain that Shakespeare had perused many
such passages more than once with no unappreciative eye.
It is no less evident that he considered that there was in
them a nucleus of what was excellent. He came later on
to laugh at his Lyly when good opportunity presented
itself, but there can be no doubt as to what book or
what passage he had in his mind when he wrote the first
draft of the memorable sentences of advice delivered by
Polonius to Laertes in *Hamlet* (I. iii.). The following is

the advice of the interminably didactic Euphues to Phil-autus, previous to their setting out for England (edit. Arber, p. 246):

'And to thee, Philautus, I begin to addresse my speach, having made an end of mine hermits tale, and if these few precepts I give thee be observed, then doubt not but we both shall learne that we best like. And these they are.

'At thy comming into England be not too inquisitive of nerves, neither curious in matters of State, in assemblies aske no questions, either concerning manners or men. Be not lavish of thy tongue, either in causes of weight, least thou shew thyselfe an espyall, or in wanton talke, least thou proue thyselfe a foole.

'It is the Nature of that country to sift straungers: everyone that shaketh thee by the hand is not joyned to thee in heart. They think Italians wanton and Grecians subtill, they will trust neither, they are so incredulous: but undermine both they are so wise. Be not quarrellous for every lyght occasion: they are impatient in their anger of any equal, readie to revenge any injury, but never wont to prefer any: they never fight without provoking, and once provoked they never cease. Beware thou fal not into the snares of love, the women there are wise, the men crafty: they will gather love by thy lookes, and picke thy minde out of thy hands. It shal be better to heare what they say, than to speak what thou thinkest. . . . Be merry but with modestie, be sober but not too sullen, be valiant, but not too venturous: let your attire be comely but not too costly : your dyett wholesome but not excessive : use pastime as the word importeth, to passe the time in honest recreation: mistrust no man without cause, neither be credulous without proofe: be not lyght to follow every man's opinions, neither obstinate to stand in your owne conceipts.'

Lyly is accused of 'playing with words and idle similes,' but the same indictment might be brought against almost all of the very greatest Elizabethans. Reminiscences of Lyly's antithetic manner are scattered profusely about Shakespeare, especially in what we may almost call the euphuistic plays, *Love's Labour's Lost, Two Gentlemen, Romeo and Juliet, Merchant of Venice, Much Ado, Twelfth Night,* and *As You Like It.*[1]

Jaques in *As You Like It* is Euphues Redivivus (with a difference!). *Rosalynde* (1590), the novel by Thomas Lodge, upon which Shakespeare's pastoral comedy is founded, purports to be written by Euphues, and to have been found after his death in his cell at Silexedra—so says the title-page. Shakespeare, adapting the story for the stage, admits a personage with a strong likeness to the supposed author, Euphues, to a place among his *dramatis personae* under the name of the melancholy Jaques, and he revives in this somewhat fantastic figure a number of the characteristics of Lyly's hero. 'Like Euphues, Jaques has made false steps in youth, which have somewhat darkened his views of life: like Euphues he conceals under a veil of sententious satire a real goodness of heart, shown in his action towards Audrey and Touchstone. A traveller, like Euphues, he has a melancholy of his own, compounded of many simples, extracted from many objects, and is prepared, like his prototype, to lecture his contemporaries on every theme.' Finally, he retires, like Euphues to Silexedra, to indulge his melancholy at the 'deserted cave.'

No less than five editions of each part of *Euphues* were printed before 1586, and seven more in the course of the next fifty years. A large school of imitators followed in Lyly's immediate footsteps. The popular outline and the characteristic manner of *Euphues* were instantly borrowed by a number of professional writers, who endeavoured as far as possible to give their productions the stamp of fashion by contriving that the word 'Euphues,' or if not Euphues 'Philautus,' should appear in a conspicuous position upon their titles. Among these 'apes'

---

[1] A remarkable list of parallelisms is given in *Quarterly Review*, January, 1896; this is based in part upon Rushton's *Shakespeare and Euphuism*. It is important to note that Shakespeare burlesques *Euphues* proper; what he *imitates* ordinarily is the refined Euphuism of Lyly's plays.

or imitators of Lyly the most prominent were **Greene, Munday,** Rich, Melbancke, Lodge, Warner, and Dickenson.

The most interesting of all Lyly's imitators, or, as M. Jusserand calls them, ' Lyly's legatees,' was the poet and dramatist, Robert Greene. His novels proper include *Mamillia* (entered in Stationers' Register 1580), *A Mirrour or Looking Glasse for the Ladies of England* (1583), a Paduan story of portentous length, the first part written while Greene was still at Cambridge, *Arbasto* (1584), *Penelope's Web* (1587), *Greene's Euphues, his Censure to Philautus* (1587), ' compiled from some loose papers of *Euphues* found in his cell,' *Perimedes* (1588), *Pandosto* (22,000 words) (1588), *Menaphon* (1589), and *Philomela* (1592), in addition to rambling productions full of moral dissertations on love, and crowded with classical imagery such as *Planetomachia* and *Morando, the Tritameron of Love* (1587) ; and all this quite apart from his coney-catching tales in which he pretends to depict actual facts of London low life, his patriotic pamphlets and his peculiar Repentances. Poor Greene, he must, in his later years, have led a terribly sedentary life ! Considering the quantity of his work, it is remarkable that the quality should be so good as it often is. But he wrote his novels, as it were, with his left hand ; and, after the original cleverness of Lyly, his output is often chargeable with being mere mechanical iteration. As page follows page of mythological allusion, and one realizes that of such pages Shakespeare's light reading was mainly composed, one ceases entirely to wonder at the pseudo-classicality of such plays as *Midsummer Night's Dream* and *Love's Labour 's Lost.*

Of Greene's novels the two most famous and popular, if not the best, were the two Arcadian romances, Greene's Novels. *Menaphon* and *Pandosto.* *Menaphon,* or ' Camilla's Alarum to slumbering Euphues ' in his melancholy cell at Silexedra, is a tedious production, enlivened somewhat by the songs of Doron in praise of his Samela and others, but chiefly known to-day by the preface addressed ' To University Students ' by Thomas Nash, in which a fierce onslaught is made on Kyd, Marlowe, and other writers for the stage, whom Nash and Greene regarded ᕁ interlopers and dunces. *Pandosto* went through many editions, was shortened down for a chap-book, versified for a ballad, and even twice translated into French. A still greater honour was its selection by Shakespeare to furnish the plot of *The Winter's Tale.* In the country of Bohemia, starts Greene gaily, 'there raygned a king called Pandosto.' Pandosto, the original of Leontes, is a puppet with one string; he represents jealousy, but as for passion of any kind, it is simply absent. Egistus is Polixenes, while the exquisite idyll of Florizel and Perdita is rudely indicated in that part of the story which concerns Dorastus and Fawnia. Autolycus and the whole scene of the sheep-shearing are Shakespeare's additions, but the dramatist takes no pains whatever to modify Greene's absurdities. He knew that *they* would not matter with a Jacobean audience. And so, as in Greene, ships sail into Bohemia, the Queen is tried by a jury panelled for that purpose, and the nobles go to consult the oracle of Apollo at Delphos. Another story of Bohemia, even more popular during the seventeenth century than *Pandosto,* was Emmanuel Ford's *Parismus* (1598), a wonderful tissue of amorous adventures and impossible wonders, which went through innumerable editions.

One of the earliest imitators of Lyly, although in strict chronology he may have been subsequent to Greene and Munday, was Barnabe Rich (1540?-1620?), a friend of Churchyard, Gascoigne, Stanyhurst, and other literary adventurers in the Low Countries. Rich turned abruptly from soldiering to *belles lettres,* and appended to his formal *Farewell to the Military Profession,* written in 1581, a small parcel of the popular sweet-meats, in the shape of stories from the Italian—in this case from Boccaccio and Bandello, through the French of Belle-forest.[1]

In the very same year appeared his more original *Don Simonides,* of which it is obvious that the plan was directly borrowed from *Euphues.* After travels in his native Spain, the hero wanders to Rome, Naples, and finally to London, where

---

[1] From the second of these stories, *Of Apollonius and Silla,* Shakespeare apparently derived the main plot of *Twelfth Night.*

he has one of those interviews with our old friend Philautus
which romanticists of that period so delighted, in Johnson's
phrase, to *feign*. The second part of *Don Simonides* appeared
in 1584,[1] and the completed narrative runs to about the length
of Dr. Johnson's *Rasselas*, which is rather in excess of the
average length of the sixteenth-century novel, though much
shorter than *Euphues* or than Nash's *Jacke Wilton*. The story
meanders, as is usual with these novels, now between banks of
dialogue and now at its own sweet will, now through a marsh
of mythology and moral instruction, and again through a mead
of miscellaneous verse. But for all the flowers in the meadows
and the pleasant conceits in its course, the Elizabethan novel
must be pronounced to be wholly unreadable by the reader of
to-day. A few of these stories claim to have been written for
the delectation of the gentlemen no less than 'the ladies of the
Court,' but in a modern view they will appear almost without
exception to have been written for the benefit of very patient
children. The only writer who has made anything out of them
is M. Jusserand, who in his *English Novel in the Time of Shakespeare* has discovered a delightful method of poking sympathetic
fun at their *naïve* and ingenious imbecility.

Among the minor 'legatees' it will be sufficient, perhaps, just
to mention Anthony Munday, whose *Zelauto, the Fountain to
Fame, given for a friendly entertainment to Euphues at his late
arrival into England*, would seem to have been issued in 1580,
that is to say before *Simonides* and in all probability even
before Greene's *Mamillia*. 'Zelauto,' another traveller, is a
Venetian prince who comes to England to see how worthily a
princess may govern, and, of course, to meet Lyly's inevitable
hero.   To Munday must be added Brian Melbancke, whose
Philotimus almost outsermonizes Euphues himself; William
Warner (d. 1609), whose *Pan, His Syrinx* (1584) was plagiarized
by Greene, and may have partly suggested the Julia and
Proteus episode in *The Two Gentlemen of Verona*; and John
Dickenson, whose *Arisbas, Euphues amidst his slumbers* (1594)

---

[1] In the same year appeared a version of the *Hystory of Herodotus*, by 'B. R.' (? Rich).

was followed in 1598 by his pastoral story of Valeria, called *Greene in Conceit*, showing the persistence of Greene's reputation for ' yarking up ' a prose story, until as many as five years after his death.   So great was the demand for these stories that we are expressly told that the printers were only too glad to pay heavily for the merest dregs of the novelist's wit, a circumstance which may serve to explain both the quality and the quantity of these extraordinary novelettes.

More important among these legatees of Lyly, a rival rather than an imitator of Greene, was Lodge's Novels. Thomas Lodge, the poet. His principal short stories or novels are *Forbonius and Prisceria* (1584), *Robin the Divell* (1591), *Euphues' Shadow* (1592), *The Margarite of America* (1596) ; but, above all, that famous original of *As You Like It*, which appeared in 1590 with the title *Rosalynde, Euphues' Golden Legacy*, found after his death in his cell at Silexedra. Chaucer had commenced to work upon the same theme, which was the mediaeval tale of *Gamelyn*. As in the play, Rosalynde and her friend put on male attire and meet their lovers in an Arcadian forest. Tame as the heroine of the novel appears beside the Rosalind of Shakespeare, and greatly hampered though the action is by meditations and monologues in Euphuistic style, Lodge's story is by no means deficient in grace, or even, thanks to the sprightly prattle of the dialogue, in liveliness, while running through the piece is a vein of freshness which has in it a certain indefinable element of pathos.

The popularity of *Euphues* and his legacies was already beginning to wane when Sidney's *Arcadia*. ney's *Arcadia* was published in 1590, and the rage for the new Romance soon seemed destined to surpass that for the old.   It was the fashion of Pope superseding that of Dryden, or the taste for

Byron eclipsing that for Scott. The ladies of the Court now began to talk 'Arcadianism,' as they had formerly talked Euphuism. The dramatist turned to it for new shades of colour and occasionally for incident.[1] Several short novels were cut out of it. Baudoin published a French version in 1624. It was passed round among the courtiers, and was regarded as the perfect representation of the best Court tone long before it actually appeared in print. Yet Sidney when he wrote it, about 1580, did not write for the public, or for posterity, but only wished, like Lyly, to write a romance for ladies, or rather for one particular lady, his sister, the famous Countess of Pembroke.[2] Her name would be a sanctuary, as he expressed it, for such a trifle—a spider's web fit to be swept away, as he

[1] Shakespeare for instance in *Lear*. The Arcadian habit, too, of ringing changes upon a single word proved specially congenial to the dramatist in his early comedy. So, too, the trick by which a man assumed female disguise, and *vice versâ*. Dekker in the *Hornbook* advises gallants to furnish their memories with Arcadian expressions. John Day called his *Ile of Guls* (1606) a little rivulet drawn from the full stream of the *Arcadia*. Shirley, as late as 1640, dramatized it for the stage, and Quarles fully avowed his indebtedness to one of the best known Arcadian episodes in his *Argalus and Parthenia* (1629). It is interesting to find the *Arcadia* still included in a select library by Addison, appealing to Samuel Richardson (who drew from it not merely the name of his first heroine) as the type of old English romance, and enshrined in *The Task* of Cowper along with its author Sidney, 'warbler of poetic prose.' With *Euphues*, *Arcadia* still stands and deserves to stand for a departed greatness.

[2] It was published posthumously from Sidney's scattered papers as *The Countess of Pembroke's Arcadia*, 1590, 4to; 1593, folio, 'augmented' (*textus receptus*); 3rd ed., 1598; 7th ed., Dublin, 1621, with additions by Sir W. Alexander; 9th ed., 1627, with a sixth book by R. Beling. See reprint of *Arcadia* (I.-III.) by Oskar Sommer, 1891. For a good descriptive account see *Retrospective Review*, vol. ii.

called his gossamer romance of 'cloud-cuckoo land.' He sent the sheets to his sister as fast as he penned them, and charged her to destroy them, never intending his romance for the public view. The explanation that it was a casual and unfinished production, in which he was enabled to deliver his young head of love fancies, fits the work much better than the theory of his friend and encomiast, Fulke Greville, that it was written with high moral and political purpose. The moral and political influence of a half pastoral, half chivalric fairy tale is not usually very great.

The literary distinction of the *Arcadia* is largely due to the fact that it combines two affectations, two strained ideals—the pastoral and the chivalric. The poetical landscape, such as the famed description of Arcadia, is derived from the pastoral of Sannazaro. The love plot is imitated from the famous *Diana* of Montemayor. The second element, on the whole, predominates, and the romantic adventures of the lovelorn Pyrocles and Musidorus are of just such a nature as Don Quixote would have doted on. Many Arcadian affectations, such as the artificiality of the cadence and the exquisite monotonous obsequiousness of courtesy, are pre-eminently Spanish. It is in the main a thorough 'coterie' piece, written by a very young and very serious literary doctrinaire. The story is extraordinarily intricate and rambling, and is encumbered by episodes gravely ludicrous and extravagant. Sidney deliberately eschews Euphuism, but he substitutes for it a style hardly less artificial than that of Lyly. Alliteration, paronomasia, repetition, and personification are all found in excess. Yet the very excess of poetic licence (for Sidney's prose is nothing if not poetic), more especially in regard to redundant ornament, is the cause and fountain of many surpassing excellences. Such are many delicate touches of imagination, and not a few phrases and passages of a noble, enchanting, and at times almost lyrical beauty. That Sidney could also upon occasion excel in perfectly direct and simple speech is nowhere better shown than in the famous prayer of Pamela (Bk. III., chap. vi.) which Charles I. is said to have used upon the scaffold. The sentences have more than a ring of the Prayer Book; and it is impossible to acquiesce in Milton's condemnation of the dying King because he used so noble a supplication, even though it was 'stolen word for word from the mouth of a heathen woman praying to a heathen god and that in no serious book.'

In conclusion, we must not study the *Arcadia* for the story, still less the purpose, but must judge it rather by detached passages, as Charles Lamb did when he wrote: 'The noble images, passions, sentiments, and poetical delicacies of character scattered all over the *Arcadia* (spite of some stiffness and encumberment) justify to me the character which his contemporaries have left us of the writer. I cannot think with the critic that Sir Philip Sidney was that opprobrious thing [referring to the hostile demeanour of the Earl of Oxford] which a foolish noble-man in his insolent hostility chose to term him.'

Barclay's once famous *Argenis* was issued at Paris in 1621, englished first by Kingsmill Long in 1625, and more adequately later as 'John Barclay, his Argenis. Translated out of Latin into English. The Prose upon his Majesties Command by Sir Robert Le Grys, Kt, and the Verses by Thomas May Esquire. With a Clavis . . . London 1629.' John Barclay was a Scot, born in
John Barclay (1582-1621). Lorraine, who came to England in 1603 and wrote a satire against the Jesuits, but left England for Rome in 1616, and shortly afterwards wrote in Petronian Latin his interminable romance of *Argenis*, imitated

in the main from the *Arcadia*, but discussing political and religious problems, and also great personages under thin disguises. Thus Meleander, father of Argenis, is Henri III. of France, Radizobanes is Philip II. of Spain, and Poliarchus, Henri IV. As an early example of the *roman à clef* it provoked intense curiosity at the time of its appearance. Charles I. was very impatient for it to be translated. Richelieu, Fénelon, and Leibniz are said to have devoured it with keen interest. It was translated into most European languages. Scott speaks of it as a 'fine old Romance.' The British Museum copy contains curious autograph annotations by Southey and Coleridge.

We resume the thread of the vernacular novel at the hands of a singularly robust and characteristic exponent—Thomas Nash.

Thomas Nash was one of the young English writers who trusted prematurely to their wits and their pens for a livelihood. Vivacious journalists, indeed, such men as Greene, Peele, and Nash would have made to-day; but at a time when London was a city of barely two hundred thousand souls, the lot of such free lances was too often that of Johnson's famous line :

Thomas Nash (1567-1600).

'Toil, envy, want, the patron, and the jail.'

Nash, however, in his time wrote a number of somewhat crude and unformed but amusing, gay, and good-humoured works. He refuses to imitate Euphues or any one else and prides himself on his independent vein.

Born at Lowestoft in the autumn of 1567, he was educated at St. John's College, Cambridge ; travelled in France and Italy ; threw himself impetuously into the Martin Marprelate controversy on the anti-Puritan side ; commenced a wordy feud with Gabriel Harvey, under the pretext of defending the memory of his friend Greene, and died apparently in 1600.

One of his first productions was a somewhat conventional satire, *The Anatomie of Absurditie*, upon the social anomalies of the capital as observed by a young man fresh from the university, with a substratum of autobiographical matter quite in the manner of Greene. In 1592 appeared his more important quasi-autobiographical satire called *Pierce Penniless*, in which good fun is made of sectaries, upstarts, depreciators of their own country, and envious detractors of poets and playwrights. *Pierce Penniless* seems to have had a considerable success. It was followed by a typical Elizabethan satire, *Strange Newes of the Intercepting of Certain Letters*, a scurrilous personal attack upon Harvey, in retaliation for a ghoulish revenge, which the latter had perpetrated in his *Foure Letters* upon the memory of the unfortunate Greene. Harvey retorted in his laboured *Pierce's Supererogation*, to which Nash made no immediate reply. In 1594 he produced what is in most respects his most notable work, a novel of contemporary life and adventure, strikingly anticipatory, in some respects, of the lesser novels of Defoe, to which he gave the title of *The Unfortunate Traveller* or *The Life of Jacke Wilton*. As a picaresque novel, if so it may be described, *Jacke Wilton* is markedly inferior to its Spanish original, *Lazarillo de Tormes*. The descriptions of low life and the adventures of the hero are greatly encumbered by the satire. Long speeches are put in the mouths of the personages at critical moments of the action, and much ridicule is expended upon the mannerisms of orators, and the absurdities of Englishmen who ape the manners of foreigners. ⸀ The moral of the whole book seems to be this: let no man for any transitory pleasure ' sell away the inheritance of breathing he hath in the place where he was born.' ' Get thee home, my young lad; lay thy bones peaceably in the sepulchre of thy fathers . . . the first traveller was Cain.' 'God had no greater curse to lay upon the Israelites than by leading them out of their own country to live as slaves in a strange land.' The adventures of Nash's hero are certainly not of a nature to stimulate his readers to seek service abroad. His adventures in Italy culminate in his being sold for an anatomy, that is, apparently, to be vivisected by a Jewish apothecary. The book ends abruptly with a long-drawn-out description of an Italian bravo's being broken on the wheel. The narrative is full of similar horrors, amongst which the passages describing the hero's intercourse with the Earl of Surrey and the fair Geraldine appear not a little incongruous. But this is thoroughly typical of the book, which is a heterogeneous compound deficient in artistic unity and possessing more historical than purely literary interest. In 1596 came the postponed chastisement of Harvey in *Have with you to Saffron Walden*, in which Nash follows up a previous inquirendo by Greene into the baseness of the 'upstart courtier's' ancestry. Nash's last work was a characteristic panegyric of the red herring in its Yarmouth home— Yarmouth was near his native place, and was a town in which he had met with a friendly reception; so Nash praised the red herring for all that he was worth in *Nash's Lenten Stuffe* (1599).

Nash was a typical quill-driver of his period—careless, jovial and dissipated, alternating between riotous excess and abject misery. A thorough Bohemian, he dearly loved a merry tale (*Aretino* was a great favourite); Tarleton and Kemp, the Dogberry of *Much Ado*, were among his friends, who also included Greene, Lodge, Daniel, and probably Dekker. He had an enthusiastic love for great literature—Rabelais, Sidney, Marlowe, but above all ' heavenly Spenser.' Incomplete artist though he was, he was full of artistic theories. His diction was deliberately

I.   K

strange and fantastic, overladen with metaphor and hyperbole. He was audacious in his quest of new figures and fresh colours. Much interest attaches to his vocabulary. He was abnormally fond of boisterous compound words. Words, he said, like winds, to have force to confute or persuade, must be swelling and boisterous. English, he thought, swarmed too much with the small change of monosyllables. Hence he craved permission to invent some long-tailed Italian words—to coin some large pieces to balance the intolerable monotony of groats. He claimed to have introduced Italianate words ending in *ize*, such as tyrannize, into English. His daring is shown to some extent in the burden of his fresh and lively spring song in his sole comedy *Summer's Last Will and Testament*, acted at Croydon in 1592, though not printed until eight years after.

> ' Spring, the sweet Spring, is the yeres pleasant King,
> Then bloomes each thing, then maids dance in a ring
> Cold doth not sting, the pretty birds doe sing
> Cuckoo, jugge, jugge, pu we, to witta woo.

> ' The fields breathe sweete, the daisies kiss our feete.
> Young lovers meet, old wives a-sunning sit,
> In every street these tunes our ears do greet,
> Cuckoo, jugge, jugge, pu we to witta woo.'

§ 4. *Satirists, Caricaturists, and others:*
Robert Burton.

The work of Nash, with its numerous eccentricities of style, subject, and point of view, serves as a convenient link between the novelists and the satirical essayists, who literally swarmed in London during the late and post-

Elizabethan periods. The prince of these pamphleteers, excelling in fluency and facetious quaintness, and a very Defoe in respect of ductility, was Thomas Dekker. More vividly even than Nash and Greene he takes us back to the crooked lanes, the gabled houses and creaking signs of old London. Human weakness and wretchedness were indeed no formulae to him. He had experienced much, and with unlimited opportunities for observing low life, he had retained a kindly, *naïf*, and withal humorous disposition. We are drawn to him, as to Steele or Goldsmith, despite the grotesque character of much that he wrote, and the blackening effect of age upon his somewhat crude system of colour. The dense verbiage in which so much of Dekker's humour is enshrouded soon rendered his books obsolete, but as a mirror of the manners of his time they are as invaluable as those of Tom Brown and Ned Ward of the age of Queen Anne, while in literary quality they are far superior. Indirectly they have formed the groundwork of almost every attempt to arrive at a clear picture of the social life of the period. Dekker's plays are full of sidelights upon the social life of the day. But even richer in this kind of material are the series of prose tracts commenced in 1603 with *The Wonderfull Yeare*. In this he describes the death of the Queen, the proclamation at the Coronation of the King, concluding with a vivid picture (with which Defoe must have been familiar) of the ravages caused by the plague. He returned to the subject in one of his last tracts, penned when people were fleeing from the city, and entitled *A Rod for Runawayes* (1625). In the same year, 1603, appeared his *Batchelor's Banquet*, a satire on different types of women suggested by the fifteenth-century *Quinze Joies de Mariage*. Among the humours which he depicts, with a whimsical ingenuity of his own, are those

Thomas Dekker (1570?-1641?)

of the woman given to pleasure, the covetous-minded woman, and the woman whose husband has gone over the sea. *The Seven Deadly Sins of London*, written against time in 1606, is a free kind of sermon embodying much grim information about the seamy side of Jacobean London. *Newes from Hell, Brought by the Devil's Carrier*, in the same year, is a fluent imitation of *Pierce Penniless*. From the sermonizing tone of *The Seven Deadly Sins* Dekker passes by an easy transition to a coarse volume of *Jests to Make You Merrie* (1607), a favourite of Robert Burton's. *The Belman of London*, which went through three editions in 1608, is largely a *rifacimento* of Harman's *Caveat for Commen Cursetors*. Dekker anticipates Vidocq in describing the different varieties of rogues, such as priggers, kinchin coves, swigmen, and others; and he followed this up by *Lanthorne and Candlelight*, describing fresh types of suburban scoundrelism, which had an even greater success than its predecessor. In 1609 appeared the most graphic of all his sketch-books, *The Guls Horn-book*. The tract is to some extent modelled on the German Dedekind's *Grobianus* (1549), a world-famous satire of bad manners, inverted etiquette, gross living, and coarse and slovenly habits. It had been Dekker's intention to turn portions of *Grobianus* into English verse, and he admits that his book retains a relish of Grobianism, but on further reflection he altered the shape, and of a Dutchman fashioned a mere Englishman. His sketch remains the most vivid picture that can be found of the manners and customs of the Jacobean gallant.

As an essayist in a modern sense Dekker is perhaps surpassed by the lighter vein and more facile touch of an even more voluminous writer, the poet Nicholas Breton. One of the best of the prose tracts that came from his versatile pen is one of the very

N. Breton.
(1545?-1626?).

earliest, an angling idyll called *Wits Trenchmour*[1] *in a Conference had betwixt a Scholler and an Angler*, 1597, in which,
but for the interminable digressions to which he was so prone,
Breton might have rivalled his successor, Izaak Walton, upon
his own ground. In the same year Breton wrote *The Figure
of Foure*, in which a great deal of proverbial small change is
served up in various ways. There is no controverting many of
Breton's propositions. He advances in fours—four good medi-
cines—abstinence, exercise, mirth, patience; four men needful
in an army: a good commander, a good scout, a good sentinel,
and a good gunner; four chief notes of a good housewife: early
rising, close gathering, safe keeping, and well bestowing.
Anticipating Caleb Whitefoord and Lamb, Breton is exceptionally fond of playing with proverbs and crossing them, as may
be seen in his *Crossing of Proverbs, Cross Answers, and Cross
Humours*, 1616. There is more humour in the *Court and
Country*, 1618, the old controversy of the debating society
between the town courtier and the rustic. The speeches are
formal and much too long; but the interlocutors are warming
towards the close when the courtier imputes an evil smell of
garlic to the countryman, who retorts that his town cousin
stinks of tobacco. In *Fantasticks*, 1626, Breton gives us com-
pact little essays on the world, money, love, harvest, Spring,
Summer, and then the months seriatim. Those on April and
May are prose pastorals, as delicate as those of Washington
Irving, and with less artificiality. After the months come the
hours, and so round the clock to an end. These charming
vignettes of Breton's are almost as rich in material for social
portraiture as those of Dekker's; they are written, too, with
much spontaneity in a racy vernacular, undefiled either by
coarseness or affectation.[2]

---

[1] Trenchmour: a boisterous dance.
[2] We should not be giving an adequate idea of the prolixity of
the Jacobean prosewrights if we omitted to mention that both
Dekker and Breton had their understudies and imitators. Among
those of Dekker, observe William Rowley, who gave to the world
in 1609 *A Search for Money*, a typical candlelight piece, illustrat-

As in *Court and Country*, contrast supplies the framework for *The Goode and the Badde*, 1616, a series of balanced types as characters, the 'worthies and unworthies' of 'this age': a good man and an atheist, an honest man and a knave, a quiet woman and an unquiet woman.

The time was now approaching—late in James's and early in Charles I.'s time—when a regular epidemic of these character-sketches broke out in England. It is not, like the sonnet-mania, to be traced directly to France, for there is little doubt that the impulse was due to the translation of the Greek *Characters* of Theophrastus into Latin, made by Isaac Casaubon in 1592. Theophrastus was the initiator of the *genre*, which is a very difficult one. Fine portraiture is not possible under its conditions. No two men are exactly alike, and a portrait cannot at once portray a class and an individual. The ideal is to hit the mean between abstract statement and details calculated to rob the portrait of all generic interest. In this Theophrastus succeeded so well that he was not surpassed in seventeenth-century England, though most of the wits, from Hall and Overbury and Earle to Butler and Halifax, put their best work into the attempt. It remains a question whether he was surpassed by La Bruyère in France.

It is true that something in the nature of the 'character' portrait-gallery had appeared in England long before Casaubon's version of *Theophrastus*, for in 1565 John Awdeley produced his *Fraternitye of Vacabondes*, followed two years later by Thomas Harman's *Caveat for*

ing side alleys of London humour, containing a reference to the Jew of Malta's nose, and not a few Shakespearean expressions. Very Bretonian is *Cold Doings in London, the Great Frost* of 1608, in a dialogue between a citizen and an old yeoman from Ripon.

Commen Cursetors, or Vagabones, a curious series of essays on various kinds of thieves, tramps and beggars, with their slang. Harman was freely imitated, not to say copied, by Dekker, in his *Belman of London*, while Dekker had independently produced something closely approximating character-sketches in his *Batchelor's Banquet* of 1603, as had several of the writers of the innumerable Touchstones, Glasses, Mirrours and Anatomies, whom we notice at the end of this section. But such productions as these could hardly have led to the Theophrastian essay, at which, as we should have expected, first attempts were made by notable scholars—to wit, Joseph Hall and Ben Jonson. Most of Jonson's plays are 'character' plays, and in the *dramatis personae* of *Every Man out of his Humour*, first printed in 1600, he condenses his conceptions into the form of a series of labels which are in effect character-sketches. Joseph Hall, who had in 1597 produced his *Toothlesse Satyrs*, and in 1605 (in Latin) his strange satirical allegory of *Mundus Alter et Idem*, allowed to appear in 1608 his noteworthy *Characters of Vertues and Vices in two Bookes*. Hall's 'Characterisms,' as he calls them, are directly modelled on Theophrastus; pithy and well-balanced, his phrasing gave the note to all his successors; but the tone of the work is too abstract, and the moralizing and balancing of good qualities against bad is unnecessarily obtruded. Yet his *Characters* may be regarded as signalling the vogue, of which the full force was felt some six years later in *A Wife, now the Widow of Sir Thomas Overbury* . . . 'whereunto are added many witty Characters & Conceited Newes.'

Sir Thomas Overbury, born in Gloucestershire in 1581, took a bachelor's degree from Queen's College, Oxford, in 1598, after which he entered the Middle Temple and then travelled. He became the adviser and 'governor' of the

favourite, Rochester, whom he had first met at Edinburgh, and perhaps subsequently abroad. His
Observations upon the Netherlands were circulated in manuscript, and Overbury obtained a great reputation for his wit at Court.
The Wife, a didactic poem, written in 1613, was soon
flattered by numerous imitations. Boswell commends it
thus : ' Sir Thomas Overbury, in his rude versification, has
very judiciously pointed out that degree of intelligence
which is to be desired in a female companion.

Sir Thomas
Overbury
(1581-1613).

> ' " Give me, next good, an understanding wife,
>   By nature wise, not learned by much art ;
> Some knowledge on her side, will all my life,
>   More scope of conversation impart :
> Besides, her inborn virtue fortifie.
> They are most firmly good, who best know why." '

The poem is stated to have been written to dissuade
Rochester from marriage with such a woman as Lady
Essex. The lady, at any rate, took umbrage at Overbury's
supposed influence over the earl. She managed to get her
enemy shut up in the Tower, where, on the 15th September, 1613, the unhappy man was poisoned. Appended to
The Wife, as issued the second time in 1614, were a
number of characters by Overbury and his friends. These
rapidly grew in successive editions from twenty-one to as
many as eighty, of which ten only were descriptive of
distinctive character. The rest are concerned with such
peculiarities as are brought out by certain occupations or
positions in life. These are curious as illustrating manners,
of which Overbury was a quick observer. But for the
delineation of character in the proper sense, Overbury and
his Court friends had no very great talent. They were
concerned primarily with tricks of speech and behaviour

rather than with moral qualities. Their portraits are frequently neither typical, distinctive, nor humorous. They are rather lively, entertaining, and quaint. Overbury sacrifices humour to epigram, and perception of subtle differences to the demands of a pretty wit. But his smartness is apt to grow monotonous and his very wit wearisome, so that it is a genuine satisfaction to find him laying aside his cleverness for once and producing a sympathetic picture like that of *The Franklin*;[1] and with this may be ranked *The Good Wife*, *The Worthy Commander*, and *The Milkmaid*. Every tiny little pamphleteer now began to place 'Characters' in large type in his shop-front. In 1615 John Stephens issued *Satyrical Essayes and Characters* (several of the latter in verse). Next year came Breton's *Goode and Badde*; in 1618 G[eoffray] M[ynshul]'s *Essaies and Characters of a Prison and Prisoners*. In 1626 a literary contortionist called Henry Parrot, author of a satire called *Springes to catch Woodcockes*, 1613, gave to the world his *Cures for the Itch*, an affected book of characters and epigrams. Two years elapsed, and the best of the bunch came from the pen of a young Oxford scholar, John Earle.

John Earle, a native of York, where his father was registrar of the Archbishop's Court, graduated from Christ Church in 1619, and became a fellow of Merton in 1620. He was a ready writer, and the fame of his 'Characters' being bruited abroad, as such things are at Oxford, they were got to the press apparently without his consent by the enterprising publisher, Edward Blount. Though issued anonymously,

John Earle
(1601-1665).

---

[1] Some of the best, however, were certainly not by Overbury, such as the witty *The Footman* and *The Tinker*, which first appeared in the 6th edition in 1616 as by Jo. Cooke, possibly the author of *A Pleasant Comedie, How to chuse a Good Wife from a Bad* (1602), and of *Greenes Tu Quoque*.

they were known to be his at the time, and many of them were probably written a year or two before publication, as we know that MS. copies were in circulation during 1627. One at least of these MS. copies (with a slightly variant text) has survived, and is now at Durham.

The first edition of the *Microcosmographie: Or a Peece of the World Discovered, in Essayes and Characters*, appeared in 1628, containing fifty-four characters; twenty-three were added during 1629.[1]   After 1629 it seems doubtful whether Earle ever concerned himself further about his 'Characters.'   He was with Chillingworth and the other Oxford men who resorted to Falkland's house at Great Tew.   During the troubles he went abroad, made a Latin version of the *Eikon Basilikè* and the *Ecclesiastical Polity*, eventually became Bishop of Salisbury, and died in the Plague year at Oxford.

Overbury and his Court friends would have been very contemptuous of the character-sketches of a raw Oxford scholar—what could such an one know either of life or of literary conceits?   But as a matter of fact Earle's scholarly aptitudes stood him in good stead.   Hall had twisted the character to purposes of edification, Overbury overburdened it with puns and epigrams.   Earle, with active literary instinct, made his sketches approximate much more nearly to the original type.   As far as he wrote from the results of his own observation, he succeeded in producing a series of life-like and at the same time generic portraits adorned not by witty antitheses, but by genuine flashes of insight into human nature.   There is no methodical arrangement of the characters.   Among the best are *The College Butler, The Church Papist, The She Hypocrite, The Meer Gull Citizen, The Criticke.*

[1] Sixth edition, 1633 (seventy-eight characters); cf. *Notes and Queries*, November, December, 1871.

They are kept within modest limits as regards length. In style they are somewhat monotonous, owing to the rather mechanical ply of the sentences; but they are pellucid, free from far-fetched conceits, and uncomplicated as regards syntax. There are singularly few obsolete words, though, as in Bacon, words are often used in senses that have become uncommon or pedantic. At their best they exhibit the work of an observer, a philosopher, a humorist, and an artist.

Such manias as this for 'characters' having reached their zenith soon commence to decline. And so the generations of English readers who interested themselves in their production may be limited down to two, occupying the first three quarters of the seventeenth century. Limited in its scope as it naturally was, the character could only be a transitional form, filling a position in advance of the familiar essay, between the *dramatis persona* in a character comedy and the elaborate character-sketch of a modern novel. After the Restoration the character as a separate literary species became relegated mainly to the sphere of the parody or the literary lampoon, though there are abundant traces of it in the character poetry of Dryden and Pope ('Zimri,' 'Sporus,' etc.). But meantime, even with the limits of our period, there appeared in 1629 *Micrologia* by R. M., containing some highly-spiced, eccentric delineations, such as a fantastic tailor, a tooth-drawer, a tobacconist, and a cunning horse courser; and in 1631 two curious examples, Wye Saltonstall's *Picturae Loquentes* and *Whimsies*, with 'a new cast,' including a coranto courier, a clergyman, an almanack maker, a launderer, a metall man, a neuter and a ruffian.

From Earle, as the master of a somewhat conventional type of humour, we pass on with a leap to Robert Burton, one of the very greatest of England's eccentric humorists.

Robert Burton, the son of Ralph Burton, born at Lindley in Leicestershire, on February 8th, 1577, passed from Nuneaton School to Oxford, becoming in 1599 a student at Christ Church, where for form's sake, 'though he wanted not a tutor,' he was placed under the tuition of Dr. John Bancroft, afterwards Bishop of Oxford. Residing at Christ Church, he drew the revenues of two livings, and there also he drew his last breath on 25th January, 1640, in the year of his grand climacteric. He lies in the north aisle of the cathedral at Oxford, and his resting-place is commemorated by a coloured bust, similar in design to the Shakespeare bust at Stratford, and the Hooker bust at Bishopsbourne, bearing the famous epitaph: 'Paucis Notus, Paucioribus Ignotus, Hic Jacet Democritus Junior, Cui vitam dedit et mortem melancholia.' He seems to have led a secluded and uneventful life as a scholar, seeking an easily found relaxation in merry tales and buffooneries. He wrote a fairly juvenile Latin play called *Philosophaster*, begun in 1606 (that is, four years before *The Alchemist*), and acted at Christ Church in 1617 (first printed 1862), dealing with the exposure of a nest of charlatans, a theme familiar to Ben Jonson. In 1621 appeared the first edition of his great work, *The Anatomy of Melancholy, What it is*, in quarto.[1] With the

Robert Burton (1577-1640).

[1] The Rylands Library at Manchester has a fine copy of the first edition 'At Oxford, 1621,' distinguished by the fact that the conclusion 'To the Reader' is dated 'from my study in Ch. Ch. Oxon, 5th December, 1620,' and signed Robert Burton. It also contains the following characteristic manuscript note by George Steevens : 'During a pedantic age, like that in which Burton's production appeared, it must have been eminently serviceable to writers of many descriptions. Hence the unlearned might furnish themselves with appropriate scraps of Greek and Latin, whilst men of letters would find their inquiries shortened by knowing where they might look for what both ancients and moderns had advanced on the subject of human passions. I confess my inability to point out any other English author who has so largely dealt in apt and original quotations.'

third edition of 1628, which was the second published in
folio, appeared Le Blanc's remarkable frontispiece, preceded by a curious description of its contents in homely
verse—verse analogous to the doggerel of the translations which adorn the text. After the

*The Anatomy
of Melancholy.* dedication to Lord Berkeley come some
Latin elegiacs of little interest, and some
English verses called the author's *Abstract of Melancholy,*
of more than a little interest, for it seems practically certain
that Milton had their theme in his mind and their refrain
ringing in his ears when he drafted his *Penseroso.* These
verses are followed by the long expository introduction,
entitled 'Democritus Junior to the Reader,' which forms
one of the most interesting portions of the book.

The Anatomy itself is carefully divided into three parts
or partitions, each part into sections, and each section into
members.

Each part is preceded by an elaborate synopsis drawn
up, it might almost appear, to parody the vast schemes of
scholastic philosophers or of Calvinistic divines. The first
partition of the book is that most strictly covered by its
title. It is, in fact, largely medical in its character. It
deals with the causes of melancholy, bodily and mental.
It attempts to define melancholy, and distinguishes three
kinds of the disorder: head melancholy, melancholy of the
whole body, and melancholy of which indigestion is the
first principle. He treats once more at great length of the
causes and symptoms of the malady, and goes on to give
instructions as to how we may prognose and diagnose it.
The second partition deals with the therapeutics of the
subject. After dismissing unlawful remedies, such as
resort to evil spirits, magicians, witches, and the like, the
author proceeds to unfold a system from which, with the
blessing of God, a legitimate cure may be fairly anticipated.

In this connection he treats at great length of physicians, dietetic, air and climate, purges, phlebotomy, and cordials; among the last-named he includes, with some diffidence, 'a strange drink which the Turks called coffee.' Among emetics he gives a distinguished place to tobacco—'tobacco, divine, rare, super-excellent tobacco, which goes far before all their panacea, potable gold and philosophers' stones, a sovereign remedy to all diseases. A good vomit I confess, a virtuous herb if it be well qualified, opportunely taken and medicinally used; but as it is commonly abused by most men, which take it as tinkers do ale, it is a plague and a mischief, a violent purger of goods, land, health: hellish, devilish and damned tobacco, the ruin and overthrow of body and soul.' The rhetorical power even of this (cf. De Quincey's apostrophe to Opium) is surpassed by that of noble passages from the Cure to Melancholy; those upon learning, the joy and the pride of it, and then again the misery and the anguish, may be cited as examples no less of Burton's plain common sense, than of his terse and vigorous style, and of his searching penetration on the rare occasions when he can be got to intermit citation. Everywhere, indeed, we see traces of highly effective artistic arrangement. The fact that Burton devotes the third partition of his work to love melancholy and religious melancholy, shows that he knew thoroughly well what he was about—two-thirds of the cases of mental aberration in all ages having been assignable (as experts tell us) to these two causes. Having dealt with unusual elaboration upon the causes and symptoms of love melancholy, he proceeds in accordance with his plan to indicate some possible remedies, though he manifestly had a very restricted faith in their ultimate success. First of all he specifies hard work, and next a judicious use of cucumber, purslane, melons, rice, lettuce, water-lilies, and other vegetables, is commended. If these fail the sufferer must avoid the occasion of love, sternly repress its beginnings, change the place of his habitation, use witty inventions, and betake himself to travelling. As to religious melancholy, Burton remarks in anticipation of Defoe, where God hath a temple the Devil will have a chapel. The Devil acts in this case by means of priests, politicians, heretics, simplicity, fear, ignorance, fasting, solitude, and the bull-bellowing Pope, for whom Burton entertained a hatred second only to his hatred for the Devil. He concludes appropriately upon this note of warning, ' be not solitary, be not idle.'

One of the most obvious and perhaps superficial remarks to make on the book is that it is typical of its age—that of the scholarly cento, the cento, or as Camden puts it, ' the patchwork quilt' of innumerable scraps of polyglot learning, and the age that of scholars like Prynne and Cudworth, Casaubon, Keckermann, and Isaac Vossius, men of an abnormal leathery physique, who sat over their desks till their eyes grew dim, whose deliberate ideal was apparently to read and abstract and summarize practically every book that had ever been written. Swift and Boling-broke, with Pope and Arbuthnot, at the beginning of the eighteenth century managed between them to laugh such a *modus operandi* out of court as the extremity of pedantic absurdity, and we have both gained and lost by the success of their *jeux d'esprit*. Smollett, jeering in his eighteenth-century fashion at the survival of the ancient scholastic diligence in Germany, said that the German genius lay more in the back than in the brain. But the English scholar of Burton's day seemed to possess both back and brain.

For brain power of no ordinary kind is surely evinced in this scheme, partial though it be, of the philosophy of human life. One out of sympathy with Burton's mood may perhaps be tempted to say that a Burton might be cut of a mind like Bacon's without much being missed. Yet Burton is much besides a scholar. If *The Anatomy* be regarded as the mere outpouring of commonplace books, with a pretext merely of unity in purpose and subject, then maybe it is no great thing. To be understood, it must be regarded at once as the exhibition of a temperament and the discussion of a case. The case is that of the seamy side of human life and its perils. The author deliberately takes up his position of detached yet watchful isolation, in order to observe and to illustrate the human comedy; and he exhibits a new variety of vanities, combining in one book, as it were, the knowledge of Solomon, and his reflections on the futility of things known and the knowing of them. 'There is nothing true, and if there is we don't know it,' said Democritus; and also, 'we know nothing, not even if there is anything to know.' We certainly know little of Democritus, save that he was 'a little wearish old man, very melancholy by nature, averse from company, and given to solitariness.' Burton modestly disclaimed any intention of comparing himself with the sage of Abdera, but urged that he too had led a silent, solitary, and sedentary life. In philosophical calibre he may have been, and probably was, inferior to his prototype; yet Burton represents admirably well the amused tolerance of the laughing philosopher, his nihilism, and his scepticism as to the possibility of attaining anything like content or happiness, 'Man never is but always to be blest.' A curious mixture was Burton, a Christian, a Protestant, and as superstitious as Montaigne, as may be gathered from his digression on Devils. So is this patchwork a curious combination of the trite and the ludicrous, of the humorous and the profound. Yet when we come to examine the texture of the writing by which it is all

woven together, we can discover not only the most remarkable literary skill, force, ingenuity, and condensing
power, but we can also discern, peeping out pretty often, the
grave waggery of a man scanning human nature for foibles,
and thereby keeping himself on the windy side of care.

The perusal of *The Anatomy* has been neglected since
the art of quotation has declined alike in press, pulpit, and
parliament; still more since the days when it fetched
Dr. Johnson out of bed two hours before his usual time
for rising. Yet Burton has lived on in Sir Thomas
Browne, in Mandeville, in Johnson and in Sterne; and
Burton was *redivivus* in some respects in Charles Lamb,
the greatest exemplar in a later day of the literary genius
and the literary virtuoso in one. And there are happily
still some such enthusiasts among us.

Allied to the character work of the period, though in its
Polonian manner it approaches nearly to the
didactic portion of *Euphues*, may here be noticed
the *Ten Precepts to his Son Robert*, written by
Lord Burghley in Elizabeth's reign, though not published
until 1637. In gnomic power—in weight of matter and depth
of judgement—still more in worldly wisdom, these *Precepts*
rival Bacon's *Essays*. They lack the wit and power of expression, but they have a homely force of their own that is impressive. The style, too, is clear, untrammelled by 'conceited'
imagery, wholly free from Italian phrasing and affectation,
which the sound Aschamite and Protestant Burghley abhorred.

Lord Burghley (1520-1598).

A place may here be found, too, for the 'witty, grave and
sententious book' of Owen Felltham, of which the poet Randolph
wrote:

> 'Thy book I read and read it with delight
> Resolving so to live as thou do'st write.'

The book so complimented was, of course, Felltham's *Resolves*
a diligent, extra-didactic, but somewhat wishy-washy under-
study of Bacon's *Essays*. Owen, son of Thomas Felltham of

I.   L

Mutford in Suffolk, of Cambridge(?) and Gray's Inn, became a dominie in the household of the Earl of Thomond, and issued the first century of his *Resolves*, 1627-8.[1]   Augmented to wellnigh two centuries, they reached a ninth edition in the author's lifetime, 1667, continued popular for two or three generations after his death, and were actually drawn upon for 'Beauties' in 1800. They resemble, in more than one respect, especially in their somewhat specious smoothness and veneer, the once-popular eighteenth-century *Meditations* of Hervey.   The prose style is for the period remarkably easy and fluent, the composition neat and accomplished; here and there may be detected an artistic finish and a proneness to literary equation and balance that suggest the manner of *The Intellectual Life*.   Very Hamertonian, too, are the various subjects or 'frames of mind': 'That the present times are not worse than the former,' 'Concealed grudges the destruction of friendship,' 'That it is difficult to be rich and good,' 'That Policy and Friendship are scarce compatible,' 'That a wise man may gain by any company,' 'That man ought to be extensively good.'   On the other hand Felltham is by no means deficient in healthy English prejudice.   Thus, in his essay 'Of Assimilation,' he remarks, 'Italy builds a villain, Spain superbiates, Germany makes a drunkard and Venice a letcher.'   It is amusing to find that this utterer of so many unexceptionable saws and wise precepts got into trouble in 1663 for an offence no less than having carried off and married in the previous year an heiress, Mary Portrey, whose relations pretended that she was not *compos mentis* at the time.   Felltham died at Great Billing, Northamptonshire, about 1678.   A rather skilfully modernized and 'amended' edition of his *Resolves* was brought out by James Cumming in 1806.

As representing a combination, characteristic of the age, of *savant*, controversialist and satirist, two well-known, little read writers of the utmost 'curiosity' may be noticed together here.

Owen Felltham (1602-1668).

---

[1] Some were written as early as 1620.   The first extant dated edition is the second, 1628.   Old editions may be picked up for a trifle at most marts of obsolete books.

Reginald or Reynold Scot, a remote descendant, it is believed, of the poet Gower, wrote in 1574 an
Reginald Scot   interesting practical treatise upon Kentish hops
(1538-1599).   called *The Hop Garden*, and it appears that
the author was an esquire, a justice, and a subsidy official of
the county of his adoption. He died at Smeeth in Kent in
October, 1599. On some points, such for instance as papal
abuses, Scot was almost as credulous as Montaigne; but in his
capacity as justice he was struck by the cruel and degrading
character of the witch prosecutions which were just becoming
frequent towards the close of the sixteenth century. He was a
born investigator, and the pseudo-erudite treatises of the learned
Bodin, and of many less distinguished students of sorcery, gave
him a splendid field for the exposure of misapplied learning
and illogical prejudice. An enlightened physician of Germany,
John Wier, had already, in 1566, raised his voice in defence of
the victims of the popular belief in sorcery. In 1584, with
more elevated views than Wier, with far more ability, and with
a boldness that no previous writer had approached, Scot in his
Discoverie of Witchcraft unflinchingly exposed the atrocious
cruelties of the witchfinders, the credulous folly of the tribunals,
by which the so-called 'witches' were condemned, and the
egregious absurdity of the marvel-mongers who filled folios
with grave details of the tricks of conjurers and the ravings
of half-demented old women. Though he is drawn by his love
for controversy into much repetition and excessive prolixity,
Scot triumphs in argument, minimizing with skill the force
of the scriptural phrases and classical precedents upon which
his adversaries mainly relied, while he points out the incon-
sistency of those who had abandoned their faith in fairies while
they retained an undiminished belief in witches. But the time
was not ripe for such enlightened views as these. His book
was denounced by the divines and answered by James I., who,
in his *Demonologie*, summed up Scot's views as 'damnable,'
and, on his accession to the throne, ordered every copy of it to
be burnt. The superstition was ratified by Act of Parliament,
and for fifty years Scot's book exercised no appreciable influence. It had some immediate effect, however, for the raw

material which Scot had gleaned with indefatigable labour was woven in the rich loom of the Elizabethan drama, notably in *Macbeth*. The *Discoverie*, translated into Dutch in 1609, was reprinted in England 1651, 1654, 1665 and 1886.

James I.'s fame as an author has undoubtedly suffered somewhat from his notoriety as a king. It may be admitted that he was a diffuse and pedantic writer, but though diffuse, there is often a pithy saying or an apt allusion to be gleaned from his furrow, and though pedantic he preferred to write in his native tongue, while he might have shone resplendent in Latin like his master, George Buchanan, or his persistent flatterer, Francis Bacon. He was naturally clever, had a tenacious memory, and a remarkable aptitude for classifying matters in his mind in accordance with the system so much in vogue among the theologians, logicians, and rhetoricians of the day. James's juvenile production, *Essayes of a Prentice in the Divine Art of Poetry* (1584), was probably written as themes for his tutors. The *Meditations on the Revelations* (1589) are indicative of his theological bent. *Demonologie* (1597), *Basilikon Doron* (1599), and *A Counterblast to Tobacco* (1604) are his best-known essays. The one subject in connection with which he approaches eloquence is the cherished tenet, the divine right of kings, of the absolute truth of which he seems to have had a sincere conviction. His prose works were collected in 1616. The *Basilikon Doron*, though teeming with quotations and references, is probably his most readable production, containing much good sense and shrewd worldly wisdom.

King James (1566-1625).

Some fragments of James's earlier writings were edited by Mr. R. S. Rait in 1902 under the title of *Lusus Regius*. These include some rather interesting items, such as an unfinished masque, several sonnets, a poem on women, a paraphrase of Psalm CI. and a letter to Du Bartas. Apart, however, from an occasional good thing (and as a royal *diseur* James was only surpassed by Charles II.), we must not look for much literature, in the higher sense, from the most erudite of our monarchs. Some of his good things were collected by Overbury and appended to later editions of his book, as *Crumbes fall'n from King James's Table*.

Still less must we look for sweetness and light among the minor humorists and satirical caricaturists of the period; and it will suffice to characterize very briefly the work of such shadowy lampooners as Robert Anton, Robert Armin, Richard Brathwaite, Henry Parrot, William Rankins, Samuel Rowlands, Philip Stubbes, Joseph Swetnam, Thomas Walkington, and Thomas Wilcox. Anton is better known for a verse satire a long way after Ariosto called *Vice's Anatomie Scourged* (1617), but he also issued a prose *Moriomachia*. Robert Armin, a pupil of Tarleton, played at the Globe Theatre and issued in 1605 his *Foole upon Foole, or Sixe Sortes of Sottes*, and as a sequel in 1608, ' to tickle the spleen like an harmless vermin,' his fantastic *Nest of Ninnies*. Henry Parrot was one of the prize epigrammatists of his day, and successfully rivalled, it was thought, such virile wits as Heywood, Bastard, Weever, Davies, Marston, and the redoubtable, though coarse, William Goddard. Like the last-named, Joseph Swetnam was an avowed woman-hater, and showed the courage of his opinions in his violent *Araignment of lewd, idle, froward, and inconstant Women* (1615), which elicited a cloud of furious rejoinders, including a very curious comedy, *Swetnam the Woman-hater arraigned by Women* (1620). Swetnam undoubtedly borrowed from the ungracious Gosson, whose *Pleasant Quippes for Upstart Newfangled Gentlewomen* had appeared in 1595; but similar satires abounded. More interesting is Thomas Walkington, a kind of forerunner of Burton, whose *Optick Glasse of Humours* (1607) treats, *inter alia*, of melancholy and its treatment. A large group could be collected of Puritanic critics and censors of contemporary manners, rude forefathers of the voluminous Prynne. Such were William Rainolds, author of the *Overthrow of Stage-Playes* (1599), and William Rankins, whose prose *Mirrour of Monsters* (1587) is also directed against the stage, and whose *English Ape* follows Andrew Boorde in denouncing the importation of foreign fashions into English dress. More individual perhaps are the scarce prose tracts of Samuel Rowlands, such as *Greenes Ghost* (1602) and *Martin Mark-all, Beadle of Bridewell* (1610), a social dredger which professes to go deeper down among vagabonds

Minor Satirists.

than Dekker himself. Will. Rowley, the playwright, attempted likewise to shed light upon the lower strata of London life in his curious *Search for Money* of 1609. Somewhat similar in tone is Brathwaite's *Solemn Joviall Disputation* (1617), anent drinking and 'smoaking.' Earlier, but more puritanic, is the unflattering *Glasse for Gamesters* (1581), a warning against cards and dice, which was echoed in George Whetstone's *Touchstone for the Time* (1586) and in James Balmford's *Unlawfulness of Cards* (1593); the depressing *Discourse for Doubters* by Thomas Wilcox (d. 1608); and the better-known *Anatomie of Abuses* (1583) by Philip Stubbes, a kinsman of the heroic loyalist, John Stubbe, who waved his left hand and cried ' God Save the Queen,' after losing his right for inditing a criticism on the Queen's French marriage project (*Discoverie of a Gaping Gulfe*, 1579). Still more lamentable jeremiads over the wickednesses and follies of the age were those of that second Zeal-of-the-land Busy, the fanatical Prynne, author of the *Unloveliness of Love-locks* and other works, the titles of which, like the posters of our halfpenny papers, are commonly more amusing than their contents. Many of these books may be found at the end of this volume in the table, which serves to show the servility with which satirist follows satirist. Literary grooves are rapidly forming and deepening. 'Mirrors,' 'Anatomies,' 'Microcosms,' and ' Looking Glasses' are all the fashion, and fashion is as compelling as it was in the days of Dunciads, Elegies, Keepsakes, and Kailyards.

§ 5. *Religious Controversialists and Theologians:* *Richard Hooker.*

In the later years of the reign of Elizabeth the spread of Puritanism, that is of distinctly Calvinistic forms of religion, indicated the approaching breakdown of the basis of compromise on which Elizabethan uniformity in religious matters rested. It was natural that one of the first symptoms should be an attack upon the Bishops. The Puritan

The Martin Marprelate Controversy.

objected to bishops both as institutions savouring of
Popery and as guardians of an Act of Uniformity which
legalized the use of the old vestments and lent itself
to Catholic interpretation.   Nor were the Puritans the
only enemies of the bishops, upon whose wealth many
of the poor clergy looked askance.   At Court also there
was a party on the look-out for more Church property.
These factors produced the Martin Marprelate controversy.

Academic controversy concerning episcopacy and vestments had for some time been going on.   The Puritan
divines, Cartwright and Travers, had been opposed by
apologists such as Jewel and Bridges.   But popular interest
was not aroused till a pamphlet war, which is as amusing
as sheer scurrility can make it, was started in 1588.   Early
in this year John Udall, a dispossessed minister of Kings-
ton, struck in with a virulent attack on bishops in a
dialogue called *Diotrephes*.[1]   This was printed by John
Waldegrave, a London printer whose press was broken
up and his licence taken in consequence.   The outraged
printer managed, however, to hide away a fount of type.
Udall seems to have soon been withdrawn from the fray,
but his place was more than filled by John Penry, a fiery
Welsh reformer, whose tract called *The Equity of a Humble
Supplication* (1587), entreating the consideration of Parliament for the miserable neglect of Welsh parishes, had
been suppressed by the Council.   Penry, who now came
forward as the Puritan champion, contributed a press
which he smuggled from London.

The Elizabethan press was, of course, under a strict cen-
sorship.   Only two printers were allowed out of London,
at Oxford and Cambridge.   In London the number was

---

[1] Diotrephes, a person who 'loveth to have the pre-eminence,'
and who 'receiveth us not' (third epistle of St. John).

limited. No press could be maintained except by a member of the Stationers' Company, and any press could be instantly confiscated by the Warden of the Company, over whom the Bishop of London had general powers of control as censor. No piece could appear without a licence, signed either by the Archbishop, the Bishop of London, or a licenser authorized by the Privy Council through the Secretary of State.

But Penry and his friends at Court and in the country managed to print what they had to say in spite of all Bishops, Archbishops, Licensers, Universities, Stationers' Companies and Privy Councils whatever. The mud really began to fly with the publication of Martin Marprelate's *Epistle* (November, 1588) directed against Dean Bridges of Salisbury, who had published in 1587 a pompous and dignified *Defence of the Government Established in the Church of England for Ecclesiastical Matters*. The scurrility of the *Epistle* drew a grave *Admonition to the People of England* (January, 1589) from Dr. Thos. Cooper, Bishop of Winchester. Martin followed up his attack on Bridges by the *Epitome* printed before the *Epistle*, but not issued until February, 1589. Then he turned on the Bishop of Winchester in *Hay any work for Cooper*. Lyly and Nash seem now to have intervened on the bishop's side with *Pappe with a Hatchet* (1589) and *An Almond for a Parrot* (1590), and the fun grew fast and furious. The object of the 'Martinist' pamphleteers was to decry episcopacy by every possible variety of personal abuse, applied to the holders and defenders of the episcopal office; and that of their opponents, the bishops' bravos, to go one better in Billingsgate and to give better than they got. The fight was fierce until 1590, and it fizzled on until 1593, when Penry and Barrow, the supposed chiefs of the Martinists (for the real writers can only be guessed at) were executed. Udall had died on emerging from prison in 1592.

The abuse throughout this quarrel was most furious, and the taste shown by both parties execrable. The tracts are little above lampoons. Their literary interest is chiefly of the antiquarian order; but their historical importance is considerable. They set a fashion. They showed what could be done by a secret press in defiance of a government so despotic, so active, and so well informed by spies as that of Elizabeth. Martin Marprelate first realized the potentialities of this guerilla warfare of pamphlets, and his *Epistle* stands at the head of a list which includes *Areopagitica*, *The Anatomy of an Equivalent*, *The Shortest Way with the Dissenters*, *Letters of Junius*, *Public Spirit of the Whigs* and *Vaticanism*. The controversy as a whole, too, may be regarded generically as a kind of rude prototype of the Jansenist, Hoadly, Middleton, and Tractarian logomachies.

'But while scenes of pride and persecution on one hand and of sectarian insolence on the other were deforming the bosom of the English Church, she found a defender of her institutions in one who mingled in these vulgar controversies like a knight of romance among vulgar brawlers, with arms of finer temper and worthy to be proved in a nobler field.' This Galahad of whom Hallam speaks was the judicious Hooker, who endeavoured in an elaborate yet moderate defence of the general ecclesiastical position taken up by the Church of England to throw oil upon troubled waters.

Richard Hooker was born at Heavitree, a suburb of Exeter, probably in March, 1554. His uncle, who was chamberlain of Exeter, heard such a good account of Richard's studies at Exeter Grammar School, that he persuaded Dr. Jewel, Bishop of Salisbury, to assist the young scholar at Oxford. When Jewel died, in

Richard Hooker.

1571, Hooker was befriended by the president of his college (Corpus), and he obtained as a pupil Edwin, son of Bishop Sandys, whose influence was of great service to him. Hooker, who was noted among the fellows of his college for his vast stores of reading, took orders in 1581. In the same year he made an unfortunate marriage, and in 1584 settled at Drayton Beauchamp in Bucks. In 1585, at the recommendation of Sandys, whose son had seen and pitied the unhappiness of his old tutor's married life, Hooker was taken in hand by Archbishop Whitgift, and through his influence was appointed Master of the Temple, in opposition to a Presbyterian champion of the name of Travers. Here began Hooker's labours in defence of episcopacy.   Travers, a bold preacher with a popular mannner, was Afternoon Lecturer in the Temple, and maintained in the pulpit Presbyterian views of Church government. Hooker preaching in the forenoon, the pulpit, as Fuller said, 'spake pure Canterbury in the morning and Geneva in the afternoon.' Travers, silenced by Whitgift on the ground of insufficient ordination, continued the war in print ; Hooker replied to the charge of latitudinarianism, but, unfit for the worry of controversy, begged from his patron some quiet post in the country, and in 1591 removed to the living of Boscombe, near Salisbury.   Here in peace and privacy he investigated the general principle involved in the position of the Church of England, and projected the eight books of his *Laws of Ecclesiastical Polity*, of which the first four were published in 1594.   Translated in 1595 to the better living of Bishopsbourne, near Canterbury, he sent a fifth book (longer than all the rest) to press in 1597.   He died at Bishopsbourne on 2nd November, 1600. A sculptured portrait bust in the chancel of the beautiful little church stands to us for a noble type of Elizabethan divine.   Books VI. and VIII. of the *Polity* were published in 1648: a seventh book appeared in 1662. Books VII. and VIII. appeared to have been edited by Gauden from notes left by Hooker. Doubts have been raised as to the genuineness of the sixth book. It does not conform with Hooker's plan, but Keble, Hooker's chief editor, had no doubt it was substantially Hooker's, though not designed as part of the *Polity*.

The great craving of Hooker's nature, as expressed in his work, is his craving, after an age of controversy, for tranquillity and peace. 'God and Nature,' says Izaak Walton, in his memorable life, 'blessed him with so blessed a bashfulness, that as in his younger days his pupils might easily look him out of countenance, so neither then, nor in his age, did he ever look any man in the face; and was of so mild and humble a nature that his poor parish clerk and he did never talk but with both their hats on, or both off, at the same time.' Every testimony, including his portrait, shows Hooker to have been an unusually shy, feeble little man, with very little activity, and very low constitutional power. He entered the controversies of his time unwillingly; and, after a short experience, begged for peace and privacy. When forced to vindicate what he had said in his sermons, he did so, not with the heat of a strongly persuaded man of energy, but with the timid charity of a retiring nature. How much he leant upon others appears in the narrative of his college life, so different from the sturdy self-reliance of Dr. Johnson. Still more does this come out in Walton's account of his visit to the Shunammite's house in London, whither he went from Oxford to preach at St. Paul's. Reaching London on a Friday on the back of a sorry horse, wet, weary, weather-beaten, numb with wind and rain, he felt that it would be impossible for him to preach on the Sunday. But Mrs. Churchman took him in and nursed him so diligently that two days sufficed entirely to cure him of his distemper. Mrs. Churchman went on to demonstrate that a man of his tender constitution needed a wife who might prove a nurse for him and make him comfortable. She even offered to provide such a wife for him, if he thought fit to marry.

'And he not considering, that the children of this world are wiser in their generation than the children of light; but like a true Nathaniel, fearing no guile, because he meant none, did give her such a power as Eleazar was trusted with, (you may read it in the book of Genesis,) when he was sent to choose a wife for Isaac: for even so he trusted her to choose for him, promising upon a fair summons to return to London, and accept of her choice; and he did so in that or about the year following. Now, the wife provided for him was her daughter Joan, who brought him neither beauty nor portion, and for her conditions they were too like that wife's which is by Solomon compared to a dripping house: so that the good man had no reason to rejoice in the wife of his youth; but too just cause to say with the holy Prophet, Wo is me, that I am constrained to have my habitation in the tent of Kedar! . . . And by this Marriage the good man was drawn from the tranquillity of his college, from that garden of piety, of pleasure, of peace, and a sweet conversation, into the thorny wilderness of a busy world; into those corroding cares that attend a married priest and a country parsonage; which was Drayton Beauchamp in Buckinghamshire, not far from Ailsbury, and in the diocese of Lincoln; to which he was presented by John Chusey, Esq., (then patron of it) the ninth of December, 1584, where he behaved himself so as to give no occasion of evil, but (as St. Paul adviseth a minister of God) in much patience in afflictions, in anguishes, in necessities, in poverty, and no doubt in long suffering; yet troubling no man with his discontents and wants.

'And in this condition he continued about a year; in which time his two pupils, Edwin Sandys and George Cranmer, took a journey to see their tutor, where they found him with a book in his hand, (it was the Odes of Horace,) he being then like a humble and innocent Abel, tending his small allotment of sheep in a common field; which he told his pupils he was forced to do then, for that his servant was gone home to dine, and assist his wife to do some necessary household business. But when his servant returned and released him, then his two pupils attended him unto his house, where their best entertainment was his quiet company, which was presently denied them; for Richard was called to rock the cradle.'

Some deductions may have to be made from this graphic picture, but it is drawn directly from Walton, who is practically the sole authority for the other facts of Hooker's life. Assuming its truth, there is hardly to be found in history, says Professor Minto, 'a more extreme instance of a man wanting in self-will and submitting himself passively to the disposal of others.'

The posthumous fame of theologians cannot as a general rule be regarded as excessive outside their own order. Yet few of our older writers have been more consistently over-praised than Hooker. Even in his own day the fame of his book reached Rome, and Cardinal Allen recommended it so strongly to the Pope that Clement VII. wanted to have it rendered into Latin. James I. was full of its praise, and rarely spoke of Mr. Hooker save with the prefix 'the judicious.' Charles I. commended it to his sons, and James II. said that the perusal of it led to his joining the Roman Catholic communion. The High Church party from Laud to Keble have highly approved of it. The Whiggish Hoadly appealed to it in confirmation of his views that Church government was a matter of expediency; Dr. Parr referred to it as adamantine; advanced Protestants have declared it to be an impregnable bulwark against heresy and unbelief; and even the sceptical Buckle eulogizes it as affording an illustration of 'immense importance' of the strides made by rationalism since the days of the dogmatic Jewel. Jewel, he says, inculcates the importance of faith; Hooker insists upon the exercise of reason. The importance of Hooker's work, as being the first great effort made in modern times to give the full theory of a great institution, to show the ideal principle upon which it was founded, and to indicate its substantial agreement with that ideal, is admittedly great. But is there not a somewhat hollow ring about the universal chorus of praise, when we reflect how few of those who as students obtain perhaps a superficial knowledge of Hooker and his work ever return to him (professional reasons apart) either for pleasure or for profit?

The objects of Hooker's work may thus be summed up. In the first book he endeavours to show the philosophical position of the Church of England, and the place of such an institution in an universal scheme. The second book is an argument to refute the Puritanical view of the Bible, as being a cyclopaedia of all knowledge and all truth. The object of the third is to prove that there is no ground for the assumption that Scripture must of necessity prescribe a form of Church government. The fourth book is a defence of the Church of England ceremonies against the charge of being Popish; and the fifth contains a long and minute vindication of the Church on all the points attacked by the Puritans.[1] The sixth book was designed to carry the war into the enemy's country, and to confute the Presbyterian theory of Church government; the seventh is an exalted vindication of Episcopalianism; and the eighth an explanation of and apology for the doctrine of the Royal Supremacy.

The plan of Hooker's treatise (for the outlines of which

[1] The fifth book is still extensively read by candidates for Anglican ordination. New edition, with *Prolegomena*, by Ronald Bayne, 1902.

he owed a considerable amount to the ecclesiastical system of the noted Spanish theologian, Francisco Suarez, his senior by six years, while many ideas in it attest his knowledge of the universal Aquinas) may be recognized as an admirable one. It is only when we turn from the plan to the book, and try to discover the solutions to the various problems raised by Hooker, that we begin to doubt whether the author had not undertaken a task far beyond his strength. A vague and poetical rather than philosophical spirit is diffused over the whole, and creates a mistiness of outline which serves to explain why Hooker ha_ been appealed to in so many different senses. For Hooker himself appeals less to the logician than to those who love the luxuries of the ear. On the other hand, it may perhaps be admitted that his shadowy ratiocination especially adapted him to be the champion of a compromise, which was deliberately calculated to give the least offence to the greater number, and in which, as a foreign critic humorously objected, the dignitaries of the Church seemed Erastian, while its liturgy was Catholic, and its articles Calvinistic. From a logical point of view it must be admitted that Hooker was in a most difficult position, between the Puritan, who referred everything to the authority of the Bible, and the Catholic, who claimed authority primarily for the Church. As compared with a trained polemical writer, such as the Jesuit Bellarmine, it may often be doubted whether Hooker perceived clearly the point of view of his opponents. In treating, for instance, of the insignificance of vestments as a cause of dissension, he might seem to ignore the fact that the sacramental theory which they symbolized was of all things most obnoxious to the Puritans. Even admitting, said they, that there was no ground for the *a priori* assumption that Scripture would prescribe a form of Church government, nevertheless, as a matter of fact, Presbyterian Church government *was* to be found in Scripture. Law was a good thing and ought to be obeyed, but Hooker, said they, appeared to make no provision for the possibility of a law being bad. The greatness of Hooker must be sought, it would seem, not in his logic, for the purposes of which his latinized style, with its long parentheses and bewildering inversions of order, is peculiarly ill adapted, but in a certain vague majesty and solemn dignified melody, adapted rather to a prayer or a rhapsody than to a close and contentious argument. Though his vocabulary is not so modern as Sidney's, his diction is singularly pure and rhythmical. But though the words, as Nathan Drake says, are for the most part well chosen and pure, the arrangement of them into sentences is intricate and harsh, and formed almost exclusively on the idiom and construction of the Latin. Much strength and vigour are derived from this adoption, but perspicuity, sweetness, and ease are too generally sacrificed.

On abstruse subjects Hooker's power of exposition is very severely tested, and his real meaning remains somewhat of a problem to this day. Clearness seems often sacrificed to the rich music of his periods. But the pathos of his demand, in the days before the rise of the conception of religious toleration, for peace and quietness in the pursuit of a *via media* is imprinted in passages of imperishable harmony upon many a page of his ever-memorable plea.

As a defender of episcopacy pure and simple many of Hooker's arguments had been anticipated by his patron, Archbishop John Whitgift (1530-1604), a rigid Church disciplinarian, whose answer to Cartwright's *Admonition to Parliament*, 1572, and defence of that argument, are characterized by clearness, terseness of expression, and logical force. As compared with Hooker he is far too intent upon refuting his adversary to devote much attention to the edification of his periods.

His opponent, Thomas Cartwright (1535-1603), the champion of Presbyterianism, had been worsted by Whitgift at Cambridge and driven from his fellowship at Trinity. In addition to his admonitions to people and parliament, he translated the *Disciplina Ecclesiastica* of Walter Travers, 1574. Protected in his long crusade against bishops by the Protestant sympathy of Burghley, he won great acceptance in the pulpit. In culture, learning, and originality, he was probably superior to Whitgift, but his style was involved, and he lacked the trenchancy and directness which made Whitgift so formidable a controversialist.

Another important light on the Puritan side was Walter Travers (1548-1635), a Cambridge student, who worked with Beza at Geneva, and there wrote his *Ecclesiasticae Disciplinae Explicatio*, printed anonymously at La Rochelle in 1574, a book which proved a great source of inspiration to the Presbyterian opposition to the Church of England.

Among English divines of this age, who crossed swords with the great apologists of the Catholic reaction, may be named Field, Whitaker, Rainolds, Featley, and Andrewes.

Richard Field (1561-1616), a famous disputant at Oxford, and a favourite of James I., who named him, on the first occasion that he heard him, 'a Field for God to dwell in,' produced his *Five Bookes of the Church* in 1606. This was mainly aimed against Romish errors and peculiarities which, it attempted to show, were of later origin than the more primitive rites of the English Church. His style often approximates to that of Hooker, with whom he was on very friendly terms.

I.   M

William Whitaker (1548-1595), master of St. John's College, Cambridge, severely criticised the Douay version of the New Testament, and opposed the Romish divines, Stapleton and Bellarmine, in his *De Authoritate Scripturae*, 1594. His learning was very great, attracting the regard of the first scholar of the age, Joseph Scaliger, while as a lecturer he was compared with 'a pillar of fire.' It is credibly reported of him, says Gataker in his *Life*, that 'Cardinal Bellarmine so esteemed him that he procured hence his Portraiture and had it hanging in his study among the pictures of other men of note, and being demanded why he should keep so near him the effigies of an adversary, made answer that though an heretick and an adversary, he was a learned adversary. . . . Only while he lived Stapleton, a peevish peece, snarled at some passages in one of his Controversies, whom he so answered that the waspish dotard had little lust to reply.' But this was a libel on Stapleton's sting.

Thomas Stapleton (1535-1598), of a good English family, entered the Society of Jesus in 1584, rendered important service to the newly founded English College at Douay, became, after Bellarmine, the first Catholic controversialist in Europe (Bellarmine subsequently adopting many of his positions), and was in high favour at Rome, though his claims to the cardinalate were overlooked, and he died at Louvain. His huge *Opera Omnia*, including his *History of the English Church* and *Apology for Philip II.* against Elizabeth, was issued at Paris in 1620. A still more famous English Jesuit of this time was Robert Parsons or Persons (1546-1610), of a Somerset family, who was sent from the Vatican as a missionary to England in 1580. His aim was a counter-reformation in England to be brought about by means of a Spanish invasion; and in this cause he was arch-intriguer and pamphleteer in general

He published in 1582 a small volume of Catholic exercises, which, reprinted as *A Christian Directorie*, had an enormous circulation.

John Rainolds (1549-1607), a nephew of Thomas Rainolds, who was Dean of Exeter and Warden of Merton College, acted for a time as tutor to Richard Hooker, became Greek reader at his college, Corpus, and lecturer in the divinity school at Oxford. Men flocked to hear his lectures, we are told, as to those of no other divine save only William Whitaker at Cambridge. He was a Low Churchman of strong Calvinistic tendencies, and is said to have refused a bishopric from Queen Elizabeth, who, when at Oxford in 1592, had scolded him for his precisian leanings. At the Hampton Court Conference his profound learning won him the lasting esteem of James I., and he occupied a leading position among the translators of the Authorized Version. He was at this time president of Corpus Christi College, to which, says Fuller, he did more good in eight years than any of his predecessors in thrice that time. He died at Oxford in May, 1607, surrounded by the fellows of his college who 'compassed his bed all about, and each did cast in his shot, which was some choice and comfortable word of Scripture.' Of his many polemical works the best remembered are his *Overthrow of Stage-Playes*, 1599, and his notable *De Romanae Ecclesiae Idolatria*, Oxford, 1596.

Another Calvinist at heart, though he defended the Church of England against the sectaries, was Daniel Featley (1582-1645), chaplain to Archbishop Abbot, who became rector of Acton in Middlesex in 1626-7, at which date also he published his *Ancilla Pietatis*, the most popular manual of devotion of the day. Of his controversial works the best known is perhaps the most aggressive, *The Dippers Dipped*, a contemptuous attack upon the

Anabaptists. In the main Featley was disposed to take a
moderate course. He spoke up boldly for episcopacy, yet
he persistently opposed Laud's innovations and finally gave
evidence against him. The harsh treatment which he received from Parliament embittered him, and on his death-
bed he uttered a fierce denunciation: 'Let them be scattered
as partridges on the mountains, and let the breath of the
Lord consume them.' Such a 'compendium of the learned
tongues and of the liberal arts and sciences was he,' wrote
Thomas Fuller, 'that you would have thought him learning itself bound up in a little volume, for he was of a low
stature, but of a convenient strength and health of body.'

Lancelot Andrewes (1555-1626), pupil of Mulcaster,
Cambridge student, and chaplain to Whitgift, was made
a bishop by James in 1605. Though a serious scholar
who 'never left his book before noon,' his wit was vivacious, and his apophthegms and happy citations made
him a great favourite in the pulpit—'stella praedicantium.'
His *Manual of Private Devotions*, as rendered into English
by Richard Drake in 1648, became famous, eclipsing in
general use the *Private Devotions* of Cosin and the
Ancilla Pietatis of Featley, both of 1627. The *Preces
Privatae*, as originally printed in 1675, have frequently
been re-issued in the Greek and Latin. Newman made a
fresh translation of some of them in one of his *Tracts
for the Times*. The prayers are constructed almost exclusively out of fragments and precious stones of ancient
devotion; but the arrangement and the setting which
give the mosaic its chief value are the good bishop's
own. During 'the evening of his life' the prayers were
constantly in his hands, and the MS., says his first editor,
Drake, was 'glorious in its deformity, being slubbered
with his pious hands and watered with his penitential
tears.' Andrewes was chiefly noted in his own day for

coming to the rescue of James I., in his notorious Latin controversy with the redoubtable Cardinal Bellarmine.

As a preacher the fame of Andrewes has been eclipsed by that of two performers of a very different style—Joseph Hall and John Donne.

Joseph Hall (1574-1656), Bishop of Norwich, a fellow of Emanuel College, was styled by Wotton ' the English Seneca,' whether for the pureness, plainness and fullness of his style, or by reason of the versatility of one, as Fuller says, ' not ill at controversies, more happy at comments, very good in characters, best of all in meditations.' His *Contemplations* on Scripture, issued in eight volumes between 1612 and 1626, are, perhaps, the best of his works. With less scholarship and wit than Andrewes, and less original power than Donne or Jeremy Taylor, he writes with great fluency and energy, and with fewer deviations from the broad path of eloquence into the quaint, the narrow, or the grotesque, than any of these writers.

John Donne[1] (1573-1631) took orders in 1615, and performed his work as a preacher while divinity reader at Lincoln's Inn between that date and 1619, and as Dean of St. Paul's, 1621-31. Many of his most important sermons were printed immediately upon delivery. Eighty were printed in a folio dated 1640, and fifty more in a second folio volume of 1649. Forty or fifty additional sermons have since been printed. As exercises in abstract subtlety, fanciful ingenuity, and classical scholarship, these sermons are wonderful. Donne resembles Andrewes rather than Hall in his fondness for quotation and fanciful turns of wit. But in power, originality, subtle distinctions, and far-fetched imagery (which must have bewildered many of his auditors), he far surpasses either. Considering the extraordinary elaboration of these sermons, says Dr. Jessopp, and the fact

[1] See p. 65.

that they form but part of their writer's works, it may be doubted whether any other English divine has left behind him a more remarkable monument of his mere industry, not to speak of the intrinsic value of the works themselves.

Donne's sermons, whatever else they may be, are astonishing as intellectual feats. Each one of wellnigh two hundred of these discourses is rather a short treatise than a brief flight of rhetoric ; first elaborated, then spoken, and then elaborately re-written. Donne's learning seems to pour out naturally from a mind stored to repletion with Aquinas, St. Bernard, and St. Augustine. His pulpit style varies widely from intricate meta-phor and frigid quibbling to the famous and dramatic appeal to the individual soul. I want you, he says to his auditor, to ask yourself whether there is a God, and I want the answer from your solitary soul. 'I respite thee not till the day of judge-ment when thou wilt call upon the hills to cover thee.' 'I respite thee but a few hours, but six hours, but till midnight. Wake then, and then, dark and alone, hear God ask thee then, and remember that I asked thee now, Is there a God ? And if thou darest, say No ! '

Upon the whole, however, as a preacher, he is steeped with scholasticism ; and the literature from which he drew his illus-trations is unable to evoke from us the slightest response. A more downright style such as that of Tillotson and South was bound to evict the subtleties of such men as Donne and Crashaw, just as the directness of Dryden and Swift supplanted the refine-ments of the Concettists in the secular sphere.

In the eyes of churchgoers from the city of the merchant and middle class, the pulpit fame and the eloquence of Donne and Andrewes was equalled, if it was not surpassed, by that of Thomas Adams, 'the prose Shakespeare of Puritan theologians,' as Southey called him, incumbent of Willington, Bedfordshire, and from 1614 to 1636 of Wingrave, Buckinghamshire, a preacher often at Paul's Cross, and a lecturer at St. Bennet's, Paul's Wharf. Among the impressive sermons which he printed separately were *The White Devil* (1615), in which there is a most eloquent passage appealing to the conviction of sin in his individual hearers, *The Spiritual Navigator, Mystical Bedlam, Sinners Passing Bell, Way Home,* and *Presumption running to Despair,* which were collected and issued in a single folio volume in 1629. Adams was a doctrinal Puritan after the pattern of Featley, but he was more inclined to jeer at than actively to resist the encroachments of the High Church party, and he spoke of the embittered communion-table controversy as a question of cupboards. In sketching a character he was hardly inferior to Earle. In the pungency or, more rarely, in the pathos with which he denounces a sin, he recalls Latimer or Baxter, while for quaint and unconventional wit he stands above Hall though below Fuller. He was very happy and abundant in verbal exposition, and was rich in puns, aphorisms, and anecdotes. 'With God,' he says, 'adverbs shall have better thanks than nouns—it is not what we do, but how we do it that matters.' Again: 'Security is the very suburb of hell.' 'An insensible heart is the devil's anvil; he fashioneth all sins on it; and the blows are not felt.' Spurgeon found the humour (' ore rotundo ') of Adams highly congenial, and it is to be regretted that he did not fulfil an intention of writing his life.

Adams was one of a very striking succession of Puritan preachers in the city—preachers whose eloquence, we may rest certain, was largely responsible for the subversion of the pagan renaissance, and eventually of the London theatres. Two names must suffice here just to give an idea of the force of this Puritan pulpit. Henry Smith (d. 1591) was in Fuller's estimation rightly termed 'silver-tongued Smith,' for his mouth was ' but one metal in price and purity beneath Chrysostom.' Smith's views were warmly patronized by Burghley. Persons of quality flocked to hear him, we are told, taking three-legged stools with them and sitting out in the 'allies ' (aisles).[1] Not less famous under James I. was Richard Sibbes (1577-1635), a famed pulpiteer of Gray's Inn, whose ministry was ' much blessed ' among

---

[1] His sermons were printed in 1592, and frequently re-issued down to 1631. The lives of these Elizabethan-Jacobean pulpiteers are grouped in the admirable *Abel Redivivus,* edited by Thos. Fuller in 1651.

the earnest cultured. He reached his zenith in 1630, when his emotional discourse *Bruised Reed and Smoaking Flax*, to which Richard Baxter traced his conversion, was published. Ten of his sermons had appeared in 1629.

Another meditation imbued with a profound devotional feeling is the prose essay entitled *The Cypress Grove*, an echo from Plato and a foretaste of Browne, which William Drummond appended to his *Flowres of Sion* (1623). This pensive discourse on Death has more poetical beauty than substance, and the beauty is evidently derived from the reflection in it of Drummond's liturgical and patristic reading.

The extreme beauty of the mould into which the devotions of the choice spirits of that age were spontaneously poured is shown in a most striking fashion in the eloquent and appealing prayers uttered by the Earl of Essex upon the scaffold on February 25th, 1601, and printed in *Lives and Letters of the Devereux, Earls of Essex*.

§ 6. *Bacon.*

Francis Bacon, younger son of Sir Nicholas Bacon, Lord Keeper, was born at York House, between West Strand and the Thames, on 22nd January, 1561. His mother, Ann, daughter of Sir Anthony Cook, was a woman of scholarly accomplishment and was the translator of Jewel's Latin *Apology* for the Church of England (1564): her sister Mildred was the wife of Lord Burghley. When Francis Bacon was born, his cousin, Robert Cecil, afterwards Lord Salisbury, was eleven years old. Francis went in 1573 to Trinity College, Cambridge, where he learned to question the authority of Aristotle. In 1576, after being admitted to Gray's Inn, he went to Paris in the suite of our ambassador, Sir Amyas Paulet, but had to return to England on his father's death in 1579. Having been called to the Bar he sat in Parliament for Melcombe Regis (1584), and during the next winter drew up his somewhat Macchiavellian treatise of Advice to Queen Elizabeth. All throughout his career the force of his advice to the great is seriously impaired by excessive obsequiousness. He avowed his pliability so frankly that everyone took him at his word; and from the beginning to the end of his career, his wise counsels were neglected, and he was little better than an instrument in the hands of the unwise. In 1586 he became a bencher of his Inn, and now sat for Taunton in Parliament. When the Marprelate controversy was raging in 1589 he sought to arbitrate between parties in his *Controversies of the Church of England.* The aggravating causes of the controversy, he says, are four. (1) Defective government of the Bishops. (2) The ambition of certain persons who love the salutation, Rabbi, Master. (3) An excessive detestation of some former (*i.e.,* Roman) corruptions leading men to think that the Church must be purged every day anew. (4) The imitation of foreign forms of Church government, whereas the Church in every country should do that which is convenient to itself. He writes with a sincere wish to mediate like a sincere Christian of Puritan inclinations, but also like a sensible Erastian with a profound indifference to small details of Church government or ceremonies. He disliked the bigoted narrowness of the Puritan, but was convinced that the Church needed some reform and much greater elasticity. In the meantime he was diligently preferring his suit with Burghley and Walsingham, but was unable to secure a post, though he was continually in debt and always in want of money. He hungered and pined after office, but he barred his own path by an independent speech in Parliament. Within two years he was craving restoration to royal favour, but in 1595 the Earl of Essex, his new patron, generously gave him an estate. In 1594, while he was still engaged in sueing, Bacon jotted down the extraordinary collection of extracts, proverbs, and happy thoughts, often of a mean and cynical character, to which he gave the name of *Promus* (*i.e.*, dispenser) of formularies and elegances. The spirit of *Promus* animates the advice which Bacon gave to Essex with a view to his more secure retention of his place as first favourite with the Queen. Essex was far too frank, according to Bacon, and lacked correspondence and agreeableness; in other words, was not half obsequious enough. He was subject in particular to five species of disparagement. The courtiers said he was too presumptuous and opiniated; to counteract this, he was to pretend to take up projects and then drop them at the Queen's bidding. Secondly, he was charged with military display; to avoid this he was to pretend to be bookish and contemplative. Thirdly, he was suspected of popularity, a dangerous impression which he was to remove as far as possible by blaming popularity in others. Fourthly, he was said to be careless in money matters, in which more prudence was necessary. Lastly, he was accused of taking advantage of his position as favourite; to remedy this unfavourable impression, he was to introduce a tool of his own into the position of a minor favourite. The same kind of cunning rather than the maturer wisdom of later instalments is apparent in the first edition of the *Essays* published in January, 1597; but the most deplorable manifestation of this same shortsighted sagacity is discerned in the part taken by Bacon in the proceedings against Essex. When Essex first returned from Ireland in defiance of the direct orders of the Queen, Bacon dilated on the indiscretion of his former patron in a speech before the Star Chamber, at York House. He subsequently intrigued to effect a reconciliation between the Queen and her former favourite; but after Essex had determined to attempt a *coup d'état* in the shape of a forcible removal of the Queen's councillors, and made his rash and despairing march through the

city, Bacon not only took part in garbling the traitor's con-
fession, but also made an elaborate speech in the capacity
of a learned counsel, in which he pressed home the charge
of a deliberate and preconceived act of treason. The ac-
cusation derived its terrible force from the fact that Bacon
had so long been an intimate friend and counsellor of the
accused : for, ignoring the earl's impulsiveness and the
misery engendered by his complete ostracism, Bacon represented his defence as a piece of carefully planned hypocrisy,
while as to the plea that he could never have planned a
revolution with so small a force, Bacon completely under-
mined it by the telling instance of the action of the Duke
of Guise on the day of Barricades at Paris. Probably
in consenting to contribute to the destruction of his
friend, Bacon acted under considerable pressure. If he
had refused the task assigned to him by the Crown, he
would have had to give up all chance of the Queen's favour,
and with it all hope of immediate promotion. Bacon was
not the man to make such a sacrifice. He had known
what it was to be under the cloud of royal displeasure,
and in his pressing necessities he was unwilling to renew
that experience. He may have felt that Essex was a reckless, wilful, incorrigible outcast from the Court, capable now
neither of helping nor being helped, doomed to inevitable
destruction. Bacon had a keen sense of the value of fortune,
of the possibilities of a learned leisure, of the importance
of his colossal plans for the benefit of the human race ; on
the other hand he had a very dull sense of the claims of
honour and friendship ; he preferred to be prosperous even
at the cost of facilitating the ruin of a friend, for whom
ruin in any case was ultimately inevitable.

Bacon completed his services on behalf of the Crown
against his old patron by penning an official declaration of
the treasons of Essex, 1601. Three years later he drew up

a palinode, or an apology for his behaviour with regard to the noble but unfortunate earl, in whose interests, he now declared, he had neglected the Queen's service and his own fortune. The whole incident illustrates but too plainly Bacon's extraordinary power of interested self-persuasion and his faculty for concentrating his attention less upon his actual deeds and utterances than upon the general rectitude of his intentions. He was paid £1,200 for his efforts in proving his friend a traitor, but he failed to secure the Mastership of the Rolls or other definite preferment. The death of the Queen brought about a complete change in his prospects. His conduct to Essex was now viewed in a disparaging light, and although he was one of a large batch of legal knights, his first overtures to the new King appear to have been rebuffed. Yet Bacon was encouraged by the conviction that the new King with his learned hobbies, his comprehensive ideas, and his aversion from intolerance, was susceptible in a high degree to philosophical advice. Hence his brief discourse touching the happy union between England and Scotland, and his treatise on the Pacification and edification of the Church. In the latter he advocates drastic Church reform in the direction of elasticity of ceremonial and conciliation of the Puritan conformists. He wrote, evidently, in ignorance of the temper of the King, who peremptorily rejected his advice. Bacon, who knew not his own mind till he knew the King's, promptly acquiesced in James's conservative views to the extent of calling in the printed copies of his treatise. In the new Parliament of 1604 he was on surer ground, and he at once assumed a prominent position of conciliation to the new sovereign, extolling the prerogative, supporting the union, advocating a subsidy, and the maintenance of the King's right of pre-emption. He at once received a pension, and devoted his leisure, previous to the re-assembling of Parliament, in working at his masterly essay on *The Advancement of Learning*, published in 1605, which contains some of his finest writing and is described as the first great book in English prose of secular interest. It is the first also of a long line of books which have attempted to teach English readers ' how to think of knowledge, to impress upon them all that knowledge might do in wise hands for the elevation and benefit of man; to warn them against the rocks and shallows of error and fallacy which beset the course of thought and inquiry, and to elevate the quest for truth and the acquisition of wisdom into the noblest aim and best assured hope of the human species.'

In May, 1606, Bacon, who was now forty-five, married Alice Barnham, the handsome daughter of a London alderman and draper. The marriage, which was unfruitful, was one of formality and convenience. Towards the end of his life, for just and great causes, Bacon revoked a will which he had made in his wife's favour.[1] In his *Essays* he remarks tersely, ' nuptial love maketh mankind, friendly love perfecteth it.' In February, 1607, Bacon spoke in Parliament with a fervour of conviction in favour of James's naturalization scheme. In the following June he was made Solicitor-General, a lucrative post with a good prospect of promotion. In 1608 he became Clerk of the Star Chamber, a long-promised reversion for which he had waited nineteen years. The ardour of the pursuit for a position having abated, Bacon underwent a period of depression, as an antidote for which he addressed himself to philosophy, and settled a plan of his *Instauratio Magna*, or great renewal of learning, to which his treatise on *The Advancement of Learning* had been intended as but a portico, a preface or statement of general principles preliminary to the great work. Bacon

[1] After Bacon's death the widow married his gentleman usher.

now composed in Latin his *Cogitata et visa* (*i.e.*, Thoughts and Judgements). In 1608 he wrote a tract expressing his sincere admiration of the late Queen, *In felicem memoriam Elizabethae*, and in 1609 *Considerations touching the Plantation in Ireland*, in which he deprecates excess of paper government, advises freedom from taxes and customs, and the addition of an Irish title to the Prince of Wales, but slurs over the great question how to treat the native population. At the same time the *Instauratio Magna* was proceeding and gaining upon his affection and desire, as he wrote to his friend Tobie Matthew. But nearer still to his heart than synthetic philosophy was the architecture of his own fortunes. In May, 1612, his cousin, Lord Salisbury, died; honours and preferments were now flying about, and Bacon was sueing for promotion in accordance with the system which he elaborated in his note-books with a thoroughness befitting an inductive philosopher. He lost no time in suggesting to the King that he should be removed to business of state; but it was not until August, 1613, that he was substantially promoted to the post of Attorney-General. His progress to the wool-sack was definitely assured in 1616, in which year he was appointed a Privy Councillor. Towards the close of the year he tendered a letter of advice to the rising star of the Court, George Villiers, soon to become the Duke of Buckingham, and in March, 1617, he received the Great Seal with the title of Lord Keeper. Buckingham early showed his appreciation of Bacon's character by sending letters to him in favour of suitors who had cases pending in chancery. Their advancement went hand in hand, for in January, 1618, Buckingham was made a Marquis, and Bacon Lord Chancellor, with the title of Baron Verulam. In October, 1620, was published all that was ever completed of his *Novum Organum*, and this date may be taken to mark the climax of his greatness. On January 27th, 1621, he was created Viscount St. Alban.[1]

Bacon rather complimented himself on his suave manners and on his knowledge of people and parliament, but he naturally excited the greatest hostility by the support he gave Buckingham and Mompesson in enforcing oppressive monopolies, and in his cold-blooded severity to the Attorney-General, Yelverton, who had incurred the spite of the favourite. In March, 1621, he was impeached for corruption, and having admitted the truth of twenty-eight of the particular charges against him, he was sentenced to be fined £40,000 and to be imprisoned in the Tower during the King's pleasure. He was also disqualified from sitting in Parliament or holding any office in the state. Of deliberately perverting justice for money Bacon was guiltless; but he had admittedly taken money from suitors; he had connived at the extortions of his servants, and had allowed himself to be brow-beaten by the King's favourite in the administration of justice to an extent which must preclude us from pronouncing him incorrupt. His disgrace procured him for the remaining five years of his life a seclusion which, though involuntary, was none the less fruitful of work befitting a philosopher and a scholar. 'Like precious odours most fragrant when incensed or crushed,' Bacon's virtues of patience, assiduity, and good temper were brought out by his adversity. Freed from imprisonment after a two days' sojourn in the Tower, Bacon pursued his philosophic studies with little interruption. The *De Augmentis*, the completed edition of the

---

[1] In an historical peerage he would be designated properly as Lord St. Alban; but he was known in his own day as Lord Keeper or Lord Chancellor Bacon, and in English literature he is generally known as Lord Bacon, a vulgar designation consecrated by the best writers.

Essays, The History of Henry VII., the *Advertisement* (dialogue-wise) *touching an Holy War*, besides the *Sylva Sylvarum* and some other fragments of the *Novum Organum*—all proceeded from his pen during his enforced retirement. He died on 9th April, 1626, owning an estate of £7,000 and debts amounting to upwards of £20,000.[1]

In 1625 appeared the solitary fruit of Bacon's devotion to the poetic Muse, his *Translation of certain Psalms into English Verse*, written in the previous year. These excursions are flat and dreary: the one poem of merit ascribed to Bacon in the *Golden Treasury* is a paraphrase of an oft-rendered epigram in the Greek Anthology. Another poem often printed as his, *The man of life upright*, is really by T. Campion.

Bacon's intellect enabled him to take large views, to judge profoundly and to appreciate certain classes of motives with extraordinary clearness and acumen. But he was deficient in that which would have compelled him to devote himself to other than personal aims. Mere intellect is but an instrument: it cannot create an object of desire, it can only aid in realizing such an object. The intellect of Bacon, owing to his defective sympathies and

Lord Bacon 'kept up his station' with a pomp and magnificence worthy of Wolsey, and this grandeur, which proved far to exceed his means, is very characteristic. The following traits are collected from that exquisite gossip, John Aubrey. His lordship would have 'musique in the next roome when he meditated.' He built an aviary at York House costing £300. 'Every meal according to the season of the year he had his table strewed with sweet herbes and flowers, which he said did refresh his spirits and memorie.' When at his country house of Gorhambury it seemed 'as if the court had been there, so nobly did he live.' His servants had liveries bearing his crest (a boar); his watermen were the best on the river. 'None of his servants durst appear before him without Spanish leather boots.' When James I. sent a buck to him he gave the keeper fifty pounds. For details see the fascinating *Francis Bacon. An Account of his Life and Works* (1885), by Dr. E. A. Abbott.

his deficient moral sense, tended to become the instrument merely of his own petty and personal ambitions and of the ambitions of persons more highly placed than himself, to whom he prostituted it. The desire of intellect, if it has any, is truth, and Bacon's scheme for the advancement of learning is the noblest thing in his life. It is just such a scheme as a man of his intellect and character would conceive and would neglect. That he did neglect it there can be no doubt. The only branch of knowledge for which Bacon really did anything is the barren knowledge of how to trade upon the folly, the vanity, the selfishness of mankind. Bacon had much in common with Chesterfield; but Chesterfield had a much higher standard of truth and honour than Bacon. In a diplomatist of the eighteenth century there is little to surprise one in the sardonic outlook of Chesterfield upon his fellow-men. In a philosopher of the calibre of Bacon one encounters with more of a shock a calculating, cold-blooded, and cynical egotism, such as we come across hardly anywhere else in the world save in a hero of Maupassant. That Bacon, with his transcendent wit, did not either rule a kingdom or found a philosophy was due to the fact that the advancement of learning interested him at bottom far less than the advancement of Francis Bacon. He never made up his mind between philosophy and politics—just as for a medium of expression he never made up his mind between English and Latin. But for this duality, however, we could never have inherited the priceless heritage of the *Essays*, in which the worldly common sense of a Franklin is combined with the culture and style of a Cicero, and the synthetic and philosophical aptitude of a Leibniz.

Of the legacies in English prose that Bacon left to the ' next ages,' the two that concern us most nearly in the twentieth century are the *Essays* and *The History of Henry VII.*

In 1597 Bacon published *Essayes. Religious Meditations.*
Places of perswasion and disswasion. The
The *Essays.*   *Essays* included in this volume were limited
to ten,[1] and were strictly aphorismic in
character. In 1612 he reprinted the original *Essays* in a
slightly expanded form, and added twenty-nine new ones.
Finally, in 1625, he again re-issued them, 'newly written,'
and now fifty-eight in number. The composition, correction, and augmentation of the *Essays* thus stretched over
a period of nearly thirty years. They were commenced
under Elizabeth, increased under James, and assumed their
final shape under Charles.[2] Such a method of composition
would scarcely commend itself to practitioners of the present day. To retouch an essay or a short story that approaches to being a work of art is generally to spoil it.
But Bacon had privileges as the founder of the *genre*. He
probably took the name Essays from Montaigne, and he
defines an essay as a ' dispersed meditation.' His essays
are, however, extremely different in character from those
of Montaigne, distinguished pre-eminently by their chatty

[1] Of Study, Discourse, Ceremonies, Followers and Friends,
Suitors, Expense, Regiment of Health, Honour and Reputation,
Faction, Negotiating. A harmony of the three editions of the
Essays was edited by Prof. Arber. The term ' Essay ' has in the
main retained its Baconian signification as a meditation upon human
life in a wide sense, while essays in Philosophy, Logic, Archaeology,
Physical Science, Criticism, Art and Politics, have been differ-
entiated severally as Dissertations, Treatises, Papers, Memoirs,
Reviews, Appreciations, and Articles.

[2] ' In the successive versions of the *Essays* we see the almost
skeleton forms of the earliest filling out, taking on trappings,
acquiring flesh and colour and complexion in the later, while in
some of the latest, the well-known ones "Of Building" and "Of
Gardens" especially, the singular interest in all sorts of minute
material facts which distinguishes him comes in with a curiously
happy effect' (Saintsbury).

irrelevance and *naïf* unexpectedness; still more from those of our greatest modern essayists, Addison, Steele, Lamb, Hazlitt and Stevenson. Bacon's *Essays* are, in fact, more like the Reflexions or *Pensées* of some of the celebrated French wits, La Bruyère, Joubert, and Rivarol, with strong occasional resemblances to the distracting flashlights of Emerson.

The earlier *Essays* in structure more nearly resemble some of the less classical pages of *The Anatomy* of Burton. Built up of detached thoughts, sentences, and maxims, they form a collection of happy epigrams, apophthegms not seldom profound, and citations both witty and apposite. The amount of thought in them is very variable, and is so 'dispersed' that the connection is often difficult to trace. The later *Essays*, especially those added in 1625, are somewhat less compressed and gnomic in form and expression, and, the style being drawn out, are more flowing and gracious in manner. Some of the famous LVIII. are rather notions or outlines, châteaux or gardens *en Espagne*, than 'meditations' proper. Their wonderful vitality is due in the main to their unusual combination of sagacity and terseness. Some of the best known sayings in the language are contained in these secular sermons, and the point is not infrequently compressed into a headline or text:

'Men fear death as children fear to go in the dark'; 'Revenge is a kind of wild justice'; 'He that hath wife and children hath given hostages to fortune'; 'Suspicions among thoughts are like bats among birds'; 'Virtue is like a rich stone, best plain set'; 'God Almighty first planted a garden.' And the tailpieces to the *Essays* are scarcely one whit less remarkable: 'Vindictive persons live the life of witches, who as they are mischievous so end they unfortunate'; 'Virtue is like precious odours, most fragrant when they are incensed or crushed'; 'In counsel it is good to see dangers and in execution not to see them unless they be very great'; 'If a man be gracious and courteous to strangers it shows he is a citizen of the world'; and 'where a man cannot fitly play his own part, if he have not a friend, he may quit the stage.' Almost every word of Essay L., *Of Studies*, has become quasi-proverbial, and even more may be said of 'Lookers on many times see more than the gamesters'; 'The remedy worse than the disease'; or of what is perhaps the finest saying in the book, 'A crowd is not company: and faces are but a gallery of pictures; and talk but a tinkling cymbal where there is no love.' Trite as the subjects are, familiar as the treatment to those who know the *Essays*, the reader is seldom unrewarded by a sensation of novelty, so multitudinous are the facets of Bacon's thought. This is, indeed, a characteristic of Bacon's writings, and may be accounted for, as Dugald Stewart impressively remarks, 'by the inexhaustible aliment they furnish to our own thoughts, and the sympathetic activity they impart to our torpid faculties.'

The *Essays* are representative throughout of Bacon's shrewd and sententious humour, his almost incomparable power of generalizing and of crystallizing the utterances of sage men of all periods. Their author was in very truth 'a discloser of lights the most overwhelming in flashes of wit.' Yet Bacon's gift for transmitting his personality is so great that they reveal with equal distinctness his too clear apprehension of the base side of human nature, his poverty in respect of genial humour, emotion, and the higher imaginative qualities, his total lack of what Milton describes as the three prime elements of poetry—the simple, the sensuous, and the passionate.

As a consistent work of art Bacon's *History of Henry VII.* has higher claims even than his *Essays*. It was written by Bacon immediately after he emerged from the Tower, between June and October, 1621. James I. is said to have recommended the reign of Henry VII. as a good subject, but Bacon had already noted the want of a history dealing with the period 1485-1603, and he had even begun a short sketch of Henry VII. before 1609.[1] He had divided histories into three classes, according as they represented a time, a person, or an action,[2] respectively shown in chronicles, lives, relations. It was this second class of history that he proposed to exemplify. He

Henry VII. was writing in this instance of James's ancestor for presentation to the King, but few of his works show less obsequiousness. Henry is commended as fortunate, a man of *virtù* in the Macchiavellian sense, a shining example of kingcraft, ' stout without and apprehensive within,' but his motives are closely analyzed, and his character anything but idealized. He is described as keen-sighted and cunning, rather than as provident or wise, and although successful in his main objects, and triumphant in his avarice, yet continually haunted by his fears and cordially detested by his subjects.

Bacon wrote this admirable narrative in a few months,[3] taking his facts from the chroniclers, and having access to few if any original documents. His peculiar merit is not accuracy, yet even if it be taken on that ground, Bacon's sagacity and knowledge of state affairs proved so true a guide that his views of the main actions have not been set aside by more patient investigators.

[1] He left a fragment of a projected reign of Henry VIII., written before 1603; and a fine characterization written in Latin.

[2] *Advancement of Learning.*

[3] The work was looked over in MS. by the King, who made one or two slight emendations, and it was published in April, 1622. Before his death Bacon executed a Latin translation.

Although the interest is concentrated upon the King it is well sustained and continuous, and the movement of the narrative as a whole is rapid. The style is singularly clear and unencumbered. Classical turns of phrase and words used in a strict classical or etymological sense (now obsolete) are much rarer than in the *Essays*. Long imaginary speeches put in the mouth of the Chancellor and others occasionally betray Latin models such as Livy and Sallust. The episodes, especially those dealing with the adventures of the two Pretenders, Simnel and Warbeck ('the King was haunted with spirits by the magic and curious arts of the Lady Margaret'), the establishment of the Star Chamber, Henry's intervention in the affairs of Britain (Brittany), and the wily diplomacy on both sides which surrounded this event, are introduced with an abundance of art. A ripple of humour, albeit saturnine, is more conspicuous than in any other of Bacon's works.[1] Pithy and poignant sayings, as is the rule in his work, keenly stimulate the zest of the reader.

[1] Henry tried to get Henry VI. canonized; but 'the general opinion was that Pope Julius was too dear.' More probably, says Bacon, 'the Pope was afraid it would diminish the estimation of the honour if there were not a distance kept between innocents and saints.' Justice was well administered in Henry's time 'save where the king was party; save also that the king intermeddled too much with *meum* and *tuum*.' Among his motives for punishing Stanley is enumerated 'the glimmering of a confiscation.' 'He knew the way to peace was not to seem too desirous to avoid war.' 'He did not care how cunning they were that he did employ; for he thought himself to have the master reach.' Perkin at Taunton is described as 'squinting one eye on the crown and another upon the sanctuary'; for 'the rebels' snowball did not gather as it went.' The king sent a complimentary embassy to Pope Innocent, 'who knowing himself to be lazy and unprofitable to the Christian world was wonderfully glad to hear that there were such echoes of him sounding in remote parts.' Very good indeed are the analysis

At the same time the reader's interest is primarily governed, as it should be, by the art with which Bacon gradually unfolds the character of his main figure, the monarch of whose nature his comprehension appears to be wellnigh perfect. Considered upon its own claims as an explanation of events by reference to the feelings and purposes of the chief actor, it is, perhaps, a better model than any history that has been published since.

The *New Atlantis* is an interesting though fragmentary example of the *voyage imaginaire*. The best specimens of this literary species are those of the wholly or semi-satirical order, such as Lucian's *Vera Historia*, More's *Utopia*, and *Gulliver's Travels*. Bacon's *Atlantis* is not satirical, but (like Johnson's *Rasselas*) speculative, and it was evidently designed to stimulate scientific speculation. The narrative, as far as it goes, is well-sustained, clear, and admirably written. An island of human paragons is discovered in the North Pacific. This is the *New Atlantis* (to distinguish it from Atlantis, *i.e.*, America), the inhabitants of which deliberately hold aloof from their corrupted fellow-men, though they follow their general proceedings with interest through the agency of secret-service spies. The island appears to be governed by a kind of Scientific Institute, known as Solomon's House. The narrator has a long interview with the head of this august body; but after a few remarks upon prehistoric times, interesting as showing the range of Bacon's thought, the colloquy degenerates into a monologue, in which the Grand Lama describes the resources of the Institute, which seems to have been a sort of combination of World's Fair, Crystal Palace, and Jardin des Plantes. Much of this seems rather tedious, if not puerile, and is only interesting as showing Bacon's real zeal for experimental studies. In the midst of the inventory of Solomon's House the fragment abruptly terminates.

---

of the motives that led Henry to spare Simnel, and the comparison of Henry, Ferdinand and Louis XI. with the *Tres Magi*. Dramatic in the extreme is the interview between Henry and the ship-wrecked Archduke Philip.

The work which Bacon regarded as the apex of his intellectual achievement, the great but unfinished *Instauratio Scientiarum*, is a sadly fragmentary and inconclusive monument. It is written in Latin, which scientific men of to-day rarely understand (so grievously is Bacon's foresight falsified), and as a scientific synthesis it is radically wrong.

The Temple to Science as conceived by Bacon in his *Instauratio Magna* was hexagonal. (1) *De Augmentis*—a ground-plan of the general scheme, showing the partition of the sciences. (2) The *Novum Organum* (fragmentary), the key, opening the new instrument or *method of inquiry*, which was to be substituted for the old instrument, the *Organon* of Aristotle (*i.e.*, observation and experiment to replace syllogistic and deductive logic). (3) *Sylva Sylvarum*, a fragment of a comprehensive experimental natural history, as Ray might have termed it, and corresponding in modern phrase to *Principles of Biology*. (4) *Scala Intellectus*, a ladder from experiment to scientific generalization (unwritten). (5) *Prodromi*, or anticipations of the Second Philosophy. (6) *Scientia Activa*. Having regard to the fact that they were never written, the tenor of the three last sections can only be described as excessively vague.

The only part of this ambitious fragment with which the English reader has direct concern is the *De Augmentis*, or rather the preliminary sketch of it as written and circulated in English under the title *Of the Proficience and Advancement of Learning, Divine and Human* (1605). It has been styled the Portico of the Baconian Systema, but in more exact Elizabethan it is a 'foule draft' of the ground-plan of the *Instauratio*, which Bacon subsequently elaborated and greatly expanded in the Latin *De Augmentis*. It contains some noble passages in vindication of the endowment of research in the widest sense of the word. But as a whole its logical, abstract, and convolute periods render it task-work to read, and its speciously logical and scientific arrangement is not only obsolete but fallacious. Like most of Bacon's writings it was esteemed by his contemporaries less for itself than as the work of a Lord Chancellor and a great patron of literature. It attained to the zenith of its fame in the eighteenth century, when it was adopted as the framework of

Diderot's *Encyclopédie*. It may be that the later twentieth century will discover philosophical qualities hitherto unsuspected in a man no less versatile and hardly less able than Lord Bacon, Lord Brougham. But the development of physical science has greatly tended to discredit Bacon's apparatus, the more so since, unlike Leibniz, Comte, Spencer, and other synthetic systematizers, of whom he was the precursor, Bacon was at no pains to keep in contact with the (far from despicable) science of his own day. Grand, therefore, as was the idea, Bacon had not the necessary equipment for its realization. He seems, indeed, to have known practically nothing of that science which he desired to advance. He made, no doubt, a few shrewd guesses of his own, but in no sense is he a pioneer of scientific philosophy. Credit is due to him for his insistence on the facts that man is the servant and interpreter of nature, that truth is not derived from authority, and that knowledge is the fruit of experience. But such facts to such men as Napier, Gilbert, Harriott and Harvey, were already axiomatic. So far from being the initiator of the inductive method, practised long before his time, notably by Roger Bacon, he did not even understand it, or at least his idea of the application of it is one that is wholly impracticable. The extent to which Bacon's claim to be an inventor of a philosophic method has been resented by advanced scientific opinion is well illustrated by a passage from an eminent American philosopher.[1] Bacon 'never produced any great practical result himself; he has indeed about as much to do with the development of modern science as the inventor of the orrery has had to do with the discovery of the mechanism of the world. Of all the important physical discoveries there is not one which shows that its author arrived at it by means of the Baconian *Organon*. No man can invent an organon for scientific inquiry any more than for the writing of tragedies and epics.' 'Few scientific pretenders have made more mistakes than Lord Bacon. He rejected the Copernican system and spoke insolently of its great author; he undertook to criticise adversely Gilbert's treatise, *De Magnete*; he was

---

[1] Draper, *Intellectual Development* (Bohn), ii. 260.

occupied in the condemnation of any investigation of final causes, while Harvey was deducing the circulation of the blood from D'Acquapendente's discovery of the valves in the veins; he was doubtful whether instruments were of any advantage, while Galileo was investigating the heavens with a telescope. Ignorant himself of any branch of mathematics, he presumed that they were useless in science but a few years before Newton achieved by their aid his immortal discoveries.'

From the genuine pioneers of scientific thought in his time, many of whom he might easily have encountered in Britain,[1] nay, from the very genius of the English language itself, there can be no denying that Bacon held himself deliberately aloof. In the interest, as he thought, no doubt, of the genuine *Scientia Activa*, he spurned the true votaries of science as masqueraders, and dismissed them from his thought with a contemptuous 'But enough of these toys.' And this brings us back once more to the contradictoriness and seeming perversity of Bacon's whole career. He had a vision of what could be achieved by men of science. He had a vision of what might be performed by wise statesmen, and of the rough places which might be made smooth by a good equity lawyer. But he was himself neither a scientist, nor a great statesman, nor even a just judge. Nor had he any clear notion of how any of the great things he thought most desirable should be actually *done.* He said that knowledge was power, and aimed ostensibly, above all, at the advancement of learning; but actually he wasted his time in the pursuit of riches and titles. Even if he had gained power instead of the shadow of it, it is far from certain that he would have known what to do with it. We come again to the solution of the problem. Intellectually capable of almost any-

---

[1] For instance, John Napier of Merchiston (1550-1617), whose epoch-making description of the Canon of Logarithms appeared in 1614; William Harvey (1578-1657); Thomas Harriott (1560-1621), the wonderful algebraist and astronomer; and William Gilbert (1540-1603), whose book on the Magnet appeared in 1600. Bacon was a little later than Tycho Brahè, but was practically of the same generation as Galileo, Kepler, De Caus, and Fabricius (D'Acquapendente), the pupil of Fallopius.

thing, Bacon entirely lacked that essential quality, which in Shakespeare dominates all his other gifts—moral capacity.[1]

§ 7. *Historians, Travellers, General Writers, and other Compilers.*

By far the greatest historical work of our period was Bacon's *History of Henry VII.* Its greatness can be estimated when we compare the finished work with the raw material out of which it was fashioned—the chronicles, namely, of Fabyan, Polydore Vergil, Hall, Holinshed, and Stowe. Poor and incomplete though these materials were, Bacon succeeded so well that he has left later historians but little to do. Subsequent researches have but confirmed and illustrated the truth of his history in all its main features. The portrait of Henry as drawn by him is the original of all the portraits which have been drawn since.

Bacon's Henry VII. The good stories of the reign, such as those of Morton's fork, Empson's fixed determination to 'cut another chop' (£720) out of Alderman Sir William Capel, Henry's rebuke to the Earl of Oxford, and Maximilian's method of marriage by proxy with Anne of Brittany, are all related by Bacon, and it is amusing to trace how certain of his statements have been borrowed, perverted, and often disfigured by subsequent historical compilers. As compared with the dull, soulless and uncritical compiling of his predecessors and contemporaries, the effect of Bacon's treatment of his materials resembled the bringing of a light into a dark room. The objects are there as they were before, but they are

[1] 'I doubt whether there are five lines together to be found in Bacon which could be mistaken for Shakespeare, or five lines in Shakespeare which could be mistaken for Bacon, by one who was familiar with their several styles, and practised in such observations' (Spedding).

now first illuminated in such a way that one can take pleasure in distinguishing them.

Bacon's *History* was written upon his emerging from two days' sojourn in the Tower. *The History of the World*, by Sir Walter Raleigh, surely one of the most remarkable productions of prison life, was compiled during an imprisonment of some twelve years, in a room which is still pointed out to the sightseer, in the same grim fortress. Other fruits of this long captivity were *The Prerogative of Parliaments*, edited by Milton in 1658, the admirably written *Three Discourses* and *Advice to his Son*, concerning choice of wife and friends, servants, flattery, quarrels, the preservation of estate, and the like.

As typical an Englishman as Sidney himself of the generation that followed Sidney's was Walter Raleigh— even more versatile, a representative of the restless spirit of romantic adventure, mixed with cool practical enterprise, that marked the times. He fought against the Queen's enemies by sea in many quarters of the globe; in the Netherlands and in Ireland against Spain; with the Huguenot army against the League in France. Raleigh was from Devonshire, the great nursery of English seamen. He was half-brother to the famous navigator, Sir Humphrey Gilbert, and cousin to another great captain, Sir Richard Grenville. He sailed with Gilbert on one of his voyages against the Spanish treasure fleet, and in 1591 he published a report of the fight near the Azores, between Grenville's ship, the 'Revenge,' and fifteen great ships of Spain, an action, said Francis Bacon, 'memorable even

Sir Walter Raleigh (1552?-1618).

beyond credit, and to the height of some heroical fable.' Raleigh was active in raising a fleet against the Spanish Armada of 1588. He was present in 1596 at the brilliant action in which the Earl of Essex 'singed the Spanish King's beard,' in the harbour of Cadiz. The year before he had sailed to Guiana, in search of the fabled 'El Dorado,' destroying on the way the Spanish town of San José, in the West Indies, and on his return he published his *Discovery of the Empire of Guiana.* In 1597 he captured the town of Fayal, in the Azores. He took a prominent part in colonizing Virginia, and he introduced tobacco and the potato plant into Europe. In 1603 his career as a courtier was blighted. Arrested for conspiring to enthrone Arabella Stuart, he attempted suicide in the Tower. Coke, the Attorney-General, set at his trial an example which was hardly eclipsed by Jeffreys, and Raleigh was sentenced to death. The death sentence hung over him until 1618, when he was sacrificed, in part as a propitiatory offering to Spain, after the failure of an impossible expedition to Guiana, which he had projected. This aspect of his case made Raleigh a popular hero. He was far from popular in his own sphere of life, in which his unscrupulous arrogance had alienated all his associates. Of all Elizabeth's courtiers he was, perhaps, the most gifted and, at the same time, the most self-seeking, headstrong, and overweeningly ambitious. His career exhibits a mixture, extraordinary even for that time, of poet, scholar, buccaneer, and spoiled child of Fortune. As Ben Jonson said of him, not unjustly, he 'esteemed more of fame than conscience.'

Raleigh's *magnum opus, The History of the World,* written by the express encouragement of Prince Henry, though some of its 'sauce' in censuring kings stuck evilly in James's throat, was published in 1614.[1] It is scarcely a history at all, in the modern sense of the word, but a series of dissertations on law, theology, mythology, magic,

---

[1] The stupendous *History* of De Thou, the first eighteen books of which appeared in 1604, may probably have stimulated Raleigh in the effort of composition.

war, and the ideal form of government, which seems in
History of the World. Raleigh's opinion to have approximated to what
we should now call a strict oligarchy. Inter-
spersed with this, however, is an extraordinarily
diffuse narrative of the rise and fall of the successive
World Empires. The briefest possible analysis of the
chapters of Book I. will give some idea of Raleigh's
emthod of progression :

Chapter I. in fifteen sections deals with the creation and preservation of the world, closely following the Mosaic account.
II. Of man's estate. III. Fifteen long sections on the position of
Paradise, with an elaborate map of the district. IV. Deals with
the trees in the garden. Query, was the tree of knowledge a
kind of fig ? V. Treats of the longevity of the patriarchs, exhibit-
ing a vast amount of reading, and citing the case of the Countess
of Desmond. VIII. Of Noah's flood.—A good example of
Raleigh's semi-rationalizing way of dealing with Scripture
history. It must be distinguished from Deucalion's and other
floods, in Egypt and elsewhere. Could it have been foreseen by
the astrologers of the day ? Where was the ark built ? What
was its motive power ? How are we to estimate its real size ?
Were common or geometrical cubits employed ? Were fish
taken in the ark ? Having settled this point to his own satisfaction, he proceeds to deal rather more briefly with such topics
as how the ark was provisioned and lighted. Rejecting with
scorn the theory that it was illuminated by a huge carbuncle,
he addresses himself seriously to the question, where did the
ark repose at the conclusion of the Flood ? It is satisfactory to
know that he had the assistance of his chaplain and of other
nice casuists and learned men in the resolution of these delicate
problems, many of which seem to befit the humour of Tom
Paine rather than that of a book informed as a whole by a
piety so genuine that it is often difficult to reconcile with the
legend of Raleigh's sceptical and ' atheistic ' early manhood.

The first book in twelve extensive chapters only takes us as far
as Semiramis. The second treats at enormous length of the
events treated in Exodus, and embraces altogether the period

from Abraham to the destruction of Jerusalem by Nebuchad-
nezzar and to the reign of Numa Pompilius. The third book
with comparative brevity takes us down to the battle of Mantinea,
and the fourth concludes in seven chapters with the death of
Pyrrhus. In the fifth and last Raleigh gives somewhat fuller
treatment to the Punic Wars (a subject upon which he had aid
from Ben Jonson), Antiochus and the conquest of Greece by
Lucius Aemilius Paulus. He had got into the middle of the
'Fourth Great Monarchy' of the world. The preface and the
conclusion are noble examples of Elizabethan prose, and the
book ends with the oft-quoted apostrophe to Death—a finale
almost as glorious and as celebrated as that of Sir Thomas
Browne's *Urn Burial.* As a monument his *History* resembles
one of those ancient, huge and fragmentary *castra,* hard to understand at a first approach and needing the archaeological
passion of a King or a Roach Smith laboriously to interpret.

A somewhat similar niche in our literary annals is
occupied by Knolles's *Turkish History*
Richard Knolles   Richard Knolles, of Cold Ashby, North-
(1550-1610).   amptonshire, graduated at Lincoln College in July, 1570, and was elected a fellow of his college,
whence he was summoned by the founder, the benevolent
Sir Roger Manwood, to take charge of the grammar
school at Sandwich. There during ten years, with Manwood to encourage him, he worked at a *Generall Historie
of the Ottoman Turks,* from the earliest times down to his
own day. This was published in folio with portraits of the
Sultans and a dedication to the new King in 1603; and
six or seven editions of this huge tome appeared during
the seventeenth century. Knolles got his information
largely from a Latin History of the Turks published at
Frankfort in 1596. His book is celebrated on account of
the eulogies which it drew from Dr. Johnson, Hallam,
Southey, and from Byron, who declared that he probably
owed his love for oriental colouring largely, in the first in-

stance, to the pleasure he derived from reading old Knolles. Pure, nervous, elevated, and clear are the somewhat random, but not wholly undeserved epithets of eulogy which Johnson bestowed upon Knolles and his prose style.

Sir John Hayward, born at Felixstow about 1564, was educated at Pembroke College, Cambridge. His *History of the First Year of Henry IV.* appeared in 1599, and being designed to some extent in support of the pretensions of Essex, got him into grave trouble with Elizabeth. But he obtained James's favour by his strong advocacy of the divine right theory, and he was, with Camden, one of the historiographers appointed to the King's College at Chelsea. He also had a good practice as a lawyer in the Court of Arches, and was knighted by the king in 1619. His best effort was probably his *Life and Raigne of King Edward the Sixt*, published in 1630. His ambition to display a brilliant literary manner, based upon study of Livy and Tacitus, exceeded his powers, and even more his grasp of the subject matter. He introduces imaginary speeches in a most reckless manner, and has no idea of perspective. But he is interesting as having made it a definite aim to get out of the track of the older chroniclers.[1] His ornate periods and antitheses come as a relief after the baldness of Holinshed and Stowe, and are a step unmistakably forward in the direction of Clarendon.

John Hayward (1564-1627).

William Camden studied at Christ's Hospital, St. Paul's School, and Oxford, until in 1575 he became second master at Westminster. His *Britannia* was completed in 1586 (englished by Holland, 1610), and its fame assured him the head-mastership at Westminster in 1593, while in 1597 he became Clarenceux King-at-Arms. His *Remains concerning Britain* appeared in 1605, and his *Annals of Elizabeth* in 1615 (Second Part, London, 1627). These materials were drawn

William Camden (1551-1623).

---

[1] The last of the *Chronicles* proper, that of Sir Richard Baker, was published rather after our period, in 1641.

largely from the Cotton Library, from the owner of which he received great assistance in his work. His short autobiographical *Memorabilia* (*apud Camdeni Epist.*) were not published until many years after his death, in 1691. He numbered among his friends nearly all the learned men of the day. Towards the close of his life he founded the Camden History Chair at Oxford, appointing as first Professor the learned Degory Wheare (1573-1647), who published in 1623 a Latin treatise on the study of history. Camden was buried in this same year with heraldic honours in the Abbey. Except for his fragmentary *Remains* he wrote habitually in Latin, but his English prose, when we encounter it, is clear, perspicuous, and good. Among the scholars whom Camden's work most directly inspired was Richard Carew (1555-1620), the translator of Tasso, who became associated with Cotton, Selden and Spelman, at the Antiquaries' Society, and who produced in his *Survey of Cornwall*, published in 1602, one of the masterpieces of our earlier topographical literature.

John Stow, the great antiquary, by original profession a tailor,

John Stow or Stowe (1525-1605). was born in London in 1525 and died there in 1605. In 1580 he brought out his *Annals of England*, afterwards known as his *Chronicle*. His *Survey of London* was published in 1598, and again in 1603. He wrote with the naked and unadorned plainness of a Defoe. He digressed freely, and devoted to the Tudor reigns nearly half the space of his *Annals* from the earliest times. He moralizes a great deal but criticises never, and he conveys without stint from his predecessors, as they had done from the older chroniclers. Holinshed had done the same. In this way Shakespeare had the benefit of a sort of Homeric tradition on which to base his *Histories*. Later chroniclers and surveyors, such as Thornbury and Knight, have followed the same sympathetic and economic plan. *The Survey of London* (1598) is an invaluable guide-book to Elizabethan London, its rivers, bridges, customs and streets. It was revised and brought up to date early in the eighteenth century.

Much of the information contained in the *Survey* was conveyed pictorially by Ralph Agas (d. 1621) in his celebrated plan of London and Westminster, executed probably about 1591.

Another tailor, another conscientious chronicler and diligent map-maker after the pattern of Stow and Agas, was the laborious John Speed (1552-1629), whose *History of Great Britaine* (1611, 2nd ed. 1623), extending to the union of England and Scotland in one monarchy under James I., was published in 1611. Samuel Daniel the poet was the compiler of a lengthy and somewhat pretentious *Historie of England* (1612-18) from the Norman Conquest to the death of Edward III. in 1377.

Most of these historical enterprises were aided and abetted, through the medium of his great learning and unrivalled library, by Sir Robert Bruce Cotton, a baronet, whose unusual distinction in those days of possessing three names was due to the adoption of the name of Bruce —a supposed ancestor—mainly out of compliment to Bruce's Stuart successor, James I. Educated at Westminster, under Camden, and at Trinity, Cotton was the moving spirit of the Old 'Society of Antiquaries,' which (founded by Archbishop Parker) flourished between 1572 and 1604, and met in close association Camden, Selden, Speed, and other scholars. He was the special patron of Speed, while Jonson, Bacon, and Camden were his frequent guests and library inmates. Cotton only published (in 1627) a *Raigne of Henry III.* His fame is due to his indefatigable zeal as a collector of old documents. His library, a veritable El Dorado to antiquarian students from Savile and Selden to Hearne and Madox, was, after many vicissitudes, lodged in the British Museum in 1753. The books of MSS. were arranged in the original library in fourteen presses, each of which was surmounted by a bust. The busts include the twelve Julian Emperors, together with Cleopatra and Faustina, and each press was

Sir Robert Bruce Cotton (1571-1631).

named after one of these personages—a system of nomenclature which is still retained.

More famous even than the 'Cottonian' is the 'Bodleian'—another imperishable monument of the love for sound learning that flourished in the Age of Shakespeare.

Sir Thomas Bodley (1545-1613) studied at Geneva and Magdalen College, Oxford, eventually becoming a fellow of Merton. He studied Hebrew, acquired several modern languages, and was extensively employed upon diplomatic errands abroad. In 1598 he wrote a formal letter to the Vice-Chancellor of Oxford, offering to found the library which is still known as Bodley's. Donations of books poured in from all quarters: the library was solemnly opened on November 8th, 1602, and the first catalogue appeared in 1605.[1] It was practically the first public library of the kind in Europe.

Sir Thomas Bodley (1545-1613).

Among the minor scholar-antiquaries may just be mentioned Alberico Gentili, the great jurist, who came from Perugia and settled in this country in 1590, and John Guillim (1565-1621), the first scholar, perhaps, thoroughly to systematize and illustrate the science of heraldry in England. Other pioneer efforts of a similar kind or upon kindred themes may be discovered by referring to our Chronological Table. Among these lesser antiquaries, who greatly stimulated each other in their researches, we must not wholly overlook Sir Simonds D'Ewes (1602-1650), a great MS.

Minor Antiquaries.

---

[1] The Tercentenary of 'Bodley' was celebrated at Oxford, 9th October, 1902. See *Pietas Oxoniensis* (Oxford, 1902). Rival collections to Bodley's were already beginning to make a distinctive mark. Thus we are told that Cecil's library was the best for history; D'Ewes's for law; Walsingham's for policy; Arundel's for heraldry; Cotton's for antiquity; and Ussher's for divinity. (See Disraeli, *Amenities of Literature*, 1859, ii. 295.)

collector and friend of Cotton, who wrote a very valuable journal of all the Parliaments during the reign of Queen Elizabeth (published not until 1682). His collections were sold to Harley and are now in the British Museum. Another figure in this particular group was John Weever (1576-1632), antiquary and verse epigrammatist, a loving scholar of Cambridge and early celebrator of the Granta, who foregathered with Cotton, D'Ewes, Spelman, Selden, and the herald Augustine Vincent, and dedicated to Charles I. in 1631 his huge and valuable folio of *Ancient Funerall Monuments* (many since his time defaced or destroyed, hence the great archaeological interest of this book). In a lower grade was John Gerard (1545-1612), noted traveller, herbalist, and gardener to Burghley at Theobalds, who dedicated his famous *Herball* (the original of Culpeper's and other more familiar compilations) to his noble patron in 1597.[1]

---

[1] Among the diarists of the period should be noted, in addition to Camden and Bodley, Sir Robert Naunton (1563-1635), whose sketches of Elizabeth's courtiers were published in 1641 as *Fragmenta Regalia*; Robert Carey (1560-1639), afterwards Earl of Monmouth, whose vivacious account of the somewhat indecent haste with which he brought the good news of the death of Good Queen Bess to her successor was committed to a little book of *Memoirs*, forgotten for many years and only published at the instance of Horace Walpole in 1759; D'Ewes, whose diaries, ranging from 1621 to 1624, were first published in 1845; Dr. John Dee (1527-1608), the famous astrologer and alchemist; John Gerard (d. 1637), the Jesuit, who wrote an account of the Gunpowder Plot; Simon Forman (1552-1611), the quack astrologer, who records in his notes afternoons spent in witnessing *Macbeth*, *Winter's Tale*, and *Cymbeline*; Sir James Melville (1535-1617), whose *Memoirs* of his own life and part in Scots history were first published in 1683; and John Manningham (d. 1622), of the Middle Temple and of Bradbourne, Kent, who listened to and reported sermons with the diligence of his great successor, John Evelyn, discussed the Queen's illness with her physician, Dr. Parry, collected gossip in the Temple Hall, retailed personal anecdotes of benchers and judges, and, not least, went to plays, making the notable entry on February 2nd, 1601-2: 'At our feast wee had a play called *Twelve Night or What you Will.*'

Three luminaries of learning, rather than *belles lettres*, come well within our period in the persons of Spelman, Ussher, and Selden. Sir Henry Spelman, of Congham, Norfolk, and Trinity, Cambridge, wrote his *Aspilogia* on coat-armour about 1595. An interest in armour indicated his early antiquarian bent. In 1613 he wrote his tract, *De non temerandis Ecclesiis*, against the lay impropriation of churches and church property—a book which produced a great impression on its appearance, and was expanded by the author into his great work (published many years later) on *Sacrilege*. These studies well illustrate his recondite learning, ecclesiastical and legal. By 1626 he had achieved the first part of his noted Old Latin and Anglo-Saxon *Glossary*. He subsequently founded a lectureship in Anglo-Saxon at Cambridge.

Sir Henry Spelman (1564-1641).

James Ussher, Archbishop of Armagh, one of the earliest scholars of Trinity College, Dublin, 1594, was known early for his patristic learning, his zeal as a book collector, and as an Irish antiquary. In 1613 he wrote a Latin work intended to carry on the argument of Jewel's *Apologia*. He did much manuscript work, and Selden calls him 'ad miraculum doctus,' while the learned Dr. Gordon says that to estimate his labours aright would be the work of a company of experts. His great books on the antiquities of the British Churches, the origin of episcopacy, on the annals of the world, and the Hebrew text of the Bible were, however, mostly issued, not in our period, but during the Commonwealth. His chronology is still the standard adopted in editions of the English Bible.

James Ussher (1581-1656).

Ussher was, perhaps, even surpassed in learning by the great jurist, John Selden, a native of West Tarring, Sussex, and a student of Chichester, Oxford, and the Inner Temple.

His learned tastes are indicated by his friends—Camden,
Cotton, Jonson, Chapman, Drayton, Bacon,
John Selden
(1584-1654). and Twysden. After some learned studies in
legal archaeology, on single combat (*Duello*)
Titles of honour, and the Jews in England (this last
for Purchas), he produced in 1617 his great work on
The History of Tythes, dealing in great detail with their
origin and development in England, and expressing doubts
as to the divine right of the clergy to exact them, which
gave serious offence in high quarters, leading to a summons
before the Court of High Commission, and the temporary
suppression of the book, though the learning which it displayed greatly interested the King. This was the beginning
of much persecution suffered by Selden for his outspoken-
ness in troubled times. He survived until 1654, but the *Table
Talk*, through the medium of which the marvellous range
and alertness of his mind can be perceived by all, was not
published until 1689. A shrewd, cynical, sarcastic, but
not unkindly observer of men and things, he went straight
to the heart of his subject, and his command of humorous
illustration and racy vernacular was scarcely surpassed by
Swift. His reply to the suggestion that the Holy Ghost
presided at general councils—to the effect that the odd
man was in truth the Holy Ghost—is a good example of
the neatness and condensation of his humour. His learning, like that of Bacon, often blossomed in the wisdom of
home truth.

Of more purely literary interest is Sir Henry Wotton.
Born at Bocton or Boughton Hall, Kent, in
Sir Henry
Wotton 1568, Wotton at New College met Gentili
(1568-1639). and Donne. His Latin was eminently good,
but Wotton himself was influenced by his
kinsman Francis Bacon, and gave the preference to scientific speculations. After Oxford, between 1590 and 1593,

he travelled, visiting Venice and Rome, where he had
acquaintance with the celebrated and formidable controversialist Bellarmine, and with the English Cardinal
Allen. During 1593 he spent some time at Geneva
under the roof of Isaac Casaubon and so mastered
French in addition to his Italian, and collected material
for his most considerable prose treatise, *The State of
Christendom*, not published before 1657. In 1600, to
escape any suspicion of complicity in Essex's dangerous
doings, he revisited Italy. While at Florence he em-
braced an opportunity which was afforded him of enter-
ing upon a career of diplomacy, being despatched on a
mission from Ferdinand de Medici to James VI., and
introduced to James at Stirling under the *incognito* of
Ottavio Baldi. In the following year, after his accession,
James gave his old acquaintance 'Baldi,' as he playfully
called him, a choice of diplomatic appointments, and
Wotton, now Sir Henry, selected the embassy at Venice—
as least likely to be ruinous. On his way out, at Augsburg,
he wrote the punning aphorism in a friend's album, that
an ambassador is an honest man sent to lie abroad for
the good of his country. (Later in life he exhorted a
beginner in his former trade to tell the truth always,
for, said he, you shall never be believed.) From Venice,
whence he was recalled in December, 1610, he wrote
many of his most interesting letters (the first really
agreeable familiar letters in English), and projected a
History of the Republic. Attacked by the unscrupulous
Scioppius, who used his Augsburg epigram as a weapon
against him with James I., Wotton had to explain his wit-
ticism to the King. In 1620 he was sent to Vienna, and it
was while negotiating there that he formed that chivalrous
attachment to the ' Winter Queen ' (Elizabeth of the
Palatinate) which was the romance of his life; and it was
to celebrate her perfections that he wrote in 1620 his lyric,

You meaner beauties of the night, the perfume of which will always cling to his name. Retired in 1622 with depleted purse to England, it was with difficulty that in 1624 he secured the Provostship of Eton—no rich post, though specially coveted by Bacon—but a quiet haven of retreat for his declining days. At Eton he was popular, the friend of that *bibliotheca ambulans*, the ' ever memorable ' John Hales, and a fellow-enthusiast of the angle with Izaak Walton, who in 1651 edited the *Reliquiae Wottonianae*. Wotton himself is said to have projected a Life of Donne, and a Book on Angling. Neither appeared, but we have of his ' Elements of Architecture,' ' A Survey of Education,' ' Characters ' of one or two historical personages, Letters, and some ' Aphorisms on Education,' said to have been collected in part by Bacon. No literary form was more suited to Wotton's genius, and these aphorisms are of rare excellence. Like the character writing of Overbury and Earle, such a form of literary exercise was in thorough harmony with the sententious tendencies of the silver age of our English Renaissance. And in Wotton's case his antecedents all combined to perfect him in the art of pithy and pregnant diction. His prose is thus interesting, though he survives more vitally as the pioneer of elegant Letters, as the author of three celebrated poems, as the enthusiast for *Comus* and counsellor of Milton in regard to *pensieri stretti*, and in the delicate traits of old Izaak's beautiful Life.

The reserve strength that was latent in our vernacular prose at the period could be illustrated almost without limit from the State Papers of Elizabeth. All we can possibly do here, merely to give some idea of the richness of the field, is to select a few of the papers dealing with one single subject, viz.: Ireland, then almost more than now the great topic of public controversy and discussion. Passing by the wonderfully vivid anonymous report on Ireland, quoted very largely by Froude (and printed first in the Irish volume of the Old Record Series of *State Papers* of Henry VIII., 11 vols., 1830-41), we come in rapid succession to Sidney's vigorous State Paper in defence of his father's administration as Viceroy; to the detailed historical reports on Irish affairs written by Sir John Davies (*A Discoverie of the State of Ireland*, 1613) and Fynes Moryson (his account of Tyrone's Rebellion in 1617); to the prose dialogue entitled *A View of the State of Ireland* by the poet Spenser; to Bacon's *Certain Considerations touching the Plantation in Ireland*, 1609, in which he deprecates excess of paper government; and to Sir Thomas Stafford's wonderfully clear, comprehensive, and impartial description of Ireland and its affairs in *Pacata Hibernia*, that is, Ireland appeased and reduced after the late wars, first printed in 1633.

The most important of these for our purpose is *A View of the State of Ireland*, 'Dialogue wise between Eudoxus and Irenaeus,' written by Edmund Spenser in 1595-6 and licensed in 1598. Eudoxus is the questioner and reasoner, while Irenaeus (Spenser himself) holds forth at length on the history, customs, and present condition of Ireland. He even gives derivations of words that puzzle his interlocutor. Irenaeus admits that the chiefest abuses are grown from the 'lawless English,' but he depicts a terrible state of affairs, and as a solution he can suggest only stern severity and a complete military settlement or plantation of the whole country, in place of scattered garrisons. The style of the dialogue is flawlessly clear, and the tendency frankly instructive: there is no florid ornament, no playing with words; the poet here shows himself master of a method of prose exposition, which gains in impressiveness from the fact of its simplicity.

Among the scholastic writers, successors of Ascham and Elyot, one of the chief places is occupied by a remarkable educational theorist, Richard Mulcaster, an Eton and King's man, first master of Merchant Taylors (1561), who brought out in 1581 his *Positions Concerning the Training Up of Children*. Mulcaster was a great enthusiast for the English tongue, though,

Richard
Mulcaster
(1531-1611).

unhappily, he was almost as conceitful in his use of it as Don Armado. But his educational theories were greatly in advance of his age. He was exceptionally enlightened on the subject of physical training. He recommends that the lowest forms should be smallest and should be handed over to the most, instead of the least, experienced masters. He would have taught his young pupils to read and write their own language, to draw, to sing, and to play some musical instrument, before they commenced Latin—a most daring innovator in this no less than in his desire to educate the Elizabethan girl as carefully as her brother. Another book of some interest on the subject of school teaching was the *Ludus Literarius* of John Brinsley, published in 1612.[1] The *Readie Way to Learne the Latine*, in which Sir Richard Carew (d. 1643) anticipates many modern language teachers by postponing grammar to much rendering backward and forward, though written at this time, was not printed until 1654.

A link between academic learning and travel is found in three interesting economic writers: Thomas Mun (1571-1641), who found a supporter in Edward Misselden, wrote several treatises on the balance of trade, Mun's first *Discourse of Trade* appearing in 1621, and Misselden's *Free Trade* in 1622. Both Mun and Misselden were merchants, and their economic ideal (which, known as the 'Mercantile Theory,' held the field until the advent of Adam Smith) was to 'sell to strangers yearly more than we consume of theirs in value.' Both contended that foreign trade should be unrestricted as long as this indispensable surplus of exports was maintained. Geffray Malynes, a mint-master of Flemish extraction, held, on the contrary, that trade and exchanges should be strictly controlled by government, and that some sort of staple system should be revived. These views he expounded at length in *Consuetudo vel Lex Mercatoria*, 1622.

---

[1] In the form of a dialogue between two schoolmasters, Spoudeus and Philoponus, with a preface by Brinsley's relative by marriage, Bishop Hall. A second edition of this suggestive book, which expands the ideas of Ascham and Mulcaster, especially in regard to 'double-translation,' appeared in 1627.

As might be expected in the first generation of English circumnavigators and seamen adventurers of every kind, the travel literature of the period is abundant. Most of it is quite outside our present range. The narratives and descriptions of Virginia and New England alone (headed by those of the redoubtable Captain John Smith) would need almost a whole chapter to enumerate. Many of these travellers' tales, as we see in the case of the *Discoverie* of the Bermudas, were eagerly absorbed by the dramatists, ever ready for new materials and fresh sensations. Tne majority of them were collected by the two arch-compilers of geographical literature, Hakluyt and Purchas. Richard Hakluyt, of Westminster and Christ Church, brought out his chief work, *The Principal Navigations, Voyages, and Discoveries of the English Nation,* in 1589, enlarged in a second edition (not without some weakening) to the three well-known volumes of 1598, 1599, and 1600. It is a vast and not unskilfully constructed edifice of borrowed records, documents, and voyagers' narratives, including such famous voyages as those of Willoughby, Jenkinson, Frobisher, Davis, Gilbert, Hawkins, and Drake.

Richard Hakluyt (1552-1616).

Hakluyt's own writing is vigorous, and his summaries are spirited and energetic, but the aims of prose style in his work are necessarily subordinated to those of research. A successor of somewhat inferior calibre was found in Samuel Purchas (1577-1626), of St. John's, Cambridge, parson of St. Martin's, Ludgate, whose great collection of voyages, *Purchas his Pilgrimes,* was published in four quarto volumes, 1625, an avowed continuation of Hakluyt, but executed with less care and judgement. In a previous work, called his *Pilgrimage,* Purchas had digested a kind of gazetteer. Four lines in this at least are famous : 'In Xaindu did Cublai Can build a stately pallace, encompassing 16 miles of plaine ground . . . . and in the middest thereof a sumptuous pallace of pleasure.' It would be interesting to expand upon the yarns of some of these seadogs; but for the most diverting and individual, and therefore the most literary, of the single narratives, we must turn to some of the landfarers, among whom preeminent stand Fynes Moryson, Thomas Coryate, and William Lithgow.

Fynes Moryson, a Lincolnshire and Peterhouse man of good family, obtained licence to travel in 1590, and after a long process of leave-taking sailed from the Thames on an extended course of travel on May 1st, 1591. Merely to enumerate the chief places in his itinerary would occupy a large octavo page.

Fynes Moryson (1566-1630).

He set out from Hamburg under somewhat unfavourable auspices, for the English, owing to commercial rivalry, were exceedingly unpopular in North Germany just then. But Moryson was not a sensitive traveller; he went on to Dresden, Nuremberg and Augsburg, then doubled back by Strasburg to Amsterdam and Leyden, where he sojourned as a student; so to Danzig, Copenhagen, Cracow, Vienna, Padua and Venice, of which he gives a plan with minute details. During 1593 he tramped from Rimini to Naples (map) and so back to Rome, where he obtained *carte-blanche* from Cardinal Allen, and did the antiquities of the place in the most thorough and conscientious manner. Like his modern successors he divides his tour of inspection into ' days.' He returns by way of Florence, Genoa (map), Verona, Berne, Geneva, where he saw Beza in 1595, Nancy, Metz, Paris (map), Dieppe and Dover. He returned almost penniless, and we have an amusing picture of a suspicious servant, tugging at the tattered cloak of the weatherbeaten Ulysses as he leaps up the stairs to his sister's apartment, until by the lady's embraces the indignant retainer perceived who the unceremonious stranger was. Whereupon, says Moryson, ' he stole back as if he had trodden upon a snake.' Next year he took a fresh route to Venice, and thence visited

Ragusa, Cyprus and Jerusalem, returning by Constantinople. In 1598 he visited Edinburgh and the North, and the first part of his travel-diary ends with a long disquisition on foreign coinages. The second part is occupied with the last three years of Elizabeth's reign, when he was drawn to Ireland by hope of preferment, and gives a full account of Tyrone's rebellion. A third part deals with travelling in general, and provides the traveller with a large choice of precepts; it compares the national traits of the various countries, and shows how many proverbial expressions are common to all. It deals with coaches, horses, and other means of transport, architectural features, varieties of diet (on which Moryson lays the greatest possible stress), apparel, and public policy. The itinerary, which was not actually published until 1617, was written by Moryson slowly and at leisure to please himself. He wrote it first in Latin, then turned it into English, and finally re-wrote and greatly condensed it. It was written professedly for unexperienced travellers, not for 'curious wits who can indure nothing but extractions and quintessences.' The result is a straightforward and clear narrative, full of queer stories and entertaining sidelights upon the social life of the day. The obstacle to the present day reader is the enormous length of the abbreviated work; Part I. containing 295 folio pages, Part II., 301 pages, and Part III., 292 pages.[1] Moryson died on February 12th, 1630.

Thomas Coryate, a son of the rector of Odcombe, near Yeovil, was educated at Oxford, but failed to take a degree, and having thus disappointed his father, who had designed him for a fat benefice in Somerset, he drifted to the Court, and became a hanger-on in the suite of Prince Henry. At Court we hear that he throve as a buffoon, and became almost a rival to 'our cousin Archie' Armstrong. His appearance was one of unrivalled whimsicality, his head resembling a sugar-cone in shape, and his style of discourse that of Don Armado in *Love's Labour's*

Thomas Coryate
(1577-1617).

---

[1] A fourth part has just been edited from a MS. at C.C.C., Oxford, by Charles Hughes (*Shakespeare's Europe*, 1903).

Lost. In 1607, in imitation of the story in Boccaccio, the courtiers shut him up in a trunk and introduced him in a Masque before the King, much to the delight of the spectators. Sweetmeats and Coryate, says Fuller, made up the last course at all Court entertainments. He was an anvil upon which the courtiers tried their wit; but sometimes the anvil returned the hammer as hard knocks as it received. By means of his compliances at Court he seems to have scraped a small sum together, and early in 1608, in accordance with a long-standing ambition, he set out to Odcombe, preparatory to leaving England for a tour of travel through Europe. Like Sterne he expatiated after his return upon the great benefit to be derived by young men of station from foreign travel.

He embarked at Dover on 14th May, 1608, and reached Calais after a seven-hour passage, but not until he remarks, 'I had varnished the exterior parts of the ship with the excremental ebullitions of my tumultuous stomach, as desiring to satiate the gormandising paunches of the hungry haddocks.' His account of what he saw in Paris and St. Denis may be compared to advantage with the descriptions of two contemporary travel-recorders—one in verse and the other in prose—Richard Corbet and Peter Heylin. He crosses Mont Cenis and observes Roch Melon, ' said to be the highest mountain of all the Alps, saving one. Some told me it was 14 miles high and it is covered with a very microcosm of clouds. The waies were exceeding uneasie, wonderful hard, all stony and full of intricate windings and turnings. So to Cremona, where he noted a very curious invention or engine. Besides fans, he says the inhabitants do carry other fine things of a far greater price, that will cost at least a ducat, which they commonly call in their Italian tongue umbrellas; that is, things that minister shadow unto them for shelter against the scorching heat of the sun. These are made of leather something answerable to the form of a little canopy and hooped in the inside with divers little wooden hoops, that extend the umbrella in a pretty large compass.' Eventually to Venice by Mantua, where he would have liked to end his days in divine meditation, but for two reasons, 'the grosse idolatry of the people' and the 'love of Odcombe, in Somerset.' His book of travel was issued in folio by Wm. Hall in 1611 as *Coryats Crudities Hastily Gobled up*, with a quaint engraved title and no less than two hundred pages of prefatory matter, mainly burlesque verses by Coryate's courtly friends and patrons, subsequently issued separately as the *Odcombian Banquet*, with other fantastic titles.

The semi-ironical applause which greeted his great folio had scarcely died away when in October, 1612, Coryate set out on his more extended voyage. He sailed first to Constantinople, visited Zante and the plains of Troy, Jerusalem, Damascus and Aleppo, whence he took a caravan to Ispahan and Lahore. He frequently toiled on foot, and must have depended largely upon alms, for between Aleppo and Agra he says (in the brief narrative of this journey printed by Purchas) that he disbursed no more than £3 in all, and ten shillings of that was filched from him by two cozening Armenians. After strange adventures in India, where he was kindly treated by Sir Thomas Roe and the English colony, and presented with money by the Great Mogul, he was carried off by a fever at Surat in December, 1617.

Coryate's book is ushered in by such a mad rout of fopperies and buffooneries that one expects to find in it scarcely even what the title suggests, but a crude prototype of the *Tramp Abroad*, with obsolete jests and archaic witticisms, and without a spark of real insight. Yet this is far from being the case. Occasionally, it is true, there is a surfeit of deliberate fooling. But nothing could be farther from the staple of the book than mere empty buffoonery. The narrative is for the most part set forth with an unvarnished simplicity, and in evident good faith. The traveller states plainly and accurately what he saw, and the marvels that he occasionally interpolates are all frankly given upon hearsay evidence alone. It is, in short, an honest book, fulfilling its purpose of telling a straightforward tale of travel— one of the first and by no means the least interesting of guide books to the Grand Tour.

More veracious in appearance, though probably not in reality, and in some respects scarcely less diverting than the *Crudities* of Coryate, is Lithgow's *The Totall Discourse of the Rare Adventures and painefull Peregrinations*, which the author dedicated to Charles I. in 1632 (a first draft had appeared in 1614). It is the narrative of nineteen years' travel, during which he claims to have tramped over 36,000 miles, beginning in March, 1610, when Lithgow left Paris for Rome. After journeying in South Italy and the Levant, he followed in Coryate's footsteps to Aleppo, thence in a caravan to Jerusalem and Cairo. Then he turned his face homewards and brought presents to James I., the Queen, and Prince Charles. In 1614 he started again, visited Tunis and Algiers, returning through Naples, Moldavia, where he was set upon by robbers and nearly killed, through Warsaw, Stockholm, and Elsinore to London. In 1620 he tramped through Spain, where at Malaga he was seized, robbed, and tortured to recant his Protestantism. The news of these cruelties reached the English consul, and through his intervention Lithgow was placed upon an English ship. His crushed limbs and racked joints were exhibited at Court, and Lithgow was twice sent by the King to Bath; but he failed to get any sympathy of Gondomar, who was so irritated by Lithgow's importunities that he assaulted him at Court. He is stated eventually to have settled at his native Lanark and to have died there after 1640. In spite of its absurd euphuistic style, the book is a valuable one for the accurate picture of manners which it contains. The author is perhaps the first to give detailed descriptions of coffee-drinking in Europe and of Turkish baths, of a pigeon post between Aleppo and Bagdad, of hookahs as smoked by the Turks, of artificial incubation, and of the importation of currants from Zante to England, 'where some liquorish lips foorsooth can now hardly digest Bread, Pasties, Broth and bag puddings without these currants.'

George Sandys, youngest son of Edwin Sandys, Archbishop of York, journeyed to Venice in 1610, and sailed thence for Egypt and Palestine, returning to England through Rome, publishing in 1615 his interesting *Relation* of his journey.

William Lithgow (1582-1645).

In 1621 he went to Virginia.   On his return, he achieved
fame in literary circles by his dexterous verse
George Sandys translation of Ovid's *Metamorphoses* ; his heroic
(1578-1644).   couplets were sufficiently smooth to commend
themselves to Pope. His travels, written in a clear, concise and
effective style, are well worth reading.   While in Palestine he
saw scores of ' sights ' denied to modern travellers, such, for instance, as the dwelling of Zebedee, the sycamore on which Judas
hanged himself, the ' Castle of Lazarus ' and the vault from which
he was raised, the house of Simon the Leper, the fount where
Bathsheba bathed her feet, the palace of Pilate, and the convent
to which the Magdalen retired from the vanities of the world.

Gervase Markham, scholar, horse-breeder, husbandman, soldier, author of all work, a writer of prodigious
Gervase   industry, has been somewhat inexactly called ' the
Markham   earliest English hackney writer.'   A country
(1568-1637). gentleman by birth, a good linguist, a fluent
compiler, and a keen man of business, he seems to have
devoted all his faculties to the service of the booksellers.   At
multiple writing he went far, writing again and again on
the same subject, and he took with alacrity to the ingenious
plan of re-issuing remainders with altered titles.   In 1595 he
published his poem on the fight of the ' Revenge,' some phrases
of which have not been wholly disdained by Tennyson.   Two
years before this he had begun a series of books on equine topics,
commencing with the *Discourse on Horsemanship* and ending
with *The Complete Farrier*.   He wrote many books on sports,
falconry, archery, husbandry, gardening, cookery, country con-
tentments, the way to get wealth, and lastly, three manuals of
military discipline, *The Soldier's Accidence*, *The Soldier's Grammar*, and *The Soldier's Exercise*.   With Markham may be compared for versatility the somewhat earlier Leonard Mascall
(d. 1589), kitchen steward to Archbishop Parker, who wrote
with a fine impartiality on pippins and how to graft them, on
poultry, on taking spots out of linen, on health, on fishing, on
trapping, on cattle, and on parish registers.   A little later came
Henry Peacham, author of *The Compleat Gentleman*, 1622.

L   P

Another light-hearted compiler, combining features of Markham and Coryate, was John Taylor (1580-1653), a waterman on the Thames, who styled himself 'His Majesty's Water Poet,' and who wrote a number of eccentric perambulations in prose and verse. When Ben Jonson set out on foot to Scotland in 1618, Taylor immediately undertook a like journey, in what was regarded as an attempt to parody the expedition of the laureate. Jonson met his needy imitator at Leith and generously gave him a gold piece. A complete list of the separate publications of this preposterous scribbler would probably not fall far short of two hundred items.

This brief notice of the journalistic activity of the period may be fitly closed by a reference to Nathaniel Butter. Butter (d. 1664) and his works. As a printer he issued *King Lear* in quarto in 1608, and Dekker's *Belman* two years later. But he soon found a more remunerative field in the publication of news pamphlets. He began by issuing little books about notorious murders, such as the famous 'Yorkshire Tragedy' of 1604-5. Later on he issued rambling notices of the *Warres of Sweden* and *Newes from Spain*. In 1622 ambition and trade rivalry spurred him to issue a regular quarto news-sheet called *Newes from most Parts of Christendom*. The titles of his sheets varied from time to time. But his 'corantoes,' whether headed *Mere Newes*, *Late Newes* or *Weekly Newes*, came out nearly every week. Butter was satirized by Jonson as Cymbal (*Staple of News*), and became a notorious character. He died a 'worn-out old stationer, very poor,' in 1664, but his enterprise virtually created the London Press.

§ 8. *Translators: the Authorized Version.*

One of the glories of the fifteenth-century Renaissance had been the surprising resurrection of classical authors. During the sixteenth century these same authors quitted the obscurity of their original tongues, and were clad in raiment of varying splendour by a whole host of vernacular translators.[1] Translations from the Latin and Greek direct, from these tongues through the medium of the French, and again from French, Italian, and Spanish authors, were executed literally by hundreds in England alone.

The opening of that wonderful treasure-house of Italian stories, Painter's *Palace of Pleasure*, made Italian tales a popular rage. Their adaptability to form plots of the romantic type of play which became predominant in England between 1560 and 1580 was soon recognized by native dramatists, and an Italian or quasi-Italian plot and scenario came to be regarded as almost indispensable.

Queen Elizabeth herself heads the host of translators with renderings from Boethius, Plutarch, and Horace. The most that her flatterers found to say of these was that they were executed in an impossibly short space of time. They are, in fact, execrable, and lead one to form a supposition that Elizabeth, like many other crowned heads, knew many languages, including her own, imperfectly.

As a whole, of course, Elizabethan prose is completely

---

[1] The importance of translations in the early development of our prose cannot easily be exaggerated. Until the end of the fourteenth century we practically had no prose literature worthy of the name. Vernacular prose, in its progress towards a standard, needs all the impetus that can possibly be obtained from the action of Court, university, and capital. But until Richard II. no monarch habitually spoke English, scholars wrote in Latin, and the merchants and lawyers were distracted between bad Norman and English dialect. English prose received its first great impulse from a translation, the Wicliffite version of the Bible, done about 1380. Under the Lancastrian kings English became predominant very rapidly not only at Court, but also in the law-courts, in the schools, and in the city. Manuals of every kind were wanted in the vernacular. The need for translators was obvious. The work went slowly on. But in Henry VIII.'s time it quickened apace, in preparation for the splendid harvest of the Elizabethan time—culminating under James I. with the Authorized Version of 1611.

eclipsed by Elizabethan poetry; but, in the special sphere
of translation, the balance is much more equally preserved; for if on the one hand we have Carew, Fairfax,
Golding, Arthur Hall, Harington, Stanyhurst, Joshua
Sylvester, and, above all, Chapman; in prose we can boast
William Adlington, Bryskett, Danett, Florio, Holland,
Mabbe, Munday, North, Savile, Shelton, Tofte, Underdown, and Whetstone, and a grand finale in Caroline
times with Urquhart. The greatest of all, perhaps, was
one of the earliest, Sir Thomas North.

Central as regards both date and importance among
Elizabethan translations stands North's *Plutarch*—Plutarch, an author singularly happy in those on whom has
fallen the task of transmitting his message to other races,
other eras, other tongues. Jaques Amyot published his
famous French version of the *Vies* in 1559—a version preeminent in its artless good-nature, and, having regard to
the standard of the time and the difference between a
young language and an aged one, far from inaccurate.

Sir Thomas North, a younger son, went with his elder
brother Roger, second Lord North, on an
embassy to Henri III. in 1574. On this
mission he probably met Amyot. Upon the
third edition of Amyot in 1567 he set to
work, and in 1579 produced his noble folio version of ' *The
Lives of the Noble Greceans and Romans*, compared together by . . . Plutarke of Chaeronea, translated out of
Greeke into French, by James Amyot, Bishop of Auxerre,
and out of the French into Englishe by Thomas North,'
which he dedicated to Elizabeth.[1]   He held a small com-

Sir Thomas North (1535?-1601?).

---

[1] Thomas Nichols, or Nicolls, had similarly rendered Thucydides
exclusively from the French of Claude de Seyssel in 1550, and
Arthur Hall (fl. 1563-1604) had translated ten books of the *Iliad*
' out of French,' 1581.

mand at Armada time, and was made a knight in 1591; but he did not apparently live to see a new (third) edition of his *Plutarch* in 1603. North's sentences are often involved and his constructions rambling; but his language is a well of English undefiled, racy of the soil, reminding one now of the Bible, now of the *Pilgrim's Progress*, now of *Robinson Crusoe*. His copious English vocabulary gives his work an incomparable vigour, so that although he owes very much to Amyot, from whom he derived not only many happy turns of phrase, but even in many cases the precise rhythm of his clauses, he must still be deemed one of the greatest of all English translators, and, in some respects, one of the greatest prose masters of the Elizabethan time. As Amyot was appreciated without stint by Montaigne (a good judge), so Shakespeare showed his liking for North in no equivocal manner. He borrowed from him in *Midsummer Night's Dream* and *Timon of Athens*, while in *Julius Caesar*, *Coriolanus*, and *Antony and Cleopatra* he incorporated whole phrases, nay, whole passages, with scarcely more alteration than was necessary to change rhythmic prose into late Shakespearean blank verse.

Adlington's *Golden Ass of Apuleius* (1566), a bravely embroidered if slightly eccentric narrative, and Underdown's vigorous and fine-sounding version of the *Aethiopian History of Heliodorus* (1569) were published a little before our period. Fenton, the translator of Belleforest and Guevara's *Epistles*, issued his last rendering, from Guicciardini, in 1579. *A Discourse of Civill Life*, translated from the educational treatise of Giraldo about 1585, though not actually published till 1606 by Lodowick Bryskett, furnishes a paraphrase of Giraldo's *Rudiments of Moral Philosophy*, but is chiefly interesting on account of its introduction, in which the translator describes the inception of his purpose at a meeting of friends at a cottage near Dublin, where the poet Spenser was present and took a leading part in the dialogue as set forth. For Spenser and Sidney, to whom he was bound by the ties of friendship and admiration, Bryskett expresses himself in befitting terms.

Thomas Danett, in addition to a *Description of the Low Countreys*, 1593, which he derived from Guicciardini, and dedicated to Burghley, produced a somewhat rude version of the *Historie of Philip de Commines*, 1601, which he also dedicated to Burghley; he manages, however, to charge with expression the often rather inexpressive dryness of his French original.

John Florio, son of a Florentine Protestant refugee, studied at Magdalen College, Oxford, paid literary court to Southampton, and was well known in metropolitan circles as a student and a connoisseur. In 1603 he became reader in Italian to James's Queen, Anne, and he died at Fulham in 1625. His Italian and English Dictionary (*Worlde of Wordes*) appeared in 1598,[1] and his famous translation of Montaigne's *Essayes* in 1603 (2nd ed., 1613). Shakespeare evidently used the translation in *The Tempest*, even if he did not possess the copy which was supposed to bear his autograph signature. It is at least interesting to know that, through Florio, Montaigne spoke to Shakespeare. And Florio, though far from accurate, is nevertheless a genuine interpreter. He represents the quaintness and *naïveté* of Montaigne as no one not of his time can. In clearness and correctness he is far inferior to Charles Cotton, whose version came out in 1686; his coxcombry, moreover, his devious quaintness and irregularity, his compound coinages, and his extreme variability—all these things are disconcerting to those whose fondness for a clear meaning will not permit them to recognize in these

John Florio (1553-1625).

---

[1] What Florio thus did for the study of Italian was done for Spanish by John Minsheu, one of Ben Jonson's aversions, whose Spanish Dictionary and Spanish Grammar both appeared in 1599.

very qualities distinctive merits. Yet at his best there is in his rendering a vital energy which gives to 'Florio's Montaigne' a gust and a character that will be sought in vain amongst more harmonious versions.

A small satellite of Florio's was John Healey (d. 1610), who rendered Bishop Hall's satire *Mundus Alter et Idem* into humorous prose and rendered Epictetus [1] from the Greek in 1610. Later in 1610 he 'Englished,' as he called his rude rendering, St. Augustine's *De Civitate Dei*.

Philemon Holland, a Chelmsford and Trinity College man, subsequently a schoolmaster at Coventry, may justly be called the 'translator general' of the period. In 1600 appeared his *Roman History* after Livy, in 1601 his Pliny's *History of the World*, in 1603 Plutarch's *Morals*, and in 1606 his version of the *Twelve Caesars* of Suetonius (one of his best efforts). In 1609 appeared his *Roman History* from Ammianus Marcellinus, and in 1610 his well-received version of Camden's *Britannia*. His longest translation was one of the last, Xenophon's *Cyropaedia*, not issued until 1632, but he also did several versions from the French. His son Henry was an eminent bookseller, 'over against the Exchange,' and published in 1618 a sumptuous illustrated folio, *Bazilωlogia, or A Booke of Kings*. Another son, Abraham, brought out in 1622 a spirited metrical description of the battle of Lepanto called *Naumachia*. Philemon's versions, as Fuller says, would in themselves furnish forth a country gentleman's library, and a shelf of 'the best Hollands' was a common adornment in an old-world gazophile, as we gather from Pope's 'And here the groaning shelves Philemon bends.' Holland was 'translated' to a better life in 1637. He went seldom abroad, we are told, drank not between meals, and never wore spectacles. He has no idea of brevity or of the economy of words, but he is a singularly graphic writer, and his *Twelve Caesars* is a rich version of an absorbing book.

Philemon Holland (1552-1637).

---

[1] The *Epictetus* bears a dedication to Florio signed 'Th. Th.' (*i.e.*, Thomas Thorpe, the literary agent).

James Mabbe, a demy of Magdalen, who went as secretary of embassy to Madrid, 1611-13, produced spirited translations from the Spanish, *The Rogue* or *The Life of Guzman D'Alfarache*, 1622, and the *Celestina* in 1631.[1]

Another prolific translator of romances was Anthony Munday,

Anthony Munday (1553-1633).

a stationer's apprentice, who travelled in Italy, and later assumed the ugly *rôle* of a spy upon the English Catholics, and a tracker of Romish priests. He was also an actor and playwright, ballad-monger,[2] librettist, and pageant writer, while as a 'hackney' he was quite as miscellaneous as Markham. He translated the *Amadis de Gaule*, 1595, *Palmerin d'Oliva*, 1597, and *Palmerin of England*, 1602, which Southey, a rare judge, describes as 'the Grub Street patriarch's worst.'

Sir Henry Savile (1549-1622).

Sir Henry Savile, fellow of Merton, acted for the Queen in the Low Countries and instructed her in Greek. In 1585 he became Warden of Merton, and in 1596 Provost of Eton. He was an intimate of Bodley and Camden, preferring the plodding scholars to the wits. His translation of four books of the *Histories of Tacitus* in 1591 was highly commended by Ben Jonson.

Thomas Shelton (fl. 1531-1620).

Thomas Shelton, apparently an Oxford man, translated the first part of *Don Quixote* from the Spanish during forty days of 1607, employing a Brussels reprint of the original, which had appeared at Madrid in 1605. His version was not published until 1612, when, as *The Delightful History of the Witty Knight, Don Quixote*, it at once became a general favourite. It was continued probably by Shelton himself in 1620. Shelton's version is vigorous and thoroughly idiomatic. As a pioneer effort it is, in fact, remarkable. But *Don Quixote* is one of the most difficult

[1] He has verses prefixed to the first Folio of Shakespeare, 1623.

[2] He was amusingly caricatured as 'Balladino' in Jonson's *The Case is Altered*.

of books to translate, and in the absence of proper glossarial apparatus and intimate knowledge of the knotty old-Spanish proverbialisms, the old English renderings, like the old French ones, are thick with perversions and inaccuracies. Shelton and Jervas (1742) are the strongest and most original of the old translators. Phillips and Smollett are very inferior, while Motteux drew most of his honey from Shelton's hive.[1]

The prose translations of Robert Tofte (d. 1620) from Tasso and Ariosto are of minor importance, and the translator himself is chiefly remembered by his complimentary poem of *Alba* in which he mentions seeing a play of *Love's Labour's Lost*.

George Whetstone (1544?-1587?), a friend of Gascoigne and Churchyard in the previous generation to that of Shakespeare, is known mainly for his *Heptameron of Civil Discourses* (1582), a collection of romances derived in large measure from the *Hecatommithi* of Cinthio, and containing the story of Promos and Cassandra, the basis of *Measure for Measure*.

Urquhart's profuse and profound yet wonderfully racy rendering of Rabelais, though full of Elizabethan vigour, was the product of a rather later generation.[2]

---

[1] The modern renderings of Ormsby and Watts leave little to be desired. Duffield, and in French Viardot, are also good.

[2] Among minor translators who can yet be distinguished from the unnumbered host, may further be included Edmund Bolton (1575-1633?), who published in 1618 a version of the *Roman Histories of Lucius Florus*. In the previous year he proposed to James I. an interesting design for a royal academy or order of men of science and literature, a scheme which was transiently in high favour at Court. Like Camden's and Cotton's Society of Antiquaries, it was in some respects a prototype of that which in a more settled literary era found a rich fruition. Somewhat similar schemes appear to have been broached by Sir Humphry Gilbert, Lord Herbert, and Sir Thomas May. Here may also be mentioned one of the chief scholiasts of the period after Scaliger and Casaubon, John Bond (1550-1612), whose valuable commentaries upon Horace appeared in 1606.

But the grandest of all the versions of the Tudor time

The Authorized Version of the Bible (1611).
is, of course, that of the Bible. The translation that we now treasure so highly was being gradually built up from 1527 onwards ; the work was being repaired and, in a measure, re-edified during the whole of our period, and the coping-stone was finally put to the edifice by the Authorized Version issued in 1611. The English version of the Bible that was due to the inspiration of Wicliffe, and which had circulated for many years among the Lollards under his name, was a translation of the Vulgate or Latin Bible, mainly the work of St. Jerome. During the fifteenth century new materials had become accessible, and the need of versions—not through the Latin, but from the original texts—had been greatly emphasized by the men of the new learning. A great edition of the Hebrew Bible had been printed, under Rabbinical influence, in 1518 and 1525.[1] The Septuagint was printed by Aldus in 1518. The Greek Testament was edited by Erasmus with a Latin translation in 1516. Luther translated the New Testament into German in 1522. Zwingli and a band of disciples issued the Zurich Bible in 1530. The new Greek and Hebrew learning met with as much obstruction from orthodox churchmen as the teaching of Galileo and Darwin in later times. The result was that men threw themselves into the study with a passion of strife. William Tyndale declared that he would cause a boy that drove the plough to know more of Scripture than the Popes had hitherto known. Nor was this an idle boast, at least as regarded some of the fifteenth-century pontiffs. The people learned to read on purpose to study the Bible ; they stayed up all night to peruse it, and relinquished in

[1] Almost simultaneously the Complutensian Polyglot (Hebrew, Latin, Greek) was brought out under Ximenes at Alcala (1502-17).

its favour their old chapbooks and tales of the Table Round and of Robin Hood. The Bible, by sheer intensity of human interest, ousted the old romances from the hearts of the generation which preceded that of Elizabethan playgoers. The age of Shakespeare intervened, and then the Bible resumed its sway with an even more exclusive and despotic power. Tyndale, the single-minded hero who sealed his work with his blood, was the man to whom more than any other we owe our Bible in its present shape, and evidence has accumulated to exhibit in the strongest light the heroic mould of his character and the originality of his work as a translator. He revised continually, thinking nothing too trifling if he could only better seize or convey to others the meaning of one fragment of Scripture; and throughout his last revision of the New Testament (1535) and the portion of the Old that he completed, it is clearly indicated that although he was acquainted both with Luther and the Vulgate, his translation is in the main an independent one framed from the original Greek and Hebrew texts. He was, for a man of his doctrinal prepossessions, singularly free from partiality in his rendering of the text, for he was a student, not of scholastic traditions, but of the original tongues and of God's Word. His achievement fixed the type according to which the later labourers worked. His influence decided that our Bible should be popular and not literary. He felt by a happy instinct the potential affinity between Hebrew and English idioms, and enriched our language and thought for ever with the characteristics of the Semitic mind. The labours of the next seventy-five years were devoted to improving his work in detail. Miles Coverdale finished what Tyndale left incomplete, and he dedicated his Bible, printed at Zurich, to the King at the close of 1535; deriving in its revision much assistance from the Zurich Bible, and depending more than Tyndale upon the Vulgate. A second edition of this appeared in 1536, and was the first Bible printed in England. The next Bible, called Matthew's Bible (1537), is a composite production based on Tyndale as regards the Pentateuch and New Testament; on Coverdale, as regards the Prophets; while the historical books are a new translation and based, to some extent, on Tyndale, but revised throughout by Tyndale's friend and kindred spirit, the reformer John Rogers. This transitional production was followed in a year's time by Coverdale's more elaborate revision of foregoing efforts, with the help of the contemporary Latin rendering of the Hebrew texts by Münster. This was corrected and re-issued with a preface by Cranmer in April, 1540, and was widely circulated in England, and known as the Great Bible. This was the Bible of the Edwardian Reformers, and the Bible presented to Elizabeth on her accession. It is the Psalter of this version that we still use as printed in the Prayer Book. Another very careful revision was issued by English exiles at Geneva in 1560, and dedicated to Queen Elizabeth. The scholars responsible for it had the advantage of highly-finished Latin versions by Castalio and Beza. The disadvantages inherent in all the sixteenth and seventeenth-century work was, of course, this; that the Greek texts used were late and faulty as compared with some of the more authentic codices to which we now have access. The Geneva version was soon imported largely into this country, and the Great Bible, as read in the churches, was subjected to comparisons that were often disparaging.

Archbishop Parker, in consequence, took in hand a new translation to be carried through by co-operative effort, and to remove all errors and obscurities from the Great Bible, adhering still, however, to the scheme of a popular and not a literary revision, retaining as much as was possible of the old phraseology. The work appeared in 1568 in a magnificent folio printed by Richard Jugge, with a portrait of the Queen as frontispiece, and the simple title *The Holie Bible*. Of the revisers (who seem as a body to have relied very largely upon the Geneva version) eight were bishops; hence the name assigned to the penultimate revision of a remarkable series—the Bishops' Bible. It soon replaced the Great Bible, and was sanctioned by ecclesiastical authority for public use, but it did not supersede the Geneva. Eighty-six editions of the latter appeared between 1568 and 1611 to only twenty of the Bishops' Bible, which was, however, carefully revised as regards the New Testament in 1572. The stimulus which prompted the setting on foot of the Authorized Version was mainly due to James I., and it is often called 'King James's Bible.' The matter was broached at the Hampton Court Conference in January, 1604. The King pressed forward the scheme during the ensuing summer, and took a prominent part in selecting the fifty-four translators and allotting the work to them.

Forty-seven scholars were eventually divided into six groups, and set to work in 1606-7. Some of them, such as Savile, Overall, Andrewes, Kilbye, Downes, Rainolds, Saravia and Bedwell, the best Arabic scholar of the day, were renowned men of learning. The translators worked deliberately, under stringent provisions. They met in six companies, two at Oxford, two at Cambridge, and two at Westminster. Beyond free commons they do not appear to have received any regular remuneration, though not a few of them earned a recognized claim to future preferment. Before commencing their labours they received a code of instructions, the more important provisions of which were: (1) The Bishops' Bible was to form the basis of their work. (2) The proper names were to be retained with as little alteration as possible. (3) The old ecclesiastical words, such as 'church' for 'congregation,' were to be kept. (4) The division of chapters was to remain. (5) No marginal notes, except for the explanation of Hebrew and Greek words, were to be admitted. (6) The following translations were to be used when they agreed with the original better than the Bishops' Bible—Tyndale's, Matthews', Coverdale's, the Great and Genevan Bibles. There were other instructions for the revision of each company's work by each other company, for the reference of disputed passages to special scholars, and finally to the general body of translators. In 1610 the whole translation was reviewed by six delegates, two from Westminster, two from Oxford, and two from Cambridge, to whom six coadjutors were soon added. After seven years' steady work the MS. was finally revised for press by Dr. Miles Smith, aided by Bishop Bilson, and in 1611 the Authorized Version was imprinted at London by Robert Barker.[1] The book was stated to be produced 'by His Majesty's Special Command,' and 'Appointed to be read in churches,' by whose authority is not precisely known.

The revisers did not attempt to render the Bible strictly into the common language of their own day. This may be seen in the quaint and highly decorative English of the dedication and in the interesting if somewhat bombastic Preface. Their great merit consists in the fact that they so fully retained the simple and racy idiom of the earlier versions. Occasionally they even replace a familiar word by one more archaic; e.g., they substitute 'charger' for 'platter.' As in the Liturgy, the Latin and old English word may be seen side by side, as in 'act and deed,' 'labour and work,' 'transgression and sin,' 'desert and wilder-

---

[1] Robert Barker (d. 1645), the King's printer, had a special licence for the printing of English Bibles. He is said to have contributed £3,500 to the expense of the translation. The title-page (engraved on copper by C. Boel, with a border, in which the figures of Moses and Aaron are conspicuous) ran : *The Holy Bible,* 'conteyning the Old Testament, and the New : Newly Translated out of the Originall tongues' . . . 1611, black letter, folio.

ness,' 'remission and forgiveness.' Upon the whole, however, the Authorized Version is marked by an unusual
predominance (greater even than in Swift) of English
words. It is in every way a complex unity, the final
product of a long series of strenuous, fortunate, converging
efforts. The result of a century of toil and study, from
the conception by Tyndale to the conclusion in 1611,
during which the researches of the ripest scholars, not of
England alone, but of Europe, were absorbed into the
work, it has been almost universally commended not only
for its fidelity, but also for its extraordinary force and
beauty. Its harmony, simplicity, and energy have drawn
panegyrics from foreigners and Catholics. Its English is,
in the opinion of all the best judges, of uncommon beauty.
'It lives in the ear like a music that can never be
forgotten, like the sound of church bells. . . . Its felicities
seem to be almost things instead of words; it is a part of the
national mind, and the anchor of national seriousness; the
memory of the dead passes into it; the potent traditions
of childhood are stereotyped in its verses; the power of all
the griefs and trials of a man is hidden beneath its words.'
A striking testimony to its essential greatness is the fact
that, instead of a cause of division, in this land of
sectarianism, it has ever been a bond between the different
sects, for it was soon adopted by the Puritans, and preferred even to the Genevan. Except the Koran it is doubtful whether any book has been more read. It has become
part of the national mind, and has permanently impressed
upon that mind some of its simplicity and directness. Its
noble figures, happy turns, and pithy sentiments are upon
every lip. It pervades the whole literature of our country.

CHRONOLOGICAL TABLE.

WORKS PUBLISHED.

1580. Gifford: *A Posie of Gillo-flowers.*

Golding: *Discourse upon the Earthquake.*

Robert Greene: *Mamillia* (Stationers' Register).

Harvey and Spenser: *Letters.*

Munday: *Zelauto.*

Lyly: *Euphues and his England.*

Jn. Stow: *Annales.*

Victories of Henry V.

COMPARATIVE CHRONOLOGY.

Newington Butts Theatre built.

Earthquake felt in England.

Elzevirs establish their press at Amsterdam.

Kepler and Tycho Brahé's Astronomical Tables.

Sir F. Drake returns to England after his circumnavigation.

Montaigne: *Essais* (i. and ii.).

Garnier: *Les Juives.*

Zurita: *Annals of Aragon.*

    Thos. Tusser died.

    Camoens died.

    Palladio died.

    Brian Twyne (the Oxford antiquary) born.

1581. Wm. Borough: *A Discourse of the Variation of the Compass.*

John Derricke: *Image of Ireland.*

Arthur Hall: *X. Books of Homer's Iliades.*

R. Mulcaster: *Positions concerning the Training up of Children.*

Th. Newton: *Seneca his tenne Tragedies* (a selection of versions by Jasper Heywood, Studley, Neville, and Nuce).

Savile: *Tacitus* (version).

Barnabe Rich: *Adventures of Don Simonides* and *Farewell to Militarie Profession.*

Tasso: *Gerusalemme Liberata.*

Bellarmine: *De Controversiis Christianae Fidei.*

Claude Fauchet: *Recueil de la langue et poésie françaises.*

Sidney's *Arcadia* finished, *Sonnets* and *Defense of Poetrie* begun.

Charles Merbury issued *Defence of Absolute Monarchy* and *Italian Proverbs.*

New Penal Laws against Papists a consequence of the Jesuit mission headed by Campion and Parsons.

Wm. Lambarde: *The Duties of Constables, Tithing Men, and such other lowe Ministers of the Peace.*

WORKS PUBLISHED.	COMPARATIVE CHRONOLOGY.
1581. T. Wilcox: *A Glasse for Gamesters.* William Hunnis: *Seaven Steppes to Heauen.*	L. Mascall: *The Government of Poultrie.* Languet died. Holinshed died. Overbury born. Ussher born.
1582. G. Buchanan: *Rerum Scoticarum Historiae.* Gosson: *Playes Confuted in Five Actions.* Hakluyt: *Divers Voyages.* Munday: *English Romayne Life.* R. Parsons: *Christian Directorie.* Watson: Ἑκατομπαθία; or *Passionate Centurie of Love* (18-line 'sonnets'). G. Whetstone: *Heptameron of Civil Discourses.*	*Rheims New Testament* (Allen and Martin). Shakespeare married Anne Hathaway. Beza presents the *Codex Bezae* to Cambridge University. Edinburgh University founded by Charter from King James. The reformed Julian Calendar is promulgated by the Pope but not adopted in Protestant countries. Della Cruscan Academy founded at Florence. Geo. Buchanan died. Phineas Fletcher born. Rich. Corbet born.
1583. Wm. Hunnis: *Seven Sobs of a Sorrowful Soule for Sinne.* Melbancke: *Philotimus.* Sir Thos. Smith: *Common Welth of England (De Republica Anglorum).* Stanyhurst: *Virgil's Aeneid* (i.-v.). Philip Stubbes: *Anatomie of Abuses.*	Scaliger: *De Emendatione Temporum.* Bruno visits England. Sir Philip Sidney married Frances Walsingham. Archbishop Grindal died, succeeded by Whitgift. William Bourne (the mathematician) died. John Heywood (the interlude writer) died about this time. Massinger born.

WORKS PUBLISHED.

COMPARATIVE CHRONOLOGY.

1583. Whetstone: *Life, Death, and Virtues of Thomas, Earl of Sussex.*

The French *Littleton* (French-English Phrase-book).
> Ld. Herbert of Cherbury born.
> Grotius born.

1584. Wm. Bathe: *Art of Musicke.*

N. Breton: *Handful of Hearbes.*

Greene: *Mirror of Modestie, Arbasto and Morando.*

John Knox: *Hist. of Reformation in Scotland.*

Leicester's Commonwealth (lampoon on the earl).

Lodge: *Forbonius and Prisceria.*

Lyly: *Campaspe* and *Sapho and Phao.*

Peele: *Araygnement of Paris.*

Clement Robinson: *Handful of Pleasant Delites.*

Reg. Scot: *Discoverie of Witchcraft.*

John Soowthern: *Musyque of the Beautie of his Mistresse Diana* ('sonnets' after Ronsard).

T. Stocker: *Civile Warres of the Lowe Countries.*

Warner: *Pan his Syrinx* (after *Euphues*).

Whetstone: *Mirrour for Magistrates of Cyties.*

Bruno: *Dell' Infinito Universo.*

Cervantes: *Galatea* (printed and approved, published at Alcalá, 1585).

Cardinal Allen: *Defense of English Catholiques.*

Dudley Fenner: *Artes of Logike and Rhetorike.*

Lyly's third play, *Gallathea,* acted.

Thos. Hudson: *Historie of Judith* (after Du Bartas).

Herodotus rendered by B. R.

Siege of Antwerp.
> William the Silent assassinated.
> Norton died.
> Sigonius (the great archaeologist) died.
> Sambucus (the great scholar and Hapsburg historiographer) died.
> John Day (one of the first Elizabethan printers) died.
> Pibrac (the French orator and poet) died.
> Selden born.
> Beaumont born.
> The 'ever-memorable' John Hales born.
> Thomas Rudd (the 'Practical Geometer') born.
> Saavedra born.
> T. Renaudot (founder of *Gazette de France*) born.

WORKS PUBLISHED.

1585. Bacon: *Advice to Queen Elizabeth* (written).

Angell Day: *Strange Sights in London*.

Sir Ed. Dyer: *A Prayse of Nothing*.

Greene: *Planetomachia*.

James I.: *Essaies of a Prentice in Arte of Poesie*.

William Smith: *County Palatine of Chester*.

Watson: *Amyntas* (a Latin version of Tasso's *Aminta*).

COMPARATIVE CHRONOLOGY.

R. Garnier: *Collected Plays* (much studied in England).

'Rose' and 'Hope' theatres built.

Guarini: *Pastor Fido* acted.

Pierre Mathieu: *Esther*.

Daniel translates Paolo Giovi's work on *Emblems*.

Thomas Tallis died.
Ronsard died.
Amadis Jamyn died.
Muretus died.
Wm. Drummond born.
Giles Fletcher born.
Richelieu born.
Tellez (Tirso de Molina) born.
Jansenius born.
Vaugelas (the French grammarian) born.

1586. Barnes: *Praise of Musick*.

Camden: *Britannia*.

Angell Day: *The English Secretarie*.

Sir John Ferne: *The Blazon of Gentrie*.

Stephen Taylor: *A Whip for Worldlings* (verse).

Warner: *Albion's England* (pt. i.).

Webbe: *Discourse of English Poetrie*.

Whetstone: *English Mirror* and *Touchstone for the Time*.

Geoffrey Whitney: *Choice of Emblems*.

Shakespeare leaves Stratford.

Cervantes' tragedy *Numancia* produced at Madrid.

Ecclesiastical Polity begun by Hooker.

Aquaviva: *Ratio Studiorum*.

Rowlands: Version of *Lazarillo*.

Patrizzi: *Della Poetica*.

Geo. Pettie's version of the *Civile Conversation* of M. Stephen Guazzo.

Chiabrera: *Rime*.

Jn. Ford born.
Sidney mortally wounded at Zutphen; died at Arnheim on 7th October.

1587. Jn. Bridges: *Defence of Church of England*.

Tasso: *Discorsi dell' Arte Poetica*.

Jean Bodin: *Démonomanie*.

WORKS PUBLISHED.

1587. Churchyard: *Worthiness of Wales.*

Angell Day: *Daphnis and Chloe.*

Ab. Fraunce: *Lamentations of Amintas.*

Greene: *Euphues, his Censure to Philautus.*

Matthew Grove: *Pelops and Hippodamia* (with epigrams and 'Sonets').

Hakluyt: *Four Voyages to Florida.*

William Rankins: *Mirrour of Monsters.*

Turbervile: *Tragicall Tales.*

1588. Wm. Byrd: *Psalmes, Sonets, and Songs.*

Greene: *Pandosto* and *Perimedes.*

Harriott: *True Report of Virginia.*

T. Hoby: Version of Castiglione's *Courtier.*

W. Hunnis: *Recreations.*

Maurice Kyffin: *The Andria of Terence in English.*

Martin Marprelate: *The Epistle.*

Munday: *Banquet of Dainty Conceits.*

Wm. Rankins: *The English Ape.*

Jn. Udall: *Diotrephes.*

COMPARATIVE CHRONOLOGY.

Mirour for Magistrates (1559), complete edition with *Induction* and 73 legends.

Misfortunes of Arthur acted.

Marlowe, Lodge, Greene, and Peele appear as professional writers for public theatres.

Marlowe's *Tamburlaine* produced.

English actors perform English plays at the courts of Hesse and Brunswick.

　　Mary Queen of Scots executed.
　　John Foxe died.
　　Vautrollier (Scots printer) died.
　　G. M. Cecchi died.
　　Nat. Field born.
　　Vondel (the Dutch poet) born.

Armada defeated.

Paris Garden opened.

Six Idillia of Theocritus in English verse.

Nich. Yonge: *Musica Transalpina.*

Timothe Bright: *Characterie* (swift and secret writing).

Baronius' *Annales Ecclesiastici.*

Montaigne: *Essais* (iii.)

　　Richard Tarleton died.
　　Speroni (Degli Alvarotti) died.
　　Paul Veronese died.
　　Salmasius (Claude de Saumaise) born.
　　Hobbes born.
　　Wither born.
　　Richard Brathwaite born.
　　John Winthrop born.
　　Ribera born.

WORKS PUBLISHED.

1589. Bacon: *Advt. touching Controversies of the Church.*

Byrd: *Songs of Sundry Natures.*

Greene: *Menaphon.*

Hakluyt: *Principal Navigations, Voyages and Discoveries of the English Nation.*

Lyly: *Pap with a Hatchet.*

Martin Marprelate: *The Epitome.*

Nash: *Anatomie of Absurditie.*

Peele: *Tale of Troy.*

Puttenham: *Art of English Poesie.*

1590. Constable: *Spiritual Sonnets.*

Richard Ferris: *Memorable Voyage to Bristow in a Wherry.*

Lodge: *Rosalynde.*

Marlowe: *Tamburlaine.*

Peele: *Polyhymnia.*

Sidney: *Arcadia.*

Spenser: *Faerie Queene* (i.-iii.).

Webbe: *Travels.*

Watson: *Meliboeus* and *Italian Madrigals Englished.*

1591. T. Bradshaw: *The Shepherds Star.*

COMPARATIVE CHRONOLOGY.

Henri IV., King of France.

Bancroft asserts High Church Doctrine of Anglicanism, Divine Right, and Apostolical Succession of English Bishops.

Lope de Vega commences his great series of dramas.

Ballad of *Faustus.*

J. Dickenson: *Shepheardes Complaint* (English hexameters) about this time.

Antoine de Baïf died.

L. Salviati (the Italian critic) died.

Thomas Carew born.

Junius (author of *Etymologicum Anglicanum*) born.

Racan born.

Campanella: *De Sensu Rerum.*

Lord Strange's Company formed (including Shakespeare and Burbage).

Peter Bales: *The Writing Schoolemaster* (shorthand; cf. 1588).

Spenser's visit to London.

John Studley (translator of Seneca) died.

G. Puttenham died.

Du Bartas died.

Robt. Garnier died.

Ambrose Paré died.

Bernard Palissy died.

Jodelet born.

Faria y Sousa born.

Ralph Agas prepares his celebrated map of London and Westminster.

WORKS PUBLISHED.

1591. Drayton : *Harmonie of the Church.*

Florio: *Second Fruits.*

W. Garrard: *Art of Warre.*

Greene: *Notable Discovery of Cosenage* and *Farewell to Folly.*

Harington: *Ariosto's Orlando Furioso* (with his *Apologie for Poetrie*).

Lodge : *Catharos* and *Robin the Divell.*

Lyly : *Endimion.*

Raleigh : *Fight of the Revenge.*

Savile: *Histories of Tacitus.*

Sidney : *Astrophel and Stella* (sonnets).

Spenser : *Daphnaida* and *Complaints.*

Robert Wilmot : *Tragedie of Tancred and Gismund.*

1592. William Alabaster: *Roxana* (Senecan tragedy in Latin, based on Groto's *Dalida*) performed.

Chettle : *Kind Harts Dreame* (apologizing for Greene's attack on Shakespeare).

Constable : *Diana* (23 sonnets).

Daniel: *Delia* (sonnets).

COMPARATIVE CHRONOLOGY.

Queen Elizabeth founds Trinity College, Dublin.

A. Fraunce : *Countess of Pembroke's Emanuel* and *Yuychurch.*

Spenser receives a pension from the Queen.

Shakespeare probably produces *Love's Labour's Lost.*

Fulke Greville's sonnet-cycle entitled *Caelica* probably begun about this time.

G. Ripley : *Compound of Alchemie.*

Sir John Smythe : *Militarie Instruction.*

> Sir Richard Grenville died.
> Henry ('Silver-tongued') Smith died.
> Ponce de Léon died.
> François de la Noue (the Calvinist historian) died.
> William Browne born.
> Herrick born.

I. Casaubon : *Theophrasti Characteres Ethici.*

Strange's men secure a theatre at Bankside, the 'Rose.'

Théâtre Français inaugurated.

Arden of Feversham and *Edward II.* produced.

Kyd's *Spanish Tragedie* (Stat. Regist.).

Montluc: *Commentaires.*

Mariana : *History of Spain.*

Bretons Bower of Delites.

WORKS PUBLISHED.

1592. Greene: *Groatsworth of Wit, Repentance, Vision, Philomela, Quip for an Upstart Courtier,* and *Friar Bacon and Friar Bungay.*

N. Gyer: *The English Phlebotomy.*

Harvey: *Foure Letters and Certaine Sonnets.*

Lodge: *Euphues Shadow, the Battaile of the Sences.*

Lyly: *Gallathea.*

Nash: *Pierce Penniless.*

W. Wyrley: *The True Use of Armorie.*

1593. Barnes: *Parthenophil and Parthenophe* (many sonnets).

James Balmford: *Unlawfulness of Cards.*

Thos. Danett: *Description of Low Countreys* (after 'Guicchardini').

Drayton: *Legend of Peirs Gaveston* and *Idea. Shepheards Garland.*

Giles Fletcher: *Licia* (sonnets).

Harvey: *Pierces Supererogation.*

Lodge: *Phillis* (sonnets).

Peele: *Edward I.*

The Life and Death of Jack Straw (farce).

The Phoenix Nest.

COMPARATIVE CHRONOLOGY.

Sylvester begins his version of *Le Semaine* of Du Bartas.

The Rialto built at Venice.

Shakespeare remodels a play, *Henry VI.,* in three parts, previously recast with the aid of Marlowe from a draft by Greene and Peele.

   Greene died.
   Watson died.
   Montaigne died.
   Wm. Elderton (the balladwriter) died.
   Quarles born.
   Gassendi (the mathematician) born.

Marischal College, Aberdeen, founded.

John Norden starts with *Speculum Britanniae* (pt. i., Middlesex), a scheme for a series of county histories.

Erdeswicke commences his *Survey of Staffordshire.*

Scaliger moves to Leyden.

Henry Locke's *Christian Passions* (100 sonnets) licensed for press.

T. Fale: *Art of Dialling.*

Marlowe's *Hero and Leander* (2 sestiads) entered at Stationers' Hall.

   Marlowe died (June).
   Philip Stubbes died.
   Jacques Amyot died.
   George Herbert born.

WORKS PUBLISHED.

1593. Watson: *Teares of Fancy*
(sonnets).
Shakespeare: *Venus and
Adonis.*

1594. Barnfield: *Affectionate
Shepherd.*
R. Carew: Version of
Tasso's *Jerusalem De-
livered.*
Jn. Dickenson: *Arisbas,
Euphues amidst his
Slumbers.*
Drayton: *Ideas Mirrour*
(sonnets).
Hooker: *Ecclesiastical
Polity* (i.-iv.).
Lyly: *Mother Bombie.*
Marlowe: *Edward II.*
Nash: *Life of Jacke
Wilton.*
Peele: *Battell of Al-
cazar.*
Wm. Percy: *Sonnets to
the fairest Cœlia.*
Sir John Smythe: *Mili-
tarie Instructions.*
Andrew Willet: *Synopsis
Papismi.*
Willobie his Avisa.
Zepheria (40 'canzons' or
'sonnets').
Shakespeare: *Lucrece.*

1595. Barnes: *Century of Spiritual Sonnets.*
Barnfield: *Cynthia, with
certain Sonets.*

COMPARATIVE CHRONOLOGY.

Father Lobo born.
Barten Holyday born.
Fulvio Testi (Ital. poet) born.

Bacon wrote his *Promus* (?).
Menaechmi translated by W.
W[arner].
Shakespeare wrote many *Son-
nets* probably about this time.
Satire Ménippée.
Odet de la Noue: *Poésie Chres-
tienne.*
Daniel: *Cleopatra.*
Greene and Lodge's didactic
play, *A Looking Glasse for
London and England.*
Kyd's version of Garnier's *Cor-
nélie.*
J. Godard: *Œuvres Poétiques.*
Spenser married Elizabeth
Boyle.
 Bp. Thos. Cooper (author of
 the *Thesaurus*) died.
 Googe died.
 Rich. Tottel died.
 William Painter died.
 Cardinal Allen died.
 Palestrina died.
 Tintoretto died.
 James Howell born.
 Balzac born.
 Gérard Sieur de Saint-Amant
 (French poet) born.

Elegies on Sidney, under title
Astrophel, by Spenser and
others, printed as Appendix
to *Colin Clout.*

WORKS PUBLISHED.

1595. Chapman: *Coronet for his Mistress Philosophie* (10 sonnets).

'J. C.': *Alcilia* (six-line 'sonnets').

Daniel: *First Fowre Bookes of the Civile Wars*.

Sir Jn. Davies: *Nine Gullinge Sonnets*.

Gosson: *Pleasant Quippes for Upstart Newfangled Gentlewomen*.

Richard Hasleton: *Strange and Wonderful Things* (his captivity).

Lodge: *A Fig for Momus*.

Gervase Markham: *Tragedy of Sir Rich. Grenville*.

Peele: *Old Wives Tale*.

Henry Roberts: *Pheander, the Mayden Knight*.

Sidney: *Apologie for Poetrie*.

Spenser: *Colin Clout's come Home again, Amoretti*, and *Epithalamium*.

1596. R. Brooke: *Discoverie of Errours in Camden's Britannia*.

Davies: *Orchestra*.

Drayton: *Mortimeriados*.

B. Griffin: *Fidessa* (sonnets).

COMPARATIVE CHRONOLOGY.

Andrew Maunsell: *Catalogue of English Printed Books* (pts. i. and ii.).

Fras. Sabie: *The Fishermans Tale*.

Wm. Fiston: *Germaine Empire*.

V. Saviolo: *Rapier Practice*.

Wm. Clerke: *Polimanteia*.

Thomas Edwards: *Cephalus and Procris*.

Daphne, opera in Florence.

Du Vair: *Traité de l'eloquence française*.

Munday's version of the *Amadis de Gaule*.

Spenser wrote his *View of the State of Ireland* in the form of a dialogue; completed in 1596, licensed 1598, but not printed until 1633.

Whitaker draws up the Calvinistic Lambeth articles.

Thomas Kyd died.

Tasso died at Rome—laureated *post mortem*.

Robert Sempill died.

Southwell died.

William Whitaker died.

Spondanus (the translator) died.

Chapelain and Desmarets born.

Essex takes Cadiz and destroys Spanish navy.

Lectures commence at Gresham College, London.

'Swan' Theatre opened on Bankside.

Lambarde's *Perambulation of*

WORKS PUBLISHED.

1596. Harington : *Metamorphosis of Ajax.*

R. Linche : *Diella* (sonnets).

Lodge: *Margarite of America.*

Nash: *Have with you to Saffron Walden.*

Raleigh : *Discovery of Guiana.*

Wm. Smith : *Chloris* (sonnets).

Spenser : *Faerie Queene* (iv.-vi.) and *Prothalamion.*

1597. Bacon: *Essays.*

Thos. Beard: *Theatre of Gods Judgments.*

Bodenham : *Wits Commonwealth.*

Breton : *Wits Trenchmour.*

Drayton: *Heroicall Epistles.*

Gerard: *Herball.*

Jos. Hall: *Virgidemiarum Sixe Bookes* (i.-iii.).

Gab. Harvey: *Trimming of Thomas Nashe.*

Hooker : *Ecclesiastical Polity* (v.).

James I.: *Demonology.*

Ri. Johnson: *Seven Champions of Christendom.*

Henry Locke or Lok :

COMPARATIVE CHRONOLOGY.

Kent (re-issued with additions from 1576).

Rainolds: *De Eccles. Romanae Idolatria.*

Mendoza's *Lazarillo de Tormes* again englished.

Edward III. printed.

P. Ubaldini : *Rime.*

Sir F. Drake died.

J. Bodin died.

Nicholas Vignier (French historian) died.

F. Sylburgius (Greek scholar) died.

James Shirley born.

Descartes born.

Henry Lawes born.

Shakespeare writes 1 *Henry IV.* and purchases New Place, Stratford.

Thomas Morley's *A Plaine and Easie Introduction to Practicall Musicke.*

Greek Anthology edited by J. Stockwood after text of Stephanus under title *Progymnasma Scholasticum.*

Jas. Rowbothum: *Chesse Play.*

The second three of Hall's ' Sixe Books ' of Satires, containing ' Biting' as opposed to 'Toothlesse' satires, appeared in 1598.

Speroni : *Canace.*

Bodley offers to bequeath his Library to Oxford University.

Marlowe's *Elegies* (Ovid's *Amores*), to which was appended (Sir) John Davies's *Epi-*

WORKS PUBLISHED.

1597. *Sundrie Sonets of Christian Passions.*

Lyly: *Woman in the Moone.*

Rob. Tofte: *Laura* (sonnets).

Shakespeare: *Richard II.*, *Richard III.*, and *Romeo and Juliet* (Quartos).

1598. Barnfield: *The Encomion of Lady Pecunia.*

Thomas Bastard: *Chrestoleros* (epigrams).

Chapman: *Iliad* (i.-vii.).

Dickenson: *Greene in Conceipt* (a pastoral tale).

Florio: *Worlde of Wordes.*

Emanuel Ford: *Parismus.*

Ed. Guilpin: *Skialetheia* (epigrams and 'Satyres').

Hakluyt: *Voyages and Discoveries* (complete edition).

T. Heywood: *Joan as Good as my Lady.*

Marston: *Scourge of Villanie.*

Marlowe: *Hero and Leander* (fragment comprised in first two sestiads).

Francis Meres: *Palladis Tamia* ('Wits Treasury').

COMPARATIVE CHRONOLOGY.

grammes, printed 'at Middleborugh' about this year (Ritson says 1596).

Peele died.

Fernando de Herrera (the Spanish lyrist) died.

Sir Roger Twysden born.

Charles Sorel (author of *Francion*) born.

Martin Opitz (the 'father of German poetry') born.

Edict of Nantes promulgated.

Globe Theatre built.

Speght's edition of Chaucer.

Mucedorus published.

The Countess of Pembrokes Arcadia, Sonnets and other works of Sidney, posthumously edited in folio.

Wilbye: *English Madrigals.*

Marlowe and Chapman: *Hero and Leander* (the completed poem); also Henry Petowe's wretched *Second Part.*

Jonson's *Every Man in his Humour* (printed 1601) acted.

Vauquelin: *Art Poetique.*

Tofte's *Alba* and version of Boiardo's *Orlando Innamorato.*

Gentili: *De Jure Belli.*

Lindschoten publishes his Voyages and Maps of the East.

Philip II. died.

Lord Burghley died.

Dedekind (*Grobianus*) died.

Thomas Stapleton died.

Jasper Heywood (the translator of Seneca) died.

WORKS PUBLISHED.

1598. William Rankins: *Seven Satyres.*

Stowe: *Survey of London.*

B. Young: Version of *Montemayor's Diana.*

Shakespeare: 1 *Henry IV., Love's Labour's Lost* (Quartos).

1599. Daniel: *Poeticall Essayes.*

Sir J. Davies: *Nosce Teipsum* and *Astraea.*

Greene: *George a Green, the Pinner of Wakefield.*

Hayward: *Life and Reign of Henry IV.*

James I.: *Basilikon Doron.*

T. Middleton: *Micro-cynicon* (vi. Snarling Satyres).

Nash: *Lenten Stuffe.*

Peele: *King David and Fair Bethsabe.*

Henry Porter: *Two Angry Women of Abingdon.*

John Rainolds: *Overthrow of Stage-Playes.*

Thomas Storer: *Life and Death of Wolsey.*

John Weever: *Epigrammes.*

The Passionate Pilgrim ('by W. Shakespeare'!).

1600. Allott: *Englands Parnassus.*

COMPARATIVE CHRONOLOGY.

Henri Estienne (the second French printer and editor of the name) died.

Serranus (Jean de Serres) died.

Voiture born.

G. Stiernhielm (the Swedish poet) born.

Thomas Carew born.

William Somner (the Anglo-Saxon scholar) born.

Globe Theatre opened with *Henry V.*

Middleton's *Old Law* produced.

A Warning for Fair Women.

Tragedie of Soliman and Perseda (? by Kyd).

Aleman: *Guzman d'Alfarache.*

Mariana: *De Rege et Regis Institutione.*

Scaliger: *De Europaeorum Linguis Diatriba* (the first classification of languages).

John Rainolds attacks and Wm. Gager defends stage-plays.

Daniel laureated.

Marston's *Pygmalion.*

Marlowe's *Ovids Epistles* and T. Cutwode's *Caltha Poetarum or Bumble Bee* burned by order of Archbp. of Canterbury.

Bellarmine made Cardinal.

Spenser died (16 Jan. ?).

Reginald Scot died.

Sir Anthony Van Dyck born.

Robert Bailey (the diarist) born.

Olivier de Serres: *La Théâtre d'Agriculture.*

WORKS PUBLISHED.

1600. Barclay: *De Regali Potestate.*

Bodenham: *Belvedere* and *Garden of the Muses.*

Dekker: *Shoemakers Holiday* and *Old Fortunatus.*

Drayton (with Munday and Hathwaye): *Life of Sir John Oldcastle.*

Ed. Fairfax: *Godfrey of Bulloigne* (Tasso's *Gerusalemme Liberata*).

Englands Helicon.

Gilbert: *De Magnete.*

Jonson: *Every Man out of his Humor.*

Wm. Kempe: *Nine Days Wonder.*

Nash: *Summer's Last Testament.*

Samuel Nicholson: *Acolastus.*

Sam. Rowlands: *The Letting of Humours Blood in the Head-veine.*

Thos. Smith: *Art of Gunnery.*

Sir William Vaughan: *The Golden Grove.*

Shakespeare: *Merchant of Venice,* 2 *Henry IV., Midsummer Night's Dream, Much Ado, Henry V.* (Quartos).

COMPARATIVE CHRONOLOGY.

Coke's *Law Reports.*

Minsheu's Spanish *Dictionarie* and *Grammar.*

Sir Clement Edmondes: *Observations on Caesars Commentaries.*

Holland's version of Livy's *Roman History.*

The Hospital of Incurable Fools (after Gazzoni).

Titus Andronicus (Quarto).

'Fortune' Theatre opened.

Thos. Middleton began to write for the 'Admirals Men' in collaboration with Munday, Drayton, Webster and 'others.'

Banks's horse goes to the top of St. Paul's.

Hooker died (November 2nd).

Giordano Bruno burned.

Thomas Deloney (the prolific ballad-writer and successor of Will Elderton) died probably in this year.

Wm. Prynne born.

Olearius (the oriental voyager) born.

Gabriel Naudé (the bibliographer) born.

Moscherosch (the famous satirist of Strasburg) born.

Puget de la Serre born.

Peter Heylin born.

Calderon born.

Francisco de Rioja (Spanish poet) born.

1601 Bacon: *Practices and* | Charles Fitzgeffrey brought out

WORKS PUBLISHED.

1601. *Treasons of Robert, late Earl of Essex.*

Campion: *Book of Airs.*

Robert Chester: *Loves Martyr* (with appendix of *Phoenix and Turtle* poems, to which Shakespeare contributed).

Thos. Danett: *The Historie of Philip de Commines.*

Heywood: *Four Prentices of London.*

Robert Johnson: *Essaies.*

Jonson: *Every Man in his Humor* and *Cynthias Revels.*

Lyly: *Loves Metamorphosis.*

Morley: *Triumphs of Oriana* (madrigals).

Munday: *Downfall and Death of Robert, Earl of Huntingdon* (Robin Hood).

Weever: *Mirror of Martyrs.*

Yarington: *Two Lamentable Tragedies.*

1602. T[homas] A[cherley]: *The Massacre of Money.*

T. Campion: *Art of English Poesie.*

Rich. Carew: *Survey of Cornwall.*

COMPARATIVE CHRONOLOGY.

a volume of Latin epigrams and epitaphs called *Affaniae.*

Charron: *Traité de la sagesse.*

Gruter and Scaliger: *Corpus Inscriptionum.*

Sir Anthony Shirley's *Travels* in Persia, enlarged from previous year: his own *Relation*, 1613.

Casaubon: *Athenaeus.*

Wm. Fulbecke: *Factions of the Romans* (a history of the later Republic).

Harward's *Phlebotomy* (against excessive bleeding).

Holland's version of Pliny's *Naturall Historie.*

Dickenson: *Speculum Tragicum Regum.*

Execution of Essex.
Nash died.
William Rankins (*Mirrour of Monsters*) died.
William Lambarde (the first county historian) died.
Claude Fauchet died.
Molina died.
Tycho Brahé died.
Earle born.
Georges de Scudéry born.
Rojas y Zorilla (Spanish dramatist) born.

Bodleian Library inaugurated.

Hamlet produced.

English version of Guarini's *Pastor Fido.*

Wm. Clowes: Treatise on the *Cure of the Evill*, touched for

WORKS PUBLISHED.

COMPARATIVE CHRONOLOGY.

1602. Daniel : *Defence of Ryme.*
Davison: *Poetical Rap-
sody* (2nd edit. 1608).
Dekker: *Satiromastix.*
Lodge: *Josephus' History.*
Marston : *Antonio and
Mellida.*
Middleton : *Blurt Master
Constable.*
Warner : *Albion's Eng-
land* (complete).
Shakespeare: *Merry Wives*
(Quarto).

by Kings and Queens of England.
Jn. Willis : *Arte of Stenographie.*
Sir Wm. Segar: *Honor, Military
and Civill.*
Poetaster and *Satiromastix* appear.
    Barthol. Griffin died.
    Passerat died.
    Chillingworth born.
    Montalvan born at Madrid.
    Mazarin born.
    Kircher born.
    Shackerley Marmion born.

1603. William Alexander (Earl
of Stirling): *Tragedie
of Darius.*
Barclay: *Euphormion.*
Breton: *A Poste with a
Packet of Mad Letters.*
Jn. Davies of Hereford :
Microcosmos.
Dekker: *Patient Grissill*
and *Batchelars Banquet.*
Drayton: *The Barrons
Wars* (completed).
Florio: *Essays of Mon-
taigne.*
H. Holland: *Pancharis.*
Knolles: *History of the
Turks.*
H. Timberlake: *Travels
of Two English Pil-
grimes.*
Shakespeare : *Hamlet*
(pirated and garbled
text).

James I. succeeded Elizabeth,
March 24th; James crowned
in July.
Heywood's *Woman killed with
Kindness* acted (printed 1607).
Wm. Fowldes: *Battell betweene
Frogs and Mice.*
Chettle: *Englandes Mourning
Garment.*
John Manningham completed
his *Diary*; in it he records
seeing *Twelfth Night* played
in Middle Temple Hall, Feb-
ruary, 1602.
Lodge's *Treatise* and Balmford's
Dialogue concerning the *Plague.*
Bacon knighted.
    Q. Elizabeth dies (March 24th).
    Pierre Charron (French moral-
      ist) died.
    Cartwright died.
    Gilbert died.
    Sir Kenelm Digby born.
    Henri de Valois (érudit) born,

WORKS PUBLISHED.

1604. Wm. Alexander : *Aurora.*
Dekker : *The Honest Whore* (pt. i.).
Heydon : *Judicial Astrology.*
James I. : *Counterblast to Tobacco.*
Francis Johnson : *Defense of the Brownists.*
Marlowe : *Faustus.*
Marston : *Malcontent.*
An. Sc[oloker] : *Daiphantus.*
Shakespeare : *The Tragicall Historie of Hamlet* . . . newly imprinted . . . according to the true and perfect coppie (Quarto).

1605. Bacon : *Advancement of Learning.*
Camden : *Remains Concerning Britain.*
Daniell : *Certaine Small Poems* (with *Philotas*).
Mich. Drayton : *Poems.*
Jos. Hall : *Mundus Alter et Idem.*
Jonson, Chapman, and Marston : *Eastward Ho!*
Marston : *Dutch Courtesan.*
Sam. Rowley : *When you see me you know me.*
Geo. Saltern : *Antient Lawes of Gt. Britaine.*

COMPARATIVE CHRONOLOGY.

Hampton Court Conference.
Lope de Vega : *Comedias* (collective edition, vol. i.).
De Thou : *Histoire.*
John Spenser's edition of the *Ecclesiastical Polity.*
Eliz. Grymeston : *Memoratives.*
Butter's tract on the 'Yorkshire Tragedy.'
    Churchyard died.
    Edward De Vere (17th Earl of Oxford) died.
    Whitgift died, succeeded by Bancroft.
    Thos. Storer died.
    Pierre de Brach died.
    Socinus executed.
    Jasper Mayne born.
    Jean Mairet (French dramatist) born.
    F. de Logau born.

Cervantes : *Don Quixote* (pt. i.).
Version of Dedekind's *Grobianus* as *The Schoole of Slovenrie.*
Vauquelin de la Fresnaye : *Œuvres.*
David Hume : *De Unione Insulae Britanniae.*
David Ormerod : *Picture of a Puritane.*
Famous History of Captain Thomas Stukeley.
Volpone produced.
    Golding died.
    Jn. Stowe died.
    Beza died.
    Pontus de Thyard (French sonneteer) died.
    Sir T. Browne born.
    Wm. Davenant born.

WORKS PUBLISHED.

1605. Arthur Warren: *The Poore Mans Passions.*

Peter Woodhouse: *The Contention betweene the Elephant and the Flea.*

1606. Richard Alison: *An Hours Recreation in Music.*

Bond: *Horatii Poemata.*

Bryskett: *Discourse of Civill Life* (after Giraldo).

Chapman: *Monsieur d' Olive.*

Jn. Day: *The Ile of Guls.*

Dekker: *Newes from Hell* and *The Seven Deadly Sins.*

Drayton: *Poems Lyrick and Pastorall.*

Ford: *Honor Triumphant.*

Greene: *Bellora and Fidelio.*

Joseph Hall: *Meditations and Vowes.*

'H. P.': *The Mous Trap.*

Hy. Peacham: *Art of Drawing and Limning.*

Sylvester: *Du Bartas his Devine Weekes.*

Rich. West: *News from Bartholomew Fayre.*

Return from Parnassus.

1607. Alexander: *Monarchic Tragedie, Julius Caesar.*

COMPARATIVE CHRONOLOGY.

Sir Wm. Dugdale born.
Thos. Randolph born.
Edmund Waller born.
Tavernier born.
P. du Ryer (the French tragic poet) born.

Scioppius: *Elementa Philosophiae Stoicae.*

Macbeth produced.

Alex. Craige: *Amorose Songes, Sonets and Elegies.*

J. Fage: *The Sickmens Glasse.*

R. Knolles: Version of Bodin's *Commonwealth.*

Philemon Holland's version of the *Twelve Caesars* of Suetonius.

Robert Barret completes his *Sacred Warr*, an epic poem in 68,000 lines extant in MS.

Daniel's *Queene's Arcadia* (after Guarini).

Bacon married Alice Barnham.

Goulart's *Admirable and Memorable Histories* (version by Ed. Grimeston, 1607).

Lyly died.
Desportes died.
Justus Lipsius died.
L. Rhodomann (the German Hellenist) died.
P. Corneille born.

A. Hardy: *Coriolan.*

Sir Francis Vere, the veteran

WORKS PUBLISHED.

1607. Wm. Barksted: *Mirrha.*
Barnes: *Devil's Charter.*
Chapman: *Bussy D'Ambois.*
Cowell: *The Interpreter.*
Daniel: *Certaine Small Workes.*
Dekker and Webster: *Westward Ho!*
R. Johnson: *Pleasant Conceits of Old Hobson.*
Jonson: *Volpone.*
Christ. Lever: *Queen Elizabeths Teares.*
Lud. Lloyd: *Jubile of Britane* and *Tragicomedie of Serpents.*
Sam. Rowlands: *Humors Ordinarie.*
Cyril Tourneur: *Revenger's Tragedie.*
Thos. Walkington: *The Opticke Glasse of Humors.*
Geo. Wilkins: *The Miseries of Inforst Marriage.*
Geo. Wilson: *Commendation of Cockers and Cock-fighting.*

COMPARATIVE CHRONOLOGY.

English commander in the Low Countries, writes his *Commentaries* (printed 1657).
Daniell: *Philotas* (first separate edition).
Edm. Howes issues his abridgement of Stow's *Chronicle.*
Ri. Johnson: *Pleasant Walkes of Moore-fields.*
Thomas Shelton began his translation of *Don Quixote.*
Whitehall commenced by Inigo Jones.
Bacon Solicitor-General.
Scioppius attacks Scaliger.
 Sir Edward Dyer died.
 Henry Chettle died.
 Thomas Newton (the translator) died.
 John Rainolds died.
 Baronius died.
 Jean Vauquelin (French poet) died.
 Mme. de Scudéry born.
 Anna Schurmann ('the Dutch Sappho') born.
 A. de Ruffi (French historian) born.
 Jean Rist (German poet) born.

1608. Wm. Biddulph: *Travels of Certayne Englishmen* (into Africa, Asia, etc.).
Chapman: *Conspiracy of Byron.*
Dekker: *Belman of London.*

Cold Doings in London: The Great Frost.
Mathurin Regnier: *Satires.*
François de Sales: *Introd. à la Vie Dévote.*
A Yorkshire Tragedy.
The Merry Devil of Edmonton.

WORKS PUBLISHED.

COMPARATIVE CHRONOLOGY.

1608. Jos. Hall: *Characters of Vertues and Vices.*

T. Heywood: *Rape of Lucrece.*

Middleton: *A Trick to Catch the Old-One* and *A Mad World my Masters.*

Ed. Topsell: *Historie of Foure Footed Beastes.*

Brian Twyne: *Antiquitatis Academiae Oxoniae Apologia.*

Shakespeare: *King Lear* (two distinct Quartos, known respectively as the 'Pide Bull' (the better) and 'N. Butter' Quartos).

R. Glover: *Nobilitas Politica et Civilis.*

Epitome of Froissart.

Rubens settles at Antwerp.

Coryate sets out on his journey.
Sackville died.
Bishop John Still died.
Dr. Dee died.
Alberico Gentili died.
Jean de la Taille died.
Milton born.
Clarendon born.
Fuller born.
John Tradescant born.
Sir Richard Fanshaw born.
Torricelli born.
Montecucculi (military memoirist) born.

1609. L. Andrewes: *Tortura Torti.*

Bacon: *De Sapientia Veterum* and *Certain Considerations touching the Plantation in Ireland.*

Daniel: *Civill Warres* (8 books).

Dekker: *The Guls Hornbooke.*

Drayton: *Life and Death of Ld. Cromwell.*

John Fletcher: *Faithfull Shepheardesse.*

Phil. Holland: *Roman Historie* (after Marcellinus).

Galileo with his telescope and Kepler began systematic observations.

Galileo and Harriott discover satellites of Jupiter.

Casaubon: *Polybius.*

Flos Sanctorum englished from Villegas.

Robt. Mason: *A Mirour for Merchants.*

Thomas Ravenscroft's Collections of Rounds, Catches and Canons: *Pammelia* and *Deuteromelia.*

Folio edition of Jewel's *Works* (ed. Arch. Bancroft).

Grotius: *Mare Liberum.*

WORKS PUBLISHED.

1609. Jonson : *Case is Alterd.*
Rowlands : *A whole crew of kind gossips.*
Alex. Gardyne : *Garden* (of ' Sonets,' etc.).
Wm. Rowley : *A Search for Money.*
Spenser : *Works.*
Topsell : *Hist. of Serpents.*
Shakespeare : *Sonnets, Troilus and Cressida,* and *Pericles* (all in 4to).

1610. Chapman : *Homer's Iliad* (i.-xii.), in heptameters.
John Donne : *Pseudo-Martyr.*
Giles Fletcher : *Christ's Victory.*
Guillim : *Display of Heraldrie.*
Philemon Holland : Version of *Camden's Britannia.*
Silvester Jourdain : *Discovery of the Barmudas.*
Ri. Niccols : *Mirrour for Magistrates* (newly enlarged).
Selden : *Duello.*
Barnabe Riche : *New Description of Ireland.*
Richard Rich : *Newes from Virginia.*
S. Rowlands : *Martin Mark-all, Beadle of Bridewell.*

COMPARATIVE CHRONOLOGY.

Garcilassa : *Comentarios del Peru.*
Sir G. Fenton died.
Barnabe Barnes died.
William Warner died.
John Dennys died.
J. J. Scaliger died.
G. Rollenhagen (German poet) died.
Arminius died.
B. Keckermann died.
Jean Rotrou (French dramatist) born.
Suckling born.

Douai Bible issued.
Keckermann : *De Natura Historiae.*
Hardy : *Marianne.*
D'Urfé : *L'Astrée.*
Robert Jones : *Muses Gardin for Delights.*
Jn. Healey : *Epictetus out of the Greek.*
Jn. Heath : *Two Centuries of Epigrams.*
Alchemist produced.
Archbp. Bancroft died, succeeded by Abbot.
Henri IV. assassinated.
Robert Parsons died.
Knolles died.
J. B. Raimondi died.
Matteo Ricci (the famous missionary to China) died.
Lupercio de Argensolas died.
Lucius Cary, Lord Falkland, born.
Scarron born.
La Calprenède born.
Antonio de Solis (the Spanish historian) born.

WORKS PUBLISHED.

COMPARATIVE CHRONOLOGY.

1611. *Authorized Version of the Bible.*

Lodovic Barrey: *Ram Alley.* A comedy (full of 'play-scraps' from Shakespeare).

Chapman: *Homer's Iliad* (xiii.-xxiv.).

Coryate: *Crudities.*

Randle Cotgrave: *Dictionarie of the French and English Tongues.*

John Davies: *The Scourge of Folly.*

Dekker and Middleton: *The Roaring Girle.*

Donne: *Anatomie of the Worlde.*

Speed: *History of Great Britain.*

Tarlton's Jests (in three parts).

Tourneur: *The Atheist's Tragedie.*

Shakespeare retires to Stratford.

James May: *Golden Legend.*

Charterhouse founded by Sutton.

Wm. Fennor: *Pluto his Travaile.*

Wither's *Abuses Stript and Whipt* (small issue, no extant copy known).

E. Richer: *De Ecclesiastica et Politica Potestate.*

Du Plessis Mornay: *Mystère d' Iniquité* (history of the Papacy).

Dr. Simon Forman (the diarist) died.

John Cowell died.

Perez died.

Pedro Ribadeneira died.

Pierre de l'Estoile (diarist) died.

Jean Bertaut (Ronsardist) died

Silvano Razzi (the Italian playwright) died.

James Harrington (author of *Oceana*) born.

Sir Thomas Urquhart (translator of Rabelais) born.

1612. Bacon: *Essayes* (2nd edition).

John Bois: *Notes on Chrysostom.*

John Brinsley: *Ludus Literarius.*

Hugh Broughton: *Censure of the late Translation for our Churches* (the Authorized Version).

L'Oratoire founded by M. de Bérulle.

Shelton's *Don Quixote* became popular (continued 1620).

Vondel: *Het Pascha.*

Savile's edition of *Chrysostom* and Farnaby's *Juvenal and Persius.*

David Rivault: *Dessein d'une Academie.*

WORKS PUBLISHED.

1612. Chapman: *Epicede on Henry, Prince of Wales.*

Daniel: *First Part of the Historie of England.*

Nat. Field: *A Woman is a Weathercock.*

Jos. Hall: *Contemplations.*

Heywood: *An Apologie for Actors.*

Jonson: *The Alchemist.*

Webster: *White Divel.*

1613. Wm. Alexander (Earl of Stirling): *Arcadia* completed.

Beaumont: *Inner Temple Masque.*

Beaumont and Fletcher: *Knight of the Burning Pestle.*

Wm. Browne: *Britannia's Pastorals.*

Corbet: *Journey to France.*

John Dennys: *Secrets of Angling* (posthumous).

Drayton: *Polyolbion* (xviii 'Songs' or Cantos).

Drummond: *Mausoleum.*

H. Parrot: *Springes to catch Woodcocks* (epigrams).

Purchas: *His Pilgrimage.*

Wither: *Abuses Stript and Whipt* (re-issue).

COMPARATIVE CHRONOLOGY.

Death of the Prince (Henry) of Wales.

Sir J. Harington died.

Bodley died.

John Bond (the Scholiast) died.

Pierre de Larivey died.

Samuel Butler born.

Bishop Pearson born.

Ant. Arnauld (the French philosopher) born.

Schottel (the German grammarian) born.

Henry VIII. written.

Sir Henry Spelman issues his *De non temerandis Ecclesiis,* a kind of first draft of his *Sacrilege.*

John Hales: *Oratio Funebris* for Sir John Bodley.

Cervantes: *Novelas.*

Suarez: *Defensio Fidei Catholicae.*

Sir R. Dallington: *Aphorismes* (after Guicciardini).

Fletcher and Massinger begin dramatic partnership.

Wadham College founded.

Wonderful Discoverie of Witches in Lancashire (by Potts and Bromley).

Constable died.

Overbury murdered.

Guarini died.

Math. Regnier (French satirist) died.

Rich. Crawshaw born.

Jeremy Taylor born.

WORKS PUBLISHED.

1613. Sir John Davies: *Discoverie of the State of Ireland.*

1614. Wm. Barclay: *Nepenthes, or the Vertues of Tabacco.*
Wm. Browne: *Shepheards Pipe* (7 Eclogues).
Leon. Busher: *Religious Peace* (a Plea for Liberty of Conscience).
Cobbes Prophecies.
J. Cooke: *Greenes Tu Quoque.*
Thos. Freeman: *Rubbe and a Great Cast* (200 epigrams).
Tobias Gentleman: *Englands Way to Win Wealth.*
Gorges: *Lucan's Pharsalia.*
Napier: *Logarithmorum Descriptio.*
Overbury: *A Wife now a Widow* and *Characters.*
Raleigh: *Hist. of the World.*
Selden: *Titles of Honour.*
Henry Smith: *Micro-Cosmo - Graphia* (or 'Map of Man').

1615. John Andrew: *Anatomie of Basenesse.*
R. Brathwaite: *A Strappado for the Devil.*

COMPARATIVE CHRONOLOGY.
La Rochefoucauld born.
Saint Evremond born.
Gilles Ménage (the great French critic and philologer) born.
Christian Rau (German Orientalist) born.

Cervantes: *Viage del Parnaso.*
F. de Sales: *Traité de l'amour de Dieu.*
Spurious 'Second Part' of *Don Quixote* (by Avellaneda).
Wm. Burrowes: Treatise *Of the Variations of the Compasse.*
Napier invents Logarithms.
Ruggle's *Ignoramus* acted.
Jonson's *Bartholomew Fayre* acted.
T. Godwin: *Romane Antiquities.*
Wm. Lithgow: *Peregrinations.*
Arthur Saul: *The Famous Game of Chesse Play.*
Richard Venner's *Apology* (an autobiography).
Capt. John Smith explores Virginia and issues his *Map.*
Lope de Vega at the zenith of his fame.
Brantôme died.
Isaac Casaubon died.
Henry More born.
Cardinal de Retz born.
John Wilkins born.

Cervantes: *Don Quixote* (pt. ii.).
Sandoval: *Hist. of the Kings of Castile.*
Cervantes: *Comedias.*

WORKS PUBLISHED.

1615. N. Breton; *Characters.*

Camden: *Annales.*

Chapman: *Odysses of Homer* (heroic measure).

Daniel: *Hymen's Triumph.*

Ford: *Sir Thomas Overbury.*

Harington: *Epigrams, both pleasant and serious.*

Heywood: *Four Prentices of London.*

Wm. Martyn: *Kings of England.*

Sandys: *Relation of a Journey.*

John Stephens: *Satyrical Essayes and Characters.*

Jos. Swetnam: *Arraignment of lewd, idle, inconstant Women.*

Sylvester: *Tobacco Battered.*

Wither: *Shepheards Hunting* and *Fidelia* (privately).

1616. Breton: *The Goode and the Badde.*

Wm. Browne: *Britannia's Pastorals* (bk. ii.).

Jn. Bullokar: *An English Expositor* (of hardest words in our language).

Chapman: *Iliad* and *Odyssey* (complete).

COMPARATIVE CHRONOLOGY.

Rowlands: *The Melancholie Knight.*

Scioppius: *Legatus Latro* (aimed at Lord Digby and James I.).

De Caus: *Raisons de Forces Mouvantes.*

Montchrestien: *Traité de l'Economie Politique.*

Sir George Buck: *The Third Universitie of England* (London).

Lathum's *Falconry.*

Thomas Tomkis: *Albumazar.*

Thomas Farnaby, the leading classical master of his day, issues his edition of Martial.

Della Porta died.

Aquaviva (the Jesuit general) died.

Etienne Pasquier (French historian and jurist) died.

Samuel Sorbière born.

Rich. Baxter born.

Sir John Denham born.

John Biddle (Unitarian founder) born.

Vanini: *De Admirandis Naturae Arcanis.*

Agrippa d'Aubigné: *Les Tragiques, Hist. Universelle.*

Holyday: Version of *Persius.*

Ben Jonson created Poet Laureate (February 1st) by Letters Patent.

Shakespeare died (Wednesday, April 23rd).

WORKS PUBLISHED.

1616. Drummond of Hawthornden : *Poems.*

Jn. Dunbar : *Epigrammaton Centuriae Sex.*

Wm. Haughton : *English-Men for my Money.*

James I. : *Counterblast to Tobacco.*

Jonson : *Works* (First Folio).

Speed : *Cloud of Witnesses.*

1617. R. Anton : *Vices Anatomie Scourged.*

Brathwaite : *A Solemn Joviall Disputation.*

Drummond of Hawthornden : *Forth Feasting.*

R. Fludd : *Tractatus de Rosea Cruce.*

Greene : *Alcida.*

Joseph Hall : *Quo Vadis.*

Fras. Holyoake : *Dictionarie Etymologicall.*

Fynes Moryson : *An Itinerary containing Ten Yeeres Travell.*

Rowley and Middleton : *Fair Quarrel.*

Selden : *History of Tithes.*

John Taylor : *Travels in Germany.*

1618. Edmund Boulton : *Version of The Histories of Florus.*

COMPARATIVE CHRONOLOGY.

Cervantes died (Sunday, April 23rd, New Style).

Francis Beaumont died.

Hakluyt died.

Philip Henslowe (theatrical manager) died.

Richard Field died.

Jn. Wallis born.

Sir Roger L'Estrange born.

Wm. Faithorne born.

Ninon de Lenclos born.

Giovanni Sagredo (the Italian historian) born.

Cornelius a Lapide : *Commentarii.*

Burton's *Philosophaster* acted.

Minsheu : *Polyglot Dictionary.*

Ed. Boulton, or Bolton, proposes an Academy to the King.

Bacon Lord Keeper.

Alex. Daniel commences his *Diary.*

Coryate died.

Ant. Loisel (the French jurist) died.

Sir James Melville (*Memoirs of his own Life*) died.

Napier of Merchiston died.

Suarez died.

De Thou (Thuanus) died.

Elias Ashmole born.

Horrocks (the astronomer) born.

Cudworth born.

Bacon Lord Chancellor.

Ben Jonson visits Scotland.

Synod of Dort.

WORKS PUBLISHED.

1618. N. Breton: *The Court and Country.*

Chapman: *Hesiod's Georgics.*

Sir Jn. Davies: *Hymnes of Astraea.*

Nat. Field: *Amends for Ladies.*

T. Gainsford: *History of Perkin Warbeck.*

H. Holland: *Basilωlogia.*

Hooker: *Ecclesiastical Polity* (vi.-viii.).

Mynshul: *Prison Characters.*

James Shirley: *Echo.*

Geo. Strode: *The Anatomie of Mortalitie.*

Jn. Taylor: *Penniless Pilgrimage.*

John Willis: *Mnemonica.*

1619. *Amadis de Gaule* (English version).

Beaumont and Fletcher: *Maids Tragedy* and *King and No King.*

Ralph Brooke: *Catalogue of Kings, Princes, etc.* (the first regular Peerage).

M. Drayton: *Poems* (collected).

Drummond of Hawthornden: *Conversations with Ben Jonson* (written).

COMPARATIVE CHRONOLOGY.

Racan: *Les Bergeries.*

Espinel: *Marcos de Obregon.*

J. Godard: *Les Déguisés* (after *Suppositi* of Ariosto).

Benedictines of St. Maur commence their historical works, comprising *L'Art de verifier les Dates, Gallia Christiana, Glossarium, Acta Sanctorum,* and *Histoire Littéraire de la France.*

Raleigh died.
Stanyhurst died.
John Davies of Hereford died.
Dr. John Bridges died.
Joshua Sylvester died.
Odet de la Noue died.
J. D. Du Perron died.
A. Morosini (historian of Venice) died.
Cowley born.
Lovelace born.
Isaac Vossius born.
Murillo born.

Sarpi: *Hist. of Council of Trent.*

Jn. Heath: *House of Correction.*

Arminius condemned by Synod of Dort.

Harvey discovers Circulation of Blood.

Decimal notation used by Napier and explained in Henry Lyle's *Decimall Arithmeticke.*

Saml. Daniel died.
Fabricius (D'Acquapendente) died.
Vanini burnt.
Lebrun born.

WORKS PUBLISHED.

1619. Henry Hutton: *Follies Anatomie* (satires and epigrams).

Purchas: *Microcosmus*.

1620. Bacon: *Novum Organum*.

Beaumont and Fletcher: *Philaster*.

Dekker: *His Dreame*.

Gervase Markham: *Farewel to Husbandrie*.

Melton: *Astrologaster*.

Quarles: *Feast for Worms*.

Thos. Scott: *Vox Populi* (the famous tract against the Spanish match).

Jn. Taylor: *His Travels from London to Prague*.

Tobias Venner: *Via Recta ad Vitam Longam* (on the Baths of Bath).

1621. Jn. Barclay: *Argenis*.

Beaumont and Fletcher: *Thierry and Theodoret*.

Burton: *Anatomy of Melancholy*.

Sir T. Culpeper: *Tract against High Rate of Usury*.

Donne: *Two Anniversaries* (of the death of Eliz. Drury).

Peter Heylin: *Microcosmus*.

COMPARATIVE CHRONOLOGY.

Olivier de Serres died.
Colbert born.
Tallemant des Réaux born.
Cyrano de Bergerac born.

Salmasius: *Historiae Augustae Scriptores*.
Villegas: *Las Amatorias*.
Campanella: *De Sensu Rerum*.
T. Stapleton: *Opera Omnia* (posthum̃as).
Holland's *Herωologia Anglica* issued.
Sailing of 'Mayflower.'
Thomas Campion died.
Thomas Tymme died.
Robert Tofte died.
Richard Carew died.
Larivey died.
Baudoin (*Les Trois morts et les Trois vivants*) died.
John Evelyn born.
A. Marvell born.
Robert Morison (the botanist) born.

Bacon ennobled and impeached; confesses to receiving money *pendente lite*, is degraded and severely sentenced, but pardoned by James I.
Donne made Dean of St. Paul's.
Thos. Williamson: *The Wise Vieillard* (after Goulart).
Jn. Barclay died.
Thomas Harriott died.
Bellarmine died.
Ralph Agas died.
John Guillim died.

WORKS PUBLISHED.

1621. R. Johnson: *Historie of Tom Thumbe.*
Mun : *Discourse of Trade.*
John Taylor: *The Praise and Commodity of Beggars and Begging.*
Tobias Venner: *On the Fume of Tobacco.*
D. Widdowes: *Naturall Philosophy.*
Lady Mary Wroth: *Urania.*

1622. Bacon: *Henry VII.*
Drayton : *Polyolbion* (in complete form).
Patrick Hannay : *The Nightingale* (poems).
Massinger: *Virgin Martyr.*
Sir Tobie Matthew: Version of St. Augustine's *Confessions.*
Peacham: *Compleat Gentleman.*
Vincent : *Discoverie of Errors in Brookes Catalogue* (Peerage).
Sam. Ward : *Woe to Drunkards.*
Wither : *Juvenilia.*
Shakespeare: *Othello* (posthum. 4to).

1623. Bacon : *De Augmentis.*
R. Brathwaite : *Shepherds Tale.*
Daniel: *Whole Workes* (8 pts., 4to).

COMPARATIVE CHRONOLOGY.

Guillaume du Vair died.
Montchrestien (French economist and poet) died.
Prudencio de Sandoval died.
Ottavio Rinuccini (Italian poet) born.
Henry Vaughan born.
La Fontaine born.
Mme. de Motteville born.
Scheffer (author of *Lapponia*) born.
P. René Rapin (the Latin poet) born.

Bourne's *Weekly Newes* and Butter's *Newes from most parts.*
William Bradford's *Diary of Occurrences.*
Thos. Robinson: *Anatomy of the English Nunnery at Lisbon.*
Edward Misselden brings out his treatise called *Free Trade,* answered by G. de Malynes.
Vermuyden commences draining operations in England.
Tassoni : *Secchia Rapita.*
C. Sorel : *Francion.*
Sir Henry Savile died.
François de Sales died.
Vaughan born.
A. Sidney born.
Molière born.

Wm. Harvey physician to James I.
Middleton's *Changeling* acted.
J. Mabbe: Version of Aleman's *Rogue* (a few copies, 1622).

WORKS PUBLISHED.	COMPARATIVE CHRONOLOGY.
1623. Drummond: *Flowres of Sion* and *The Cypresse Grove.* Massinger: *Duke of Milan.* Webster: *Dutchesse of Malfi.* Shakespeare: *Comedies, Histories, and Tragedies* (the First Folio).	Campanella: *Civitas Solis.* Marini: *Adone.* Buxtorf: *Hebrew Grammar.* Velazquez settles at Madrid. Wm. Camden died. Giles Fletcher died. Wm. Byrd (the composer) died. Du Plessis Mornay died. Pietro Sarpi died. Robt. Thoroton (the antiquary) born. Pascal born.
1624. Fletcher: *Rule a Wife and have a Wife.* John Gee: *The Foot out of the Snare* (anti-Jesuit treatise). *Loves Garland* (posies and love-tokens). Lord Herbert of Cherbury: *De Veritate.* Massinger: *Bondman.* Norden: *View from London Bridge.* Capt. Jn. Smith: *General Historie of Virginia.* W. Udall: *Life of Mary Stuart.* Ussher: *Answer to a Jesuit.* Wotton: *Elements of Architecture.*	Vossius: *De Historicis Graecis.* Middleton's *Game of Chess* produced and printed. Baudoin's French version of *Arcadia.* J. Bingham: *Historie of Xenophon* (*Anabasis* englished). Edm. Gunter: Books on *Dialling.* Perrin's *Luthers Forerunners* (englished). Sir Henry Wotton made Provost of Eton. Mariana died. Jakob Boehme (the mystic) died. Geo. Fox born. J. Regnauld de Segrais (the French poet) born. Scheffler (Angelus Silesius) born.
1625. Bacon: *Essays* (final form) and *Translation of Certain Psalms into English verse.* Camden: *Annales* (ii.).	Charles I. succeeds James I. (March 27th). Grotius: *De Jure Belli et Pacis.* Nich. Ferrar at Little Gidding. Voiture: *Pyrame et Thisbé.*

WORKS PUBLISHED.

1625. Dekker: *A Rod for Run-*
      awayes.
      Jonson: *Staple of News.*
      Purchas: *Pilgrimes.*
      Shirley: *Love Tricks.*
      Thos. Tuke: *The Holy*
      Eucharist.
      Geo. Wither: *Scholars*
      Purgatory.

1626. N. Breton: *Fantasticks.*
      Walter Cary: *The Pre-*
      sent State of England.
      Donne: *Devotions upon*
      Emergent Occasions.
      Daniel Featley: *Ancilla*
      Pietatis.
      Flecknoe: *Hierothala-*
      mium.
      Fletcher: *Fair Maid of*
      the Inn.
      H. Parrot: *Cures for the*
      Itch.
      Sandys: *Ovid's Metamor-*
      phoses (completed ren-
      dering in heroic verse).
      Sir H. Spelman: *Glos-*
      sarium Archaiologicum
      (i.).

1627. Bacon: *New Atlantis* and
      Sylva Sylvarum.
      Cosin: *Private Devotions.*
      Drayton: *Battaile of*
      Agincourt and *Nim-*
      phidia.
      Phineas Fletcher: *Lo-*
      custae vel Pietas Jesu-

COMPARATIVE CHRONOLOGY.

Long's version of *Argenis.*
      James I. died (March 27th).
      John Fletcher died.
      Lodge died.
      Thomas Dempster died.
      Herrera y Tordesillas died.
      D'Urfé (French romancist)
      died.
      Marino died.
      Pierre Nicole born.

Robert Carey finishes his *Me-*
      moirs (publ. 1759).
Jardin des Plantes inaugurated
      at Paris.
      Bacon died (April 9th).
      Bp. Andrewes died.
      Sir J. Davies died.
      Purchas died.
      Cyril Tourneur died.
      Augustine Vincent died.
      N. Breton died.
      Edward Alleyn (the actor)
      died.
      Théophile de Viau (French
      critic and dramatist) died.
      Jn. Aubrey born.
      Mme. de Sévigné born.
      Claude Chapelle born.
      Francesco Redi (Italian poet)
      born.

Grotius: *De Veritate.*
Dempster: *Historia Ecclesias-*
      tica Gentis Scotorum.
Cotton: *Raigne of Henry III.*
Mendoza: *Guerra de Granada.*
Nich. Sanson: *Galliae Antiquae*
      Descriptio Geographica.
      Middleton died.

WORKS PUBLISHED.	COMPARATIVE CHRONOLOGY.
1627. *itica* (Latin and English). Grimstone: *A Generall Historie of the Netherlands.* *A Looking - Glasse for Drunkards.* George Peele: *Merrie Conceited Jests.*	Richard Barnfield died. Sir Henry Goodyer died. Gongora died. Joannes Gruter (the philologist and friend of Scaliger, died. Robert Boyle born. Bossuet born. Mlle. de Montpensier born.
1628. Brabourne: *Discourse on the Sabbath Day.* Coke: *On Littleton.* John Earle: *Microcosmographie.* Owen Feltham or Felltham: *Resolves.* Wm. Harvey: *De Motu Sanguinis et Cordis.* Rob. Hayman: *Quodlibets, Epigrams and other small Parcels.* Robert Norton: *The Gunner.* Prynne: *Unloveliness of Lovelocks* and *Sinfulnesse of Drinking Healths.* Selden: *Marmora Arundelliana.* Wither: *Britain's Remembrancer.*	Scioppius: *Grammatica Philosophica.* Le Jay's *Bible Polyglotte* (commenced, printed by Antoine Vitré). Cyril Lucar, the Patriarch, presents *Codex Alexandrinus* to Charles I. Castelli: *Misura dell' Acque Correnti* (this and De Caus helped to found hydraulics). *Robin Goodfellow. His Mad Pranks.* John Owen: *Certaine Epigrams* (englished). Taj Mahal built. Daborne died. Malherbe died. Fulke Greville killed. Sir Wm. Temple born. John Ray born. Perrault born. P. Lambeck (German historian) born.
1629. Thomas Adams: *Sermons.*	Mairet: *Sophonisbe.* P. Corneille: *Mélite*

WORKS PUBLISHED.

1629. Sir J. Beaumont: *Bosworth Field*.
Davenant: *Albovine*.
Fletcher: *Faithfull Shepheardesse* (2nd edit.).
Ford: *The Lover's Melancholy*.
Hobbes: *Translation of Thucydides*.
Fras. Lenton: *The Young Gallants Whirligig*.
R. M.: *Micrologia* (eccentric character portraits).
Quarles: *Argalus and Parthenia*.
Sir Thos. Ryves: *Historia Navalis*.
Shirley: *The Wedding*.

1630. Davenant: *Cruel Brother*.
Drayton: *Muses Elizium*.
Wm. Freake: *Doctrines and Practices of the Jesuites*.
Hayward: *Life and Raigne of Edward VI*.
Massinger: *Renegado*.
Quarles: *Divine Poems*.
Ruggle: *Ignoramus. Comoedia*.
H. R.: *Mythomystes*.
Sibbes: *The Bruised Reed and Smoaking Flax*.
Capt. John Smith: *True Travels*.
John Taylor: *Works* (63 titles).

COMPARATIVE CHRONOLOGY.

Alarcon: *Comedias*.
Carleton: English *Life of B. Gilpin*.
Maxwell: Version of *Herodian*.
Fras. Malthus: *Treatise of Artificial Fireworks*.
J. Parkinson: *Paradisus of Pleasant Flowers*.
Le Grys's version of *Argenis*.
Descartes retired to Holland.
    Speed died.
    Bérulle (French theologian) died.
    Anastasio Pantaleon (Spanish poet) died.
    Spanheim (Swiss scholar) born.
    Christian Huygens born.

Renewed grant of Laureateship to Jonson.
G. Herbert at Bemerton.
Davila: *Storia delle Guerre civili di Francia*.
    Agrippa d'Aubigné died.
    Gabriel Harvey died.
    Fynes Moryson died.
    Henry Briggs (Napier's collaborator) died.
    Kepler died.
    Jean Godard died.
    Barrow born.
    Tillotson born.
    Daniel Huet (the great French scholar) born.
    Jean de Santeul (Latin poet) born.
    Carlo Maggi born.
    Charles II. born.

WORKS PUBLISHED.

1631. Andrewes : *Sermons.*

Done: *Polydoron* (maxims).

Fuller: *David's Heinous Sin.*

George Herbert : *The Temple.*

Heywood: *Fair Maid of the West.*

Martin Parker : *True Tale of Robin Hood.*

Wye Saltonstall: *Picturae Loquentes* and *Whimsies.*

Shirley : *The School of Compliment.*

COMPARATIVE CHRONOLOGY.

Harriott's *Praxis of Algebra,* to which the science owes its present form.

May : *Lucan.*

Mabbe's version of the *Celestina,* from Spanish of Ferdinando de Rojas.

Chettle : *Tragedy of Hoffman.*

Renaudot founds the *Gazette de France.*

Drayton died.

John Donne died.

Cotton (the antiquary) died.

Davila died.

Alexandre Hardy died.

Richer (French theologian) died.

Dryden born.

INDEX TO VOLUME I.

[An attempt is made in the Index to give a rough indication of editions most accessible to the student. Grosart stands for the late Dr. A. B. Grosart's limited issues and reprints ; Nat. Libr. stands for Morley's *National Library* (Cassell); Univ. Libr. and Carisbrooke for the *Universal Library* and *Carisbrooke Library*, also edited by H. Morley (Routledge); Bohn for the *Bohn Library* (Bell) ; Tudor for *Tudor Translations* (Nutt); Muses' for *Muses' Library* (Bullen) ; Arber for Professor Arber's *English Reprints* and *Scholar's Library* (Constable); and English Garner or Garner for Messrs. Constable's *An English Garner*.]

I.   T